Coaching Kasparov,
Year by Year and Move by Move

Volume II: The Assassin (1982-1990)

Alexander Nikitin

Coaching Kasparov, Year by Year and Move by Move

Volume II: The Assassin (1982-1990)

Author: Alexander Nikitin

Translated from the Russian by Ilan Rubin

Chess editors: Grigory Baranov and Anastasia Travkina

Typesetting by Andrei Elkov (www.elkov.ru)

Versions of this book were published in German, French and Spanish over 1991-1996

Front cover photo: Nikitin and Kasparov with Norik Grigorian, Kasparov's fitness coach

Photos provided by 64 Publishing House

Analysis of the twenty Kasparov vs Vladimirov and Kasparov vs Timoshchenko training games was carried out by Grandmaster Dorian Rogozenco in 2020 using modern computer engines. The author and publisher wish to express their gratitude to the Kasparov family for providing these games especially for this book, in which they are published for the first time. Analysis of the other games has generally not been updated since it was completed by the author in the early 1990s, although a small number of corrections have been made, as the main purpose of the analysis is to explain the thought process of Kasparov and his opponents in the context in which they played

Follow us on Twitter: @ilan_ruby

www.elkandruby.com

ISBN 978-5-6041769-9-3

CONTENTS

INDEX OF GAMES

At the beginning of my career as a coach I promised to do my utmost, using all my strength, knowledge and experience, to bring up a challenger capable of replacing Karpov on the throne. I am proud that I kept my promise and achieved my aim

Chapter 1. Reaching the Summit (1982-1984)

Garry's rapid chess progress not only threatened Karpov's reign but also created masses of problems for the people working with him. The lad had to cope with a number of painful trials, each of which could have broken him. World fame was growing even more rapidly than his chess ability. The praise gushing from newspaper pages and television screens blurred his thinking. A boy whom the System had taught to live in the crowd had now been hoisted far above it on the crest of the wave of public recognition, before he had time to digest his true significance. His stunning victories at chess tournaments, his famous victims – all this started to create a superiority complex within him, and he turned out to lack immunity against celebrity disease. Moreover, he had to handle the first signs of a cold war launched against him by the sporting functionaries and which took the form of measures incompatible with the concepts of honesty and fairness that had embedded in the lad's mind after graduating from school. Only a strong personality could protect himself in such circumstances, one with a tough character and the wisdom of a philosopher capable of fighting against fate itself.

So what was Garry like prior to the start of these new serious trials? He was a tall, handsome lad with thick, black hair and an athletic figure. He liked sport due to his love of risk. He hence willingly ran around with a football at his feet, swam like a fish in the Caspian Sea, and would try to run a hundred meters in just 12 seconds. His passion for reading was as strong as ever. His ability to read entire pages at once, rather than just line by line as we lesser mortals are used to, enabled him to read a thick book from beginning to end in an evening. His excellent memory resembled an endless chest from which he quickly and accurately extracted dates, figures, facts, and large pieces of poetry. Although Garry spurted information of an unusually large range – from chess to politics – he constantly strived to learn more and more.

At the base of his spiritual qualities stood kindness and a striving for justice. However, while the latter is typical of the majority of young people, the former is a quality that far from everybody possesses. Even then, we could trace the lad's creative nature, which he had inherited from his father. From an early age he stopped fearing the full audiences of the playing halls and, as the crowd's interest grew, he felt increasingly self-assured and inspired. He not only felt his chess strength, but he knew his own worth and what he needed to achieve in life.

By then, his energetic nature drove him to live an active public life. He presented with pleasure before audiences, and carried out missions for the Komsomol. As had long been the tradition in our country, the majority of young people were involved within the orbit of the Party's youth organization. This was where future candidates for party roles were selected, and where the rest were educated in the spirit of blind adherence to the communist dogma and the Party's appeals. Garry didn't avoid such an outcome, and didn't even attempt to resist. However, public service wasn't something that he enjoyed; moreover, he didn't have the time to perform it seriously. He simply liked to make presentations, to be seen among a charmed audience. This striving, fed by the gasps of delight, gradually developed into a drug that came to explain some otherwise incomprehensible decisions.

His clever brain was still a mess from the amalgamation of authorities telling him what to do, opinions and facts. He should have been surrounded by serious and clever people in order to correctly and soberly think through, evaluate and develop his convictions. However, he preferred people who were close to him in terms of temperament and youthful spontaneity. His mother became his main support and they were inseparable. She shaped his world-view, his attitude to people, and did so in a very smart way, in accordance with her life philosophy and experience. Garry would learn at an early age how to handle the powers that be, what to say to them so that they liked him, even though deep inside him his feelings were quite different. The life philosophy of people crippled by our society started to cripple him, too. Soon he would come across cynical treachery of several representatives of the Party's central power. This would not only embitter and harden the lad, but it would destroy the last remnants of communist dogma in his psyche. In order to achieve his main goal, to realize his abilities, he would adopt "their" rules of the game and double standards, and, like his predecessor, he would succeed admirably in this.

1982 began with an important event for the Kasparovs: they were again invited to meet Geidar Aliev, the all-powerful head of the Azerbaijan Party. The purpose of the reception, which was widely trumpeted by the local newspapers, was obvious – to emphasize top-level support for Garry in the republic, and that proved to play a key role in his ascent to the summit. Actually, the lad's stunning victories were important for Aliev, too, given he was at the time a member of the Soviet Politburo, the country's supreme decision-making organ. His colleagues were always proud of home-grown sportsmen, and Kasparov was promising to become the brightest flower of the somewhat modest bouquet of Azeri sporting stars.

Klara Kasparova's behavior soon changed sharply. Her gentle and kind manner gave way to judgement based on cold calculation and bossing the coaches around. It became clear that the Azeri leadership had by now decided to keep tight control over Kasparov's career progress and the development of his personality. The role of team "pseudo-leader" was invested in his mother, whom the leadership had no difficulty in managing.

Zhenya Vladimirov, a very strong master who at the time had taken a genuine liking to Kasparov, flew in from Almaty to our first training session of the year. He possessed an unusually subtle and deep understanding of chess at a good GM level, was independent in his judgement and would not give in to pressure. His chess brain was always fresh and he came up with many valuable ideas. He blended in with our team straight away, which significantly eased my burden as a coach, taking on the main role of challenging Garry's analysis, both at the table and during walks in the park where our analysis would continue, only without a board. Zhenya even strengthened our football team, fighting for the ball with a serious and sometimes comically imperturbable expression. When he first showed up in our camp, his appearance was anything but sporty, with a weight exceeding 100 kilos. He at first accepted our jogging routine and then toughened it. In a couple of years, he managed to shed 25 kilos, transforming into a tall, handsome, athletically built young man.

Two months of intensive training in Zagulba brought returns. Garry's chess ability grew notably, and the strong tournament in the Yugoslav city of Bugojno, to which Garry had been invited by the organizers, was meant to demonstrate that. However, complications unexpectedly arose. Garry was informed out of the blue from Moscow that the USSR Sports Committee expected him to fly to Dortmund where he would compete with average masters, rather than strong grandmasters. That said, Garry was prepared for such a turn of events and knew what moves to make in this unchess-like variation unveiled by the Moscow-based sporting functionaries.

Shortly before we received official notification about the change in Garry's tournament itinerary we heard that after Garry's victory in the Soviet championship a "directive opinion" had formed somewhere at the top of the Party that all available levers should be pulled to keep Karpov on the throne, as a champion who fitted the System well. Above all, the plan involved pulling the rug from under Kasparov's chess progress, given that he was considered the most likely challenger. The chosen strategy was simple. From now on, Karpov and Kasparov should not meet over the board in the same competition in order to avoid a repetition of the consternation seen at the previous year's tournament of generations, when the world champion finished with fewer points than Garry. Moreover, to avoid Garry achieving further victories in major foreign tournaments that would have quickly driven his rating up towards Karpov's level, they decided that it made sense to lower the level of tournament to which the young national champion would be sent by our federation.

Our sporting bosses, carrying out this directive, were following a simple calculation: Garry would kick up a fuss and quickly become known as a scandal maker who was too big for his boots, or, even better, he would collapse in the face of such obvious unfair treatment, or, as many others did, he would accept his lot in life and become a good soldier. Well, Garry neither accepted his lot in life nor kicked up a fuss, but turned to Aliev for help. The level of people who had organized this hidden resistance to Kasparov was below that of Politburo members, and just one phone call by Aliev to that mysterious office proved to be sufficient to enable Garry to fly to Bugojno.

Yugoslavia had a special motivational impact on Kasparov, and he always put in stellar performances in that country. In was in Belgrade in 1990 that he reached a record rating of 2800! Of the 14 grandmasters invited to Bugojno, nine were rated above what was then the super-grandmaster level of 2600, while the strong play of certain others (M. Najdorf, S. Gligoric, and B. Ivkov) didn't need to be confirmed by any rating number. Yet among this gathering of stars Garry's play stood out, as expected, for being particularly brilliant and inventive, but by now we could add the qualities solid and deep. Many of his ideas and entire games drew exultant praise from his vastly experienced opponents. The lad from Baku achieved six wins and no losses – a great achievement in a tourney of such a high level. Only once at the very end did Garry find himself on the verge of defeat after a careless opening. Yet he managed to befuddle Timman so expertly that the latter was unable to achieve more than a draw despite being a rook ahead. Botvinnik, reporting on the tournament, expressed the thought that Kasparov could even become Karpov's challenger in the recently begun championship cycle. The Moscow interzonal was just two months away...

The government of Azerbaijan continued to sponsor Garry's prep. We held our next training session at a government dacha in picturesque mountainous surroundings. Our coaching team had strengthened further – Grandmaster Gennady Timoshchenko, a stern Siberian with a matter-of-fact approach but somewhat prickly character, now became a permanent member. He improved the way we organized and planned our work, and brought a more rigorous approach to our analysis.

July 1982 should be considered the starting point of the work of our powerful, creative team that would work with Kasparov for nearly four years. For a month and a half, Garry and his coaches (me, Shakarov, Vladimirov and Timoshchenko) worked in the mountains far from temptations and populated areas. In this serene atmosphere we made massive progress. We sorted out his opening repertoire taking into account the tastes of his future opponents and planned Garry's optimal tournament strategy. The latter was no pointless exercise, as the other interzonals demonstrated that those who qualified for the next stage were the players who retained energy and strong nerves at the finishing line. At the end of the session Garry played a training match against Vladimirov. Its unexpected result (3:3) proved to be great medicine for his big head before the upcoming interzonal tournament, whose result no expert was prepared to predict in advance.

As it happened, the Moscow interzonal was the strongest of that cycle's interzonals, and, like in the two others that had already finished, only the top two players progressed to the candidates matches. This fact meant that the battle would be particularly fierce. Thanks to the draw, Garry built up early a decent set of points that determined his overall success: the series of draws in the middle of the tournament, which was when he faced the strongest opponents, didn't create the concerns we had in previous tourneys. Rather, by startling everybody with his relentless aggression even in drawn positions, he was driven to fight even harder. Having sensed his powers, Garry managed to preserve his nervous energy and was unstoppable at the finishing line.

Garry was seconded at the tourney by me, Shakarov and Valery Chekhov. Botvinnik as always limited himself to general advice and long, deep telephone conversations with Garry and his mother. I don't recall any occasion when the Patriarch gave his pupil or coaches specific chess advice or helped to select a plan when analyzing adjourned positions. However, his general instructions and advice were of great use for Garry, even when he was fighting Karpov for the throne. Firstly, his advice was based on his vast and carefully analyzed experience as a great player. Secondly, Garry was quite impressionable and constantly sought approval of his decisions and actions. The mentality of a man from the south means that approval had to come from a universally respected person, and Botvinnik was an ideal figure for that. Conversations with the teacher were effective psychotherapy for Garry for about five years, but then they transposed into more of a ritual.

Kasparov's success, achieved with confident play and without any evident overexertion, once again worried the people tasked with ensuring that Karpov remained on his throne. I discovered that the latest chess material delivered to the Central Chess Club (games of completed tournaments and foreign chess magazines) would first be passed on to the champion's coaching team, and only later (sometimes with parts missing!) would be made available to other GMs. So we urgently had to arrange our own information channel. However, the main military maneuvers were still to come.

Once again, no place was found for me in the large delegation accompanying the Soviet team to the next Olympiad in Switzerland, despite my pupil's participation. So I had to give Garry written advice, which he promised to follow. This is what I wrote for him:

1)   Above all, play solidly. That way the team won't get nervous about your games, and, further, solid play will prove to be extremely important in the upcoming candidates matches. Well, Garry didn't lose a single game and, apart from one deliberately assumed risk in a crazy duel with Korchnoi, never stood worse.

2)   Try to score more points than the player one board above you in the team. Let him worry about it. Well, Garry played more games than anybody in the team, 11, and picked up 8.5 points. Karpov played the fewest number, just 8, scoring 6.5 points.

3)   Don't play like an open book in the opening – our novelties will be needed for the candidates matches. Try to play more games with complicated strategic middlegames. This request was fulfilled.

4)   Don't take part in analyzing other players' games and, in particular, don't demonstrate the depth of your opening knowledge when giving advice to your team mates. The delegation has appointed special coaches for opening prep against the other teams, but the depth of your opening knowledge will be best appreciated by your own coaches who have stayed at home. Garry told me that he acted with care here, too.

5)   Don't be surprised if, the greater the gap in points versus the chasing teams grows, the leadership takes increasingly strange decisions, in particular, about who will play which matches. Karpov's people, who head the delegation, won't hesitate to use any chance available to erode the nerves of a dangerous challenger. Therefore, you should act calmly and smile throughout. Above all, you should say nothing... The effect will be powerful! Garry told me upon his return that this is exactly what happened, even the effect...

Not only have Karpov and Kasparov long been listed next to each other in the rating lists, but they have neighbored each other on the Olympiad team sheets, too. Well, the two players tried to keep up with one another during that tournament, and their personal rivalry benefited the team. The joke went round that the Soviet chess ship now possessed a powerful "*KarKas*" (a word used to mean the hull of a ship in Russian).

It was only at the end of the Olympiad, once victory of the Soviet grandmasters had been assured, that Karpov committed an error in suddenly refusing to play against Switzerland, as had been originally planned. In doing so he really did leave Kasparov in a tricky situation, who now had just a few hours to plan how he would take on Korchnoi with black. Even though this was Kasparov's eighth game in a row without a break, his duel with Korchnoi would go down in history as one of the most exciting games ever seen at an Olympiad. When the excited winner relayed the moves to me in Moscow I was spellbound by the events that had taken place on the board, and then I spent ages with my own chess pieces trying to figure out what had happened. Garry flew back and we met up with Botvinnik, exchanging our impressions and evaluations, but some hidden force seemed to mix up the new chains of moves in our heads and forced us to return time and again to that battle.

Karpov's miscalculation cost him a prestigious prize that he had been used to winning year after year. The effect exercised on the chess world by the lad's astounding win was so powerful that global chess journalists awarded the Oscar for 1982 to the youngest ever winner in its history. The vote, held two months later, assigned Garry 1,021 points, which was 78 ahead of the world champion.

The draw for the candidates matches was held during the Olympiad's closing ceremony. It was conducted by the FIDE President in quite an overelaborate manner, from which the dumbstruck GMs could clearly see how one group of four candidates contained the most ambitious and, probably, the strongest among them, while the other four consisted of players whose ambitions could hardly have extended beyond the semi-finals. So Garry's first opponent on the narrow candidates path was the young, ambitious and well trained Alexander Beliavsky (February to March 1983).

Adaption to the specifics of short candidates matches promised to be as tough a challenge as any. The fact that Garry's opponent was a newbie to the candidates stage was a further disadvantage. We had our own problems to resolve. Kasparov's first candidates match was his first official match in his life. We needed to study everything that had been written about such competitions in order to grasp how important the role of psychological preparation was in them and how to distribute energy so that it would last the entire candidates cycle. Long conversations with ex-world champions who willingly shared their rich experience helped us profoundly.

We were warned that the first candidates match would be particularly tough for the debutant as he would quickly need to get used to the empty stage and the monotony of playing the same opponent over and over. We were especially struck by the warning that the peak time when expending strength and nervous energy would be during the second, semi-final match. By the time of the candidates final we would have already built up enough experience of match play for it to run automatically. Strange as they may have sounded, these observations by the chess matadors proved to be a prophesy for Garry and helped significantly in our battles.

Knowing that Beliavsky attached particular importance to the opening, we decided to prepare a surprise for him. Vladimirov and I spent half a year analyzing the subtleties of the Tarrasch Defense to death. We decided that the isolani in the center, which ensured good places for the black pieces, would prompt Garry to play as actively as possible, thereby fully exploiting his playing strengths. At first, Garry was unimpressed with our initiative, but we convinced him by demonstrating refutations to the unflattering evaluations of this classical opening contained in the textbooks. Eventually, his eyes began to sparkle at the notion and he joined in with our investigations, contributing a number of interesting ideas.

Garry certainly didn't expect an opening setup so criticized by theory to bring him such a large number of victories and to essentially solve the problem of the black pieces in all matches of the candidates cycle. During those two years (1983-84) Kasparov deployed the Tarrasch in twelve games in official tournaments and matches, and on no occasion did he obtain a worse or unpromising position, no matter how well prepared or strong his opponents were. Time and again, the grandmasters playing white would attempt to exploit the weakness of the d5 pawn and miss the turning point when they should have started to think about how to equalize. He scored six wins and six draws – a fantastic 75%! Such a result would have been impressive for an aggressive white opening, yet he'd achieved it as black in a classical defense to the Queen's Gambit! However, time was to confirm that Kasparov didn't like openings "imposed" on him. The fact that the idea of deploying the Tarrasch didn't come from him made this somewhat a "Cinderella" of an opening in his repertoire – a poor cousin deprived of trust and affection. The two defeats that Garry recorded at the start of his first match with Karpov, in games that began with the Tarrasch but which were actually lost in the middlegame while the opening wasn't responsible, conclusively turned him away from that defense.

The effect from the first application of our secret weapon, in the second match game against Beliavsky, exceeded all expectations. Our opponent was shaken up badly and lost without making any fist of the game. However, Garry lost his next game as black after deciding to change openings... when in the lift taking him down to the playing hall. It was a curious feature of his thought process that prompted that decision.

It would be about an hour before the game was due to begin, after he had eaten lunch and was putting on his evening suit, that opening variations would incessantly spin in his head and completely unexpected ideas would occur to him. I termed this intensification of his thought process "unfortunate insight". It was then that he would find slip-ups, most often than not imaginary, in our analytical work. This would last about half an hour and was an unpleasant trial for his coaches' nervous systems. Without looking at a board, none of us was capable of maintaining a meaningful argument with a supergrandmaster, as the speed of the computer in his head was incomparable to our arithmometers. Usually, we would wait silently for him to leave for the game, and then about an hour later, after calmly moving the pieces around the board, we would find the necessary counter arguments, though by then it was too late...

What happened was that just before we left for the fourth game against Beliavsky he suddenly asked a question and, not getting a concrete answer immediately, flew into a temper and claimed that his coaches had again(!) left him without an opening, having foisted a faulty defense on him. Actually, he came fine out of his improvised opening, but, as he couldn't get his anger at his evil coaches out of his head, he lost the ability to think calmly and failed to accurately assess the resultant complications, taking fright at phantom threats and falling under attack. He steered his next game as black to a draw with ease, deploying that very same Tarrasch Defense.

Although the match ended with a victory for Kasparov with several games to spare (6:3), our coaching team was diminished by serious losses. The young and hard-working Chekhov, who had briefly joined our team for the candidates' cycle, would have been very useful on our subsequent journey, and at this match we had a chance to get to know each other better. Valery found it tough to bear the nervous, negative tension that pierced relations between the coaches and a player even during a successful battle, and he desired to play a role no more. Moreover, he was "unexpectedly" invited to join the army sports club of which Karpov was also a member, plus he was offered well paid work abroad. We had no ace to trump that offer. Playing in German tourneys, Chekhov soon gained the grandmaster title.

Another loss occurred when the great sports psychologist Rudolf Zagainov turned away from Garry. This was somebody with solid experience of top-level chess matches, and at a critical moment, with the score at 2:2 and an upset Garry having taken a time-out, I asked Rudolf to visit us. He turned up bearing a placard with the then unknown slogan "If not you, then who?" We hung the placard in Garry's bedroom so that those words were the first thing he saw when he woke up. The same slogan was to glare into his eyes during the first two matches against Karpov. During that tough period in the first match none other than the legendary pop-star Alla Pugacheva wrote her sprawling autograph on that same placard. It now hangs in my home as a relic of times past. Zagainov had managed to get Garry, at the time a bag of nerves, to listen to him and the three of us spent an entire day among stars of Soviet figure skating. The candidate's mental tranquility was restored and Garry confidently won game five. The experienced psychologist realized the reason for the tension in our team and made a series of critical comments to Klara Kasparova about her approach to "leadership" and her son's attitude to those around him. By then, Garry had built up a decent lead, and the Kasparovs didn't want to go back over the recent crisis and circumstances connected with it. For many years after I retained the warmest of relations with Zagainov and was delighted at any opportunity to work alongside him. He's a true, top-level professional psychologist.[1]

After a short break, we began to prepare for a much more serious test. A couple of months later Garry was supposed to play Korchnoi, although we were unaware that this match was being actively managed by a group of people from the Sports Committee. Headed by the Minister of Sport Marat Gramov, they were responsible for arranging a scenario written out by the Party Central Committee and the KGB.

This was the first time that we had experienced the Sports Committee's involvement behind the scenes of a match, and it turned us cold. The goal of the quite unchess-like maneuver that they had initiated was to break off the match, and in such a way that only one participant would appear to be guilty and, hence, get punished – Garry, the world champion's most dangerous opponent. Azeri and "other" party leaders of course noticed the start of these strange goings-on, but they had their own problems in their relations with the Moscow bosses, and so they decided to remain on the sidelines for the present.

The crafty politician Florencio Campomanes immediately grasped what this was all about. Being a longstanding friend of Karpov, the FIDE president also got involved and became a noticeable figure in our show, although he was really only a stooge. And while he knew what role he was supposed to play, he really needed some incident that would increase his popularity. Now a coming scandal was inevitable, and it promised to burst onto the pages of the world's biggest newspapers.

---

[1] Born in 1940, Zagainov died in 2014 (publisher's note)

Events kicked off with the State Sports Committee sending Garry a list of cities which had agreed to hold the match. Garry was recommended to mark Las Palmas as his first choice, with Rotterdam second. By that time it was already common knowledge that Korchnoi had selected only Rotterdam. Had Garry named the Dutch city first, which, by the way, is exactly what he would have liked to do, the problem would have disappeared. However, the Moscow bosses persuaded him ("for political reasons"!) to select the Spanish city as his preferred choice. "In any event, Rotterdam will be in both lists and the issue will be thus solved," they assured him. However, they were lying and setting a trap. They knew that once the list reached the FIDE president, the next act in the show would begin – Campo would instead select Pasadena, the third bidding city, which had been rejected by both players, on the grounds that these "idiot players" were unable to agree on anything. Garry, surprised but calm, accepted this decision, too. Why not play in America? Oh, how naive we were!

After Korchnoi agreed to play in Pasadena ten or so days later, the invisible authors of the show opened a new page in their drama. Moscow dispatched a refusal by the Soviet Chess Federation to send Kasparov to Pasadena on the grounds that it was impossible to assure his safety there! Our press, obeying a whispered order, took to criticizing the FIDE president and wrote out in detail the dangers facing Kasparov. The fact that at that very time star Soviet swimmers, led by the brilliant Vladimir Salnikov, had already been in California for the last week, and nobody had kidnapped or murdered them, deserved no mention.

Now, to complete the mission, the Soviets had to officially have an argument with Campomanes in front of witnesses and thereby cut off any path to a compromise. To this end, the FIDE president was invited to Moscow, where the final act in the show was put on in the presence of all interested parties. This time, the authors of the drama appeared on stage, one of which was a KGB general. The FIDE president was set conditions for starting the match which probably only the president of the United States was capable of arranging. Campo was already aware of these conditions and rejected them, but only after he had flown back from Moscow. So that was it – the bridges were burnt and the show had ended. Garry Kasparov was left scratching his head in disbelief at the suddenly emptied negotiating table.

Several days later, the FIDE president announced that Kasparov was disqualified for failing to turn up at the match and thereby knocked out of the cycle. The shaking candidate went to see the senior party leader Stukalin, who just a few days earlier had assured the lad that nobody would cause him any grief. Garry now heard what was effectively a sentence: "You're still young, you can wait another three years." It was only then it dawned on him that he had been tricked like a child.

Like in fairy tales, Garry was left with one final chance – to ask Aliev, one of the five most powerful officials in the country, for help. I don't know what the latter did, what he said or to whom, but those bosses who were so fervently cutting Garry down changed their opinion in an instant and in a panic did all they could to cancel Kasparov's disqualification. The wily Campo realized that his hapless partners in this operation had found themselves in a ridiculous situation, and, in order to save his fellow plotters from punishment, agreed to a compromise, albeit not without decent financial compensation for himself. Mutual accusations, appeals to the public and public petitions – all of these levers were used to their fullest in the USSR with one aim: to maneuver the embarrassed authors of this drama out of their important jobs. Their job descriptions didn't allow them to make mistakes, and even less so to admit them.

While our chess federation waged its pretend battle with the FIDE president to restore Kasparov's place in the candidates final, the latter found time to play in a major tourney in Yugoslavia. His unplanned participation brought joy to the organizers and fans alike, but not to the other players. The candidate, anxious to demonstrate what he was capable of, unleashed the full might of his prep for the semi-final match on his grandmaster opponents in Niksic. At our brief training session in Moscow we had marked out the range of openings that he should show in Niksic, and, most importantly of all, Garry agreed to play all the games to the very end, as his future opponent Korchnoi was prone to do, in other words to continue to play for as long as the slightest possibility of maintaining the struggle remained on the board. As a proper professional, he needed to get used to fighting on in boring, technical positions, rather than offering a draw as he did previously. He consented, but I think he was secretly sure that no such games would occur at that tournament. Yet in the very first round, the effort by Yasser Seirawan to simplify led to an equal pawn endgame which Garry played until the end and managed to win! He then won another game against Petrosian, in a subtle positional style. It was already clear who was going to win the tournament by the end of round four, when Garry tore the experienced Lajos Portisch apart. His great performance of 11 points out of 14 together with his unusually strong play added powerful weight to the view that the candidates cycle would be quite damaged were Kasparov to be excluded from it thanks to skullduggery.

By the way, Karpov's protectors did their charge a disfavor here too. After that tournament, the ratings of the two Ks finally equalized, albeit not for long. Garry soon permanently surpassed his rival.

When the tournament ended, Viktor Korchnoi also showed up in the tournament hall and took part in a double-round robin grandmasters blitz tournament. Kasparov was unstoppable here, too. With a score of 13.5 out of 16, he was three points ahead of second-placed Korchnoi, whom he defeated in both head-to-heads. However, far more important for Garry and Viktor were the negotiations they were to hold on the match conditions. Both fighters, passionate about the game, were anxious to get on with it and were perfectly aware of the underlying cause of all these events. Therefore, their discussions were short and fruitful. As a result, the Soviet Chess Federation lifted the embarrassing, seven-year old boycott of Korchnoi by our players and even agreed to pay him a sizeable dollar-denominated fine. The chess federation never had either power or money, so it was of course the Sports Committee that paid out. Yet none of the functionaries taking part in this show that had ultimately so dishonored them was punished for it.

For the first time ever, Garry was accompanied abroad by a person whose role was to support the young candidate. However, this was neither a professional coach, nor his "chief coach", as he called his mother, but KGB Colonel Viktor Litvinov, who from then on would accompany him and his mother on all foreign travels. This was Aliev's doing – he had risen to the crest of power after a KGB career. Against the background of the slow but sure disintegration of our society that was already underway by then, the KGB was the only civilian (on outward appearances!) structure where guidelines were replaced by orders that had to be followed. This organization was more powerful and agile in Azerbaijan than anywhere else. And indeed, all organizational matters concerning Kasparov's life and career got to be resolved in Baku in a minimum of time and without obstruction. The Kasparovs felt real and powerful support. Himself a former sportsman, Litvinov never interfered in our professional matters, and never attempted to give us orders. He was soothing and very friendly, never boasting about being a member of our team, let alone its unofficial head. The last match he accompanied us to was Seville in 1987, but upon his return he was sent to the Armenia-Azerbaijan war zone. He helped Garry to evacuate from Baku in 1990 with the minimum of losses, but from then on Garry travelled without him. For Kasparov, he turned out to be a truly kind genius.

Don't think, of course, that the KGB only watched over Kasparov. Karpov enjoyed just as much protection, going back to when he was a candidate. Since 1975, he had been accompanied like a shadow on all his foreign trips by Vladimir Pishchenko, whose rank was no lower than Litvinov's.

Today we are able to attack the KGB. However, far from all of that organization's staff were bad people. Some KGB agents whom we encountered were perfectly friendly and skillful, possessing a greater intellect than that of the sports functionaries, who would often find themselves shunted to sport after failing in a Party or Komsomol role, and who could not be relied upon to tell the truth. All of the country's leading chess players and coaches would have held conversations with the KGB, indeed, all those playing a noticeable role in the chess community and who might be sent abroad. I'm sure some people enjoyed the attention. That's a matter for them and their conscience. There was nothing surprising in the KGB's attempt to control everything the chess stars did. Members of that organization were (and I've no doubt still are) to be found in all the sports federations. Sport, as part of our culture, was meant to showcase abroad the success of our type of society, and so somebody had to ensure that our sportsmen behaved abroad appropriately and said all the right things. The pre-screening of people allowed to travel abroad and the presence of KGB staff in all travelling delegations helped to hide the boorish behavior ingrained in our culture. For many years we portrayed a heavily embellished image of our life and only sent people to other countries who stood out from the average, "homo-Sovieticus" masses. Yeah, we didn't show the West the shitty side of our lives. Now that restrictions on travel abroad have been lifted a huge number of Soviet people have crossed the border, and it's turned out that many of them don't follow social norms that are generally accepted throughout the world, and they have no self-respect or sympathy for their homeland, which is suffering so badly.

Finally, the start date of the candidates semi-finals was agreed, and that they were to be held in London. The second semi, between Smyslov and Ribli, was viewed from the very beginning as an appendage to the first, as it was clear that neither of these grandmasters had any chance of winning against the victor of the main semi-final.

Garry's stunning success in Niksic together with his victory in the behind-the-scenes battle over the match also had a negative side. A month before the match began, the candidate's nerves were already worn out, while the waves of delight that had risen in Azerbaijan eroded any remaining objective chance of self-evaluation. It became impossible to convince him of anything – I was not one of the "respected" persons with whom he had got used to socializing in recent months.

He flew to London, as I saw it, with the aim of wrapping up just another match win as quickly as possible and tasting another portion of glory and eulogies. Success is also a form of stress, and you need to learn how to cope with it. However, Garry was now surrounded by people who endlessly high-fived with him. He was unable to slow down and encouraged himself with the belief in his immense superiority over his opponent. Such a psychological state is vulnerable to a situation where if the person suddenly experiences a recognition of reality, it doesn't last long enough to incite a sharp re-evaluation of one's opponent's potential and strength. Such a thought only occurred to Garry a few hours before the match began, when he suddenly figured out that it would still be some time before the winner would be announced – he had a whole match to play and victory was anything but a foregone conclusion. Garry swooped back down to planet Earth in an instant, and his tiny, almost imperceptible opponent transformed into a mythical titan, devoid of weaknesses. The lad finally grabbed the protection of his coaches, hoping to hear assurances that his anxiety was in vain and that he was sure to win. Yet for some reason the latter were calm – "Of course, it's not them who have to play the match!" – and they stubbornly knocked it into his head that he had to stop talking nonsense and start to work, and that would deliver a victory as he was objectively stronger. The Azeri, and not the coaching half of our team, having noticed the change in his mood, piped down and attempted to avoid being noticed by their young chief. Klara, meanwhile, was stirred no less than her son, while Litvinov and the team doctor rushed around incessantly, trying to calm down the key players.

It's not for nothing that I invoked the term "team". Yes, first three and then four professional chess coaches accompanied Kasparov to his matches, as well as a translator and a doctor who was responsible for the fitness of all other team members. Coordination of this team was formally the responsibility of both the official delegation head, Azer Zeynally, whose functions were mostly symbolic, and the effective delegation head, Litvinov, whose decision was final on any matter that did not require chess expertise. Klara Kasparova also tried to take charge of all matters, which sometimes caused unwanted tension, especially during her interaction with the coaches or during her attempts to find a psychologist, which the team lacked at the time. Kasparov's psychological preparation was our team's Achilles' heel. Gasanov, who had been Garry's doctor for over ten years and who was also part of our delegation, was also capable of acting as Garry's psychologist, but only in Baku, in a peaceful environment.

There was nothing original in putting together such a team of specialists. Karpov's teams since 1975 sometimes reached 25-30 people, as had been the case in Baguio City in 1978, and his team never counted fewer than ten members. All sorts of organizations were engaged in financing this huge machine, which functioned all-year round, whether or not a match was upcoming.

We didn't manage to restore Kasparov's calm by the start of the first game, and he messed that duel up. Above all, it was his thought process that was disturbed – he had lost both discipline in calculating variations and the ability to carry out a plan. After he rightly lost that opening game, the following four resembled each other in the lad's nervy and uninspiring play. We coaches got quite down when, after the third game, Klara, a bag of nerves, uttered that it could make sense to resign the entire match. We didn't see any reason to panic, as there was no sign of any dominance by Korchnoi in the games played. However, with both mother and son in such a fragile mental state we could only continue to do our work and wait for a change.

Well, it was actually Korchnoi who pulled us out of this mess. He saw perfectly well that Garry was playing without confidence and going awry, and, soberly assessing his energy reserves, decided to go for all-out warfare at the match's half-way stage. In game six, exploiting his opponent's indecision, he managed to grab the initiative. Just as the threat of a second loss became a reality, Garry's instinct for self-preservation forced him to take evasive action, and as he approached the adjournment he had not only liquidated the danger, but also gained chances of winning. Another mistake by our charge, this time perhaps from exuberance, meant that the game was adjourned in a double-edged position. However, we weren't too disappointed by that, as we noticed a miraculous transformation in Garry's state of mind. The fact that he had not only wriggled out of an impending disaster, but had also managed to outplay his opponent for the first time in the match, changed the lad beyond recognition in an instant. It was as though his previous strength and confidence had returned by magic. During our analysis, he once again showered out variations and provided deep assessments of the positions on the board.

From the adjourned position, Korchnoi could have simply brought the game to a draw had he wanted to. However, having studied his way of playing matches, we correctly guessed that Viktor would take a risk and first attempt to try his luck with some unexpected line – so it was the unexpected lines that we analyzed the most thoroughly. Indeed, Korchnoi immediately steered away from the obvious path at the resumption and headed for a double-edged ending – but one that we had analyzed deeply. Garry played confidently and outplayed his opponent for the second time in the game. This time, he didn't let victory slip from his grip. Despite such a sharp turn in the match Korchnoi didn't take a time out, and without having calmed down he sat down at the board just 20 hours later for the next game. That was a fatal mistake. Garry successfully deployed the Catalan Opening and managed to achieve a second consecutive victory in game seven, this time thanks to subtle positional play.

By then, we had introduced a special strategic weapon that our creative team had developed – playing the same opening for both colors, starting in the drawn game five. I discuss the purpose of this ploy, the so-called "cross-fire", in my notes to game No. 25.

The next day, Kasparov played out another Catalan with black and achieved an easy draw, but then again played the same opening in game nine with the colors reversed and pulled off a confident victory. Such a Catalan "inquisition" could have broken any warrior, not only Korchnoi. The fight in the match was now over.

When the score was still 2:3 our sporting bosses consulted with Petrosian on whether to strengthen the team of seconds. Ultimately, I don't know what prevented the appearance of an unwanted guest. Most probably, nobody wanted to take responsibility for a case whose happy ending seemed to many people to be quite unlikely. We, though, had only one request – that they didn't interfere with our work! The seconds were planning a turning point in the match with daily intensive work, constantly trying to bring their charge into fighting shape. I believe that the new creative chess team withstood its baptism of fire honorably, despite serious obstacles. The team was sent home straight after the match, while the winner and his mother remained in London to reap the laurels and go sightseeing. Well, we all have our likes and dislikes.

Victory in the London match brought Kasparov to the final of the candidates cycle. The world champion showed his nerves and bitterly hastened to declare Korchnoi a "spent force" and "a king with no clothes", conveniently forgetting that just two years earlier he had demanded that the country's sports leadership mobilize the best chess minds of the USSR to help him take on this "king with no clothes" who was in poor form at the time.

As though a reward for the pains that we had endured, the candidates final was the easiest and most enjoyable match in the cycle for Garry. Both he and, all the more so, the wise 63-year-old Vasily Vasilievich Smyslov were aware that only one outcome was possible from their match. Karpov also realized this, even correctly predicting the score before the match. Yet all foretellers were outdone by a Kievan club player who sent a letter to Klara Kasparova before the start in which he correctly predicted the outcome of each of the thirteen(!) games. At first we coaches laughed as we observed coincidence after coincidence, but we stopped laughing after game 11 in which Garry failed to mate his opponent's king and complained that he was unlucky, whereupon his mother showed him the letter.[2]

---

[2] According to Kasparov's book *Garry Kasparov on Garry Kasparov: Part I,* Garry was shown the letter before the match began and the letter was sent by a "prominent arbiter" called Leonid Ostrovsky (publisher's note)

The Lithuanian organizers of the match attempted to turn the clash between the grandmasters into a grand celebration of chess, and in this they succeeded. The finalists enjoyed a great time and played a number of wonderful games. The team of seconds also functioned like clockwork, and we tried to forget about how we had faced interference in London. Moreover, Garry's victory led us to completely forget all the affronts delivered to us and our thoughts of withdrawal – as seconds we really wanted to test our abilities in the big match. We now faced carrying out a completely new project. Those who had been there told us that this work would be incomparably tougher than anything we had yet experienced – and this encouraged us on.

From our match in Vilnius I still recall the unusual hospitality of the organizers, the touching respect that the two players had for each other, and attending concerts by Alla Pugacheva. The players and seconds stayed at the same hotel, but this didn't cause any inconveniences. On the contrary, on Smyslov's 63rd birthday Garry sent him a card that morning with a message that he was specially taking a time-out to mark the occasion and invited the Smyslov couple to the opera. Moreover, Garry's 21st birthday came just as the match ended and was close to Alla Pugacheva's (15 April), who was still performing in Vilnius at the time. The pop star cancelled her concert that evening and instead showed up at our hotel with some friends. We held a fantastic party – a sea of flowers, singing and laughter. During our first match against Karpov, Pugacheva was a faithful supporter of Garry.

I also remember Vilnius because that is where we improved our play as black in the Tarrasch. The players fought a true theoretical duel in this opening. The ex-world champion had specially prepared a major opening novelty which initially frightened Garry, who again accused us of foisting a faulty opening on him, which really offended Vladimirov and me. We soon found a worthy response to Smyslov's interesting idea, and during the final three games as black Garry tested the quality of the emergency work of his aides. Two draws and one victory were a decent return on our efforts in an argument with such a revered chess theoretician as Smyslov.

We were sad to leave such a wonderful city. The spring sun shined brightly, locals smiled around us, but our thoughts had already turned to Moscow in autumn and the upcoming big match.

Chapter 2. Disaster Canceled (Match 1, 1984-1985)

Garry and his mother spent around a month in a state of euphoria after the candidates final ended, whereas as soon as I returned from Vilnius I began to think about the process of preparing for the title match.

For me, this was a match of life or death. Many years had passed since Karpov and I parted ways. I had now found my true calling as a professional coach and time could well have healed the wounds. However, certain manifestations of the champion's character, certain actions that he took, led me to think of nothing but the upcoming battle. The Karpov of those years was for me a symbol of the injustice imposed in our country by the communist regime. So my wish to help Garry overthrow the world champion was not only a desire to keep my promise of years earlier, but also a quiet protest against our society's way of operating.

I was not naturally vengeful. Normally, I would wipe people who had caused me damage from my memory. Karpov, though, was an exception, as for me he was a symbol of the system that had destroyed the country. Having gained the title of world champion in 1975 he had made smart use of possessing the title. Immediately accepting the rules of the game prevalent in the Party's upper echelons, Karpov gained strong support from the country's leaders. He became a true national champion, "proving" with his results the superiority of our political system. There is no doubt that he had no equal over the chess board in those days and he was a formidable world champion. Seeing this, the country's leadership did all they could to ensure him a long stay on the throne, and to make any challenge to his pre-eminence dangerous and pointless.

Our preparation for the match was huge in volume and incredibly meticulous. Everything that we had put together during the candidates cycle was just a small part of the immense building that we needed to raise in the few remaining months. All ex-world champions gladly gave me detailed advice, which meant that we didn't miss any important points in our preparation. However, we had to carry out the main work ourselves. Only Tigran Petrosian agreed to take part directly in our preparation: "Health permitting," he added. Unfortunately, his health didn't permit. He managed to meet me and Garry only a couple of times before his terminal illness took hold of him.

His death in 1984 was also a huge blow to me, because it left me to hold the lessons in the by now famous Spartak school by myself. Tigran's memory forced me to carve out time to hold the next school sessions even when it seemed that I could not possibly have any free time during the endless stream of matches. I am proud that the Petrosian school regularly trained kids who came from all over our vast country. Even those kids who never made it big in chess retained a love for our wise game and remembered our school fondly.

When we began preparation for the match, Kasparov's team contained four coaches: Timoshchenko, Vladimirov, Shakarov and me. Lvov grandmaster Iosif Dorfman joined us before the match began. Our forces were clearly insufficient to carry out the full volume of work that we had planned in the few months left, but nobody else was available – other potential seconds were afraid of incurring the wrath of the reigning champion and his backers.

At the same time, the list of grandmasters and coaches involved in aiding Karpov was a veritable nightmare: grandmasters Vaganian, Geller, Zaitsev, Polugaevsky, Balashov, Tamaz Georgadze, Lerner, Mikhalchishin, Makarychev. The list of masters began with the highly experienced Podgaets and Kharitonov, followed by young masters serving in the so-called sporting squadron and carrying out heavy lifting such as choosing Kasparov's games or putting together game selections in the opening repertoire that Karpov planned for the match. This monster-sized preparation was financed by the state, Moscow and army sports committees, as well as the Komsomol leadership, which provided a country house to their favorite at a resort in Latvia.

Our most important work during our preparation involved drawing up creative and sporting portraits of both players that were as detailed as possible. This was to devise an effective match strategy taking into account each player's strengths and weaknesses. The second most important part of our prep was to improve his opening repertoire, a task with which we were all familiar. In our case, this challenge was particularly complicated as we needed to create a repertoire that would withstand critical attacks from the country's best chess analysts and which would still be useable during an unusually long match.

We had so much work to do that I turned down a trip to London to the USSR versus Rest of the World match. There, Kasparov was "helped" by Litvinov, who was proud of the fact that while in his presence the future rivals walked about together, thereby delighting the journalists and photographers. However, I wasn't interested in delighting anybody – the smart Karpov was simply twisting both men from Baku around his fingers. As he soon admitted to his friends, he extracted a lot of useful information from chatting to the naive lad at close quarters which would come in useful in devising his own match strategy.

Meanwhile, in Azerbaijan the local KGB made a real effort and our prep was hidden from outside and overly curious eyes, while we worked in fantastic conditions. We worked extremely hard, and only took breaks when our brains ceased to function. Eight hours of mental work per day comprised a perfectly normal workload, and we withstood such a tough regime thanks to intensive physical exercise, including swimming, football and running barefoot along the sandy beach. In inviting the Hungarian grandmaster Andras Adorjan to our final training session, Garry decided to repeat Karpov's experiment with involving a foreigner in the coaching team. I don't know how useful Uhlmann proved to be in Karpov's prep in his matches against Korchnoi, but Adorjan's genuine desire to help Garry wasn't matched by the use he brought. All he managed to do was to convince the challenger that black had a strong position in the Keres Attack, and Garry successfully applied his recommendation in the first game of the match but subsequently forgot about this opening variation, worried about certain features. Adorjan didn't want to persuade the challenger, and from then on nearly all of his advice was rejected. He found our work methods and regime to be unusual and tough, and the role of an ordinary member of the coaching team was burdensome for him. Neither could he get used to the friction in Garry's relations with his coaches, especially during the match. Further, his character, demanding tactful treatment of each other at all times, was also unsuited for this atmosphere, especially when we were under stress. He frequently and justifiably took offense at times when we coaches, united by a common cause, put up with everything, clenched our teeth and said nothing.

It was probably only Kasparov's physical preparation that we honed to perfection, yet this proved decisive at the end of the match. We had thought that our chess prep was good enough, too, but the match demonstrated that we were wrong. The real failure was in psychological preparation, but the coaches weren't particularly responsible for that. Garry proved to be quite unprepared for a long and heavy battle. All the excitement generated in Azerbaijan around his name reached a peak just before we left for Moscow. His and his mother's constant interaction with "highly respected" people in the republic had made the Kasparovs in their own eyes remarkable personas, and it was a huge honor for ordinary mortals to get to meet them. Klara, who had really been pushed aside by the coaching team by the start of the match but who enjoyed the confidence of the republic's leadership, fought us desperately to maintain influence over her son, and in so doing made our job far more difficult. She rejected the notion that everybody should do their own job, given that the republic's leadership, not trusting the coaches as we were outsiders, demanded that she be informed on all matters, even coaching ones. We were powerless to do anything about it, as we knew that the ultimate reason for her sometimes inexplicable actions was her fierce motherly love for her son and her striving to protect him at any price from looming woes. It was unfortunate for us that she was massively conceited and believed that only she knew how to avoid such woes. Nobody was to be found in Azerbaijan capable of convincing her to step back or at least to get involved only in matters which she grasped properly. While those who had at least some influence over her simply used it to achieve their own goals.

The discord in our team began to grow as soon as the match started. The coaches were categorically opposed to Garry carrying out the usual post-mortem with Karpov after each game ended. And although our view was supported by all the ex-world champions consulted, the Kasparovs wouldn't listen to us. During those "chats" on the stage of the Hall of Columns Karpov reaped a huge amount of information about defects in the young challenger's way of thinking, while giving away nothing in return. The coaches could laugh, show their disgust, demand he stopped – but it was all in vain. Photos in the newspapers showing how Garry could simply natter away with the world champion had an irresistible impact on these proud people from the south. "I didn't want to appear impolite," Garry would say later, trying to justify himself. It was an unpleasant surprise for Karpov when Garry revised his original concept of politeness in the next match and ended these post-mortems. Anatoly's source of valuable information had dried up.

I was also totally against holding the entire match in the Hall of Columns. With its huge, glistening chandeliers, the hall was perfect for staging balls, concerts, formal receptions and the funerals of great leaders. It would have been worth following the experience of the 1974 Karpov versus Korchnoi match and holding the first couple of games or so there, after which the rest would have been played in more modest premises that were conducive to hard, daily work. However, my opinion as the first second was pooh-poohed by the Kasparovs – they wanted to make history in this highly prestigious government events hall.

Well, to say they were making history there was an understatement. After nine games Garry was being crushed with the score at 0:4. Given that, according to the rules, the champion would be the first to win six games with draws not counting, the battle for the throne risked turning into one huge embarrassment. The truth of the matter was that the world champion only had a vague role in creating this huge points gap.

Kasparov's troubles began in game three, when, after he had only managed to salvage a draw in game two despite having been on the verge of winning it, he decided to deploy an opening novelty of his own which only he had effectively analyzed. No, he didn't fear that his enemies would outsmart him. For some time by then, Garry had started to demonstrate incredible vanity, and he considered anything his mind came up with in terms of new ideas to be brilliant. Any objection we raised would be met by a nervy and sometimes angry defensive reaction. Therefore, when analyzing with Garry, we coaches usually preferred to adopt a role of tight-lipped, bit-part actors.

Karpov quickly detected a defect in Kasparov's plan and won the game with ease. Suddenly, the fun event to which the challenger had arrived was over. He lost heart and troubles piled on top of one another. In his first three white games, Garry enjoyed a large and sometimes decisive advantage, yet he was unable to play any of those positions at a grandmaster level and managed only two draws from them.

In game seven, Karpov started with 1.d4 for the first time in the match. This was no surprise as such, but our meeting to choose Garry's opening had been a languid one. With the situation already difficult (Karpov had by now won two games, including the last one), none of the grandmasters present wanted to appear insistent and impose their view on Garry. I on the other hand managed to convince the despondent lad to deploy his elite battalion in the match – the Tarrasch – which had so far not betrayed him. Well, the opening fulfilled its purpose this time, too, bringing him equality. However, an inexplicable mistake just before time control, when Garry was not in any time trouble but suffering from despondency, delivered his third defeat.

I then had to make a massive effort to convince Garry to employ the same opening in game nine. Although Karpov had prepared perfectly for the game, that was only sufficient for him to gain a microscopic advantage, which he only just managed to preserve by adjournment. The adjourned position was viewed by everybody as a draw, but Garry's sealed move was a poor one and black now faced unexpected difficulties.

We coaches searched for a draw all night, but we were unable to find either a clear path to a draw or a clear path to a win for Karpov. At this critical point in the match we lacked a cool-headed leader for such brain storming. Our analysis was unusually nervy, disorganized and hence of little effect. Garry left for the second session in an angry state of mind and played very weakly that evening. He missed his last opportunity for a draw about five moves before he resigned.

The young challenger had to pay the penalty of four defeats for his conceit, and definitely not for his lack of experience of top-level play. When Fischer played the still very strong Boris Spassky in 1972, such a lack of experience didn't prevent him from capturing the throne from our grandmaster. The boasts that Garry had made before the match in interviews and during "important" meetings had come back and squashed him into the ground after his first failure, leaving him devoid him of confidence. At the time, nobody thought of allowing the disappointed and psychologically broken challenger any unplanned rest days, yet he needed a break like oxygen.

Garry now talks about a decision that he took in this situation to hold on at any price. But actually he was so crushed psychologically that he was incapable of taking any such decisions. SOS signs were dispatched from the apartments in the Hotel Rossia where the Kasparovs were staying. In response, as it later transpired, the Azeri leadership sent their court psychic Tofik Dadashev, who had long worked for the KGB. It was his job to instill confidence in Garry... by predicting the results of each game for him. The Kasparovs said nothing about his forecasts to the coaches. It was only several years later that Dadashev publicly acknowledged his involvement in the match and claimed that all of his predictions were correct. Well, we can only admire his unusual talent and regret that we didn't learn any of his forecasts in advance. Had they really existed then the work of the coaches would have been superfluous. Whereas each of us could have competed with this "specialist" from Baku in foreseeing events that had already taken place.

The coaches, meanwhile, quite understood the reasons for the tragedy taking place before their very eyes. The obvious disparity between the score and the players' ability forced us to seek ways to save the match. We advised Garry to switch to a method of cynically "preparing" quick draws with either color, in order to try and hold on for a week or two and restore his mental well-being in that time. There was no other way. We had to exclude from his repertoire all aggressive or insufficiently safe opening setups (including the Tarrasch), replacing them with systems that took the sting out of the game and which we had prepared earlier "just in case". In a few days we managed to polish a couple of super-reliable systems, which Garry then started to deploy in each game. Even though we worked like dogs, our idea would probably not have worked. Yet Garry was saved, not by Dadashev, but by... his opponent.

Karpov's preparation for the match was aimed at delivering a win with as big a score as possible – so that after the match Kasparov would not be seen as a realistic challenger for a long time to come. Much was undertaken to make this goal easier for Karpov to reach. I don't know the fine details of that plan, especially its chess part, but I was struck by the psychological war that broke out in the Hall of Columns and its foyer. Of particular note was the large number of people dressed in civilian clothing strutting around the foyer with a marked military poise, as well as the multitude of silent individuals intensely looking non-stop at the grandmasters up on stage. Then, after we had got used to these permanent residents of the hall, we were informed that numerous psychics were attending the match. In the hall we constantly felt an oppressive and tense environment, as did lots of spectators. I think that the secret service was carrying out experiments on wielding psychological influence over the crowd in the Hall of Columns and testing how to manage them.

It's known that Karpov constantly adjusted his match strategy, and now, having been handed a huge advantage on his plate by his opponent, he decided to finish Kasparov off with a 6:0 score. All he had to do was play slightly more actively, make his play more complex and dynamic, and he would gain a quick win, as the challenger, already crushed, would be incapable of solving even moderately complicated problems. However, you needed to know Karpov's character – he decided not only to win 6:0, but to achieve this result solely due to Kasparov's errors, in order to further humiliate him and make him consider himself worthless. Karpov decided to wait for Kasparov to blunder, and to wait manifestly. In this cruel game of cat and mouse, the cat would suddenly stop running after the condemned victim. This, as it turned out, was his key mistake.

Garry began to draw the games, one after another, with increasing confidence. He drew 18 in a row. In game 16 he even missed a win, but that was a chance event testifying most probably to Karpov's complacency, rather than to the resurrection of Kasparov's fighting qualities. The environment in our camp remained nervy, and when Garry was unable to calculate a rather simple winning variation, which just six months earlier would have been dead easy for him, I said right there to Klara in the Hall of Columns that if he was incapable of winning such positions, then maybe we should resign the match and go home. However, no such discussion was ever held: the Kasparovs had long since stopped listening to the seconds' opinions.

That said, the coaches did manage to beef up Garry's opening repertoire, which helped to reel off the draws (sharp-wits even made a joke in Russian about him being a "long-playing record player", given that the Russian word for "record player" was similar to the word for "loser"). Yet Garry stubbornly refused to play aggressively, as he panicked at the thought of losing another game and standing on the edge of the precipice. The psychic Dadashev then supposedly forecast that Garry would soon find himself 0:5 down. Only the coaches had no idea what was going to happen. Devoid of such psychological support, we know from experience that the fear of losing in such a situation would give rise to frustration and inevitably bring on a fifth defeat.

That defeat eventually occurred after a calm series of draws lasting a month and a half that had bored everybody senseless. Another vegan draw was on the cards in a stale position in game 27 and I'd even told our driver to go and warm up the car. However, Garry suddenly began to play with a lack of sureness, and his opponent noticed this straight away. The white pieces slowly crawled in the direction of a lonely black pawn and eventually exterminated it.

Obviously this fifth loss didn't add to the challenger's confidence, yet it miraculously relieved him of any fear of defeat. He now acquired the attitude of a person with nothing to lose and it even became easier to talk to him. We managed to convince him that with the match result considered by almost everybody to be a foregone conclusion, he should make an effort to save his honor over the board and play some games in an aggressive mood, even if only at half of his normal intensity. Not only the coaches, but Botvinnik and Tal said much the same to him. Garry listened to us conscientiously, but he was in no rush to leave his now familiar work at the drawing factory. Indeed, he still didn't have the energy to do so.

Well, Karpov again helped us, suddenly deciding at a very late stage to begin active play. His highly-place protectors had begun to get bored of this drawing standoff and had ordered the champion to take quick and decisive action.

We soon learned that the decisive storm was penciled in for game 31. Everybody had begun to talk about that day – the information leak had been deliberate, with the aim of frightening Garry and even demoralizing him. Oddly enough, though, this information only encouraged the challenger. He was glad that a tense fight towards which his coaches had been pushing him, but which he had been incapable of instigating, would now be imposed by his opponent.

The first thing that struck us as we entered into the Hall of Columns that evening was the formal attire worn by Karpov's team. There was also an unusual number of TV cameramen who had long since lost interest in this languid, drawn-out match. A hall administrator whom I knew showed me the laurel necklace hidden in a corner behind the stage that had just been delivered from Sukhumi. Garry's head would clearly not have fitted in it, but it was just the right size for his opponent's.

Karpov played the first half of the game strongly. However, once his advantage became tangible, the approach of this great and long awaited victory knocked him off-balance. The champion suddenly showed nerves, and, with a couple of energetic moves, Garry managed to drum up a strong counter attack that changed the picture of battle. Karpov was saved from a nasty outcome, and with his flag hanging, by none other than his opponent, who unexpectedly offered a draw. Although Garry was very self-critical in the hotel for his second of weakness, it was this game that liberated his thought process, similar to what happened in the match with Korchnoi. A desire to fight finally awoke in him, and he launched a fierce battle in the next game that he brought to a victorious conclusion.

His first defeat was a real shock for Karpov – his dashed dreams of a "Fischer-style" 6:0 victory gave way to self-reproach for choosing the wrong match strategy with the score at 4:0. In the next game, Kasparov's important opening novelty effectively excluded 1.d4 from the champion's opening repertoire, which had been the main source of his wins. Karpov lost heart, and seemed to abandon interest in the game. Signs of his mental tiredness and physical exhaustion shone through with increasing starkness.

A fourth month of nervous and exhausting struggle was now upon us. According to our calculations made before the match began, the champion would no longer be capable of withstanding the burden. The young challenger, on the other hand, was by now long used to this endless struggle, as though it were part of his everyday life. He hadn't forgotten his collapse at the beginning, but the stress had gone – his years of training, the care of Doctor Gasanov, his excellent health and his youth all made themselves felt. Garry was clearly in fighting spirit and the future no longer appeared so gloomy. He had already saved his honor over the board, and a thin but alluring glimmer of hope flickered on the horizon.

There was no change in the scoreline at New Year, but the initiative was firmly in the challenger's hands. In the last game of 1984 only a miracle saved the physically faltering champion from a second defeat. The players saw in the New Year with differing moods. Karpov, with his five victories, was gloomy and all at sea, as he didn't know from where to draw the strength for a final storm. His young opponent, on the other hand, who had by now fully recovered his composure, waving his single point like a baton, felt more vigorous and confident – and many people saw this. Garry didn't know when he would record his next win, but he couldn't now imagine losing a sixth and final game.

When Karpov the chess king blessed the idea of a world championship match with no maximum number of games he surely couldn't have imagined that this would not only drive himself into a trap, but also cause serious harm to chess. By the fourth month, most fans had lost interest in this extremely long-drawn sporting event. The match instead became of greater interest to cartoonists and sharp wits. The intrigue was only maintained by the sudden likelihood of the world champion's defeat, with him publicly losing confidence and strength. Each new January day was torture for him. Even non-playing days failed to soothe him, as sleeplessness and irritation didn't leave him be. He wanted this nightmare to go away and for everything to end as quickly as possible, but with the crown remaining on his head.

The challenger had preserved more strength. The crisis was over, although it occasionally reminded us of itself in his frequent changes of mood. But we coaches were long used to that. Garry became more willing to deploy new opening systems, and in three games in a row even played an opening "cross-fire" against Karpov.

The champion lost all belief that he could win after game 41, played in the middle of January. That morning, our coaching team had come to the conclusion that the opening we had planned the previous evening needed some refinement, and for the first time we suggested to Garry that he play the Petroff as black, which Karpov had himself successfully deployed previously. We had studied this cast-iron defense during the match and were convinced of its soundness. Garry, as always, pooh-poohed our proposal, but I cut short the verbal volcano that he was about to unleash and told him that come what may there would be a Petroff on the board that evening, so it would be more useful for Garry to spend time on refreshing his memory with variations rather than on kicking up a scandal.

Kasparov's opening choice was an unpleasant surprise for the champion. In a situation where he needed just one win to retain his title, he had unexpectedly been provided with a chance, moreover, his opponent had provided it especially. The price of the game was too high, and to play for a win Karpov would have to choose a continuation that he considered strongest of all for white. However, he realized that if he failed to win the game on this occasion and the match continued, then he would be deprived of a solid defense as black. So of course Karpov did choose the strongest line, but gained too little an advantage and then lost it. The game was heading towards another draw, but the challenger, as happened in game 27, suddenly lost his way and Karpov could have won the game and the match by finding the right move. However, he missed that opportunity.

And just to punish him, Caissa sent him one more trial in this game. It was adjourned in an ending where Karpov had an extra pawn promising some chances of victory. Garry, upset that he had almost gifted his opponent a sixth and final win, at first wanted not to show up to the next session – his nerves weren't made of steel, either, and he felt sick at the thought of playing a worse adjourned position. He had no energy left for analysis. Two of his coaches, Dorfman and Vladimirov, came to his rescue. They found a new and brilliant method of defense in a tough technical endgame that guaranteed Garry a draw. All the next evening, Karpov attempted without success to gain that win. After the game, we had this momentous premonition for the first time that Karpov was destined not to win the match. He had spent his last drops of energy in this dramatic and so disappointing game. Hesitations in the opening, torture over his missed win, and unsuccessful attempts to win in the final session all comprised an unbearable burden at the end of the match. I think it was this game that finally broke Karpov.

After that, the exhausted champion succumbed to sporting agony as he struggled like a fish out of water. Garry missed fairly simple wins in two white games, but eventually won game 47 with black. Karpov played that game lethargically and in an inconsistent manner. After two hours of play Garry saw his opponent's face suddenly turn grey – his energy was visibly disappearing. Some people were surprised at the fact that after Karpov stopped the clocks he proposed analyzing the game with Garry. An ovation broke out in the hall that not only irritated but also humiliated the champion, yet he continued to sit on his chair and moved the pieces around unhurriedly. To us it was clear that he simply didn't have the energy to stand up from the table. I decided that the match would be over in another six games. However, everything ended much more abruptly and unexpectedly than that.

Once game 47 finished Karpov suffered a nervous breakdown that prompted interference by sporting and other officials of various ranks who were somehow involved in the match. They rushed around like headless chickens, not knowing what to do. The sports leadership then came up with the odd proposal of subjecting both players to a medical exam. The obvious purpose of this absurd novelty was to grant Karpov more time to recover, on which the leading lights of Soviet space medicine were now intensively engaged.

We waited nine whole days to play the next game, number 48. That was the amount of drawn out time that the organizers spent on relocating the chess table and demonstration boards from the Hall of Columns a whole ten kilometers away to the modest conference hall of the Hotel Sport. During that time Karpov had managed to take a course of recovery in the decompression chamber of the Institute of Space Medicine.

It was obvious that the proposal to carry out medical exams of both players was a trap for Garry. Had they convinced him to agree, the search would have begun to find authoritative medics to join the commission, with debates on the merits of each candidate and the drafting of a program and criteria. The medical exam could hence have been drawn out for as long as anybody wished. It would surely have taken at least three weeks and granted Karpov the energy to play another two or three games. Meanwhile, the stroppy challenger would have spent this time in an environment of uncertainty, surrounded by rumors about when the battle was to resume. The risk that he would blow a fuse was too high, and so Garry and the official team doctor naturally refused to take part.

Our opponents were by then so bewildered that during the negotiations the president of the Soviet Chess Federation, Vitaly Ivanovich Sevastyanov, and the real head of chess in the country at the time, Nikolai Krogius, attempted to move Garry to tears by telling him the doctors saw danger in Karpov's state of health. Even the Minister of Culture Demichev, in his role as head of the match's organizing committee, asked Garry in a phone call "not to kick a man lying on the ground".

Evidently, Karpov really was in a miserable state, and they needed to save him. However, they had to do so in a fair manner. The duel needed to be cancelled and doctors were required to pull the trigger, issuing a conclusion that Karpov was incapable of fighting on due to poor health. Naturally, he would be recognized as having lost the match. The law of sport is strict and harsh: if you can't continue then you have to withdraw from the competition and admit defeat. However, Kasparov could not of course claim the title of world champion, as Karpov was formally ahead in the match. Therefore, he would agree to play a new match a year later. Chess would have to go without a world champion for a short time, but Karpov would regain the love and support of millions of chess fans, which would hasten his recovery. This option was far from favorable for Garry, but it turned out to be totally unacceptable for the "ailing" champion as well, whose title was by then a prefix to his name.

Having no energy to continue the fight, Karpov begged influential friends to end the match while allowing him to remain champion. Experienced political insiders solved this problem in just a few moves! A decision to end the match was taken at the level of the Party Central Committee, and unchess-like maneuvers began. The head of our delegation was ordered not to interfere in the following events, which had been authored by experienced script-writers. After that, some dubious-looking fuss began around our doomed match – discussions, meetings and phone calls with delegation members and the players themselves were held every day. All this was necessary to create chaos which could only be ended by extraordinary measures – a well-known and quite unsporting scenario.

Game 48 again depressed Karpov's supporters. He again lost limply, without a struggle, and plainly forcing himself to play despite having nothing left in the petrol tank. This turned out to be the last game in the near half-year long battle between the titans. The once disastrous score gap had narrowed to just two points, and we all felt that the outcome of the match was hanging in the air. The wise Botvinnik provided the best assessment: "There are three ways the match could end. The first alternative, the least likely, is that Karpov will break his three-month spell without victory and finally win another game to remain champion. The second is that Kasparov, who won the last two games easily, will win another three and thereby become champion. This alternative is more likely than the first. And it's because of that that the most likely alternative is the third one... the match will simply be cancelled in the coming days."

However, the champion's protectors were still holding out for a miracle similar to that which happened in Baguio City in 1978. Back then, Karpov managed to return to a fighting state after a rest day and won the decisive game against Korchnoi with the score at 5:5. Now, the next game was also due to be played after a rest game, and again Karpov had his favorite white pieces. This favorable combination of signs drove the champion and his protectors to taking an extreme step.

All discussions about exhaustion suddenly ended. It became clear that a final charge was being prepared. We had some general idea of the methods with which the champion was being "prepared" for the new game. Therefore, the surprise that Kasparov delivered to him on Monday 11 February, just hours before the start of play, was incomprehensible to chess fans, but extremely unpleasant for the champion: Garry informed the arbiters that he was taking his final time out. This was a calculated risk that not only messed up Karpov's "preparation" for a last game, but which made a repeat of such preparation impossible. We realized that in the 50 hours left before the start of the next playing period the champion would be unable to restore his strength.

Karpov's circle panicked as soon as we announced our time-out. That very same day, Campomanes was urgently summoned to Moscow, flying in late in the evening. He was evidently unhappy at such a summons, and in order to demonstrate his independence from the State Sports Committee, he told the heads of both teams as soon as he arrived at the hotel, where they were waiting for him, of his plan to end the match. The first clause in his document would be to end the match after sixty games if neither player had obtained six wins by then. He added that he was going to meet the players the next day.

However, the next day he only went to meet the champion, and, realizing the full seriousness of the situation, made an unusual move – he switched the playing day from the planned 13th of the month, thus taking a "presidential" time out. Thus a new match participant appeared on the scene, who had begun with fast and decisive action.

The FIDE president only appeared in the Kasparov camp the afternoon of the 14th, in the company of chief arbiter Gligoric. Garry was asleep and the president didn't insist on meeting specifically with him. Instead, he began to address the head of our delegation and the seconds. Now he was no longer talking about ending the match after a certain number of games were played. Campo told us how "many people" were unhappy at such a long match, about the players' extreme tiredness and the threat to their health were play to continue. Finally, he showed us a shocking document. It was a letter from the president of the Soviet Chess Federation asking the FIDE president to temporarily halt the match for three or four months, naturally, "to preserve the health of the match participants". Campo spoke rather half-heartedly with us and wouldn't get into an argument. We realized that much of what he had said wasn't his own view and hence he had no desire to defend his view. So it was a purely formal visit in a situation where everything had already been decided.

Campo simply wanted to warn us of his next steps. He took no pleasure in the mission entrusted to him to become the match's executioner. Seeing that we were insisting on resuming the match in the very near future, Campo stood up and said that he would announce his decision the next day. He left unanswered our question: "Does that mean there will be no game tomorrow?" So Botvinnik's forecast was beginning to materialize.

Later, as we strung together individual facts, we came to understand what happened to Karpov in those days. In declaring a time-out, the president saved the champion. Karpov was incapable of playing. Far from all people in his circle enjoyed the experience and were so disappointed that they couldn't keep their mouths shut after the match ended. The day of the presidential time-out the chief organizer Demichev again attempted to convince Garry to take into account his opponent's poor health and not to appeal to "influential people" for help. Garry took the hint and didn't ask Aliev to intervene. The young challenger quickly calculated the variations and decided that the now planned end to the match would accord him and his protector a large amount of goodwill.

Before the start of the match almost nobody had focused on the new and unusual clause in the regulations granting the FIDE president the right to make any decisions with respect to the match. The players were occupied with other business – they needed to play, and not to study FIDE documents. Well, the author of the regulations turned out to possess considerable foresight. Campo opted to make use of his exclusive right to cancel the match without waiting for game 49 to begin!

He decided to announce his decision at a press-conference convoked in the playing hall the day that the next game was due to start. Nobody invited Kasparov to that press-conference. Moreover, the head of our delegation received the order to prevent Garry from traveling to the meeting between the FIDE president and journalists. However, the coaches attempted to persuade Garry to accompany them to the playing hall of the Hotel Sport where the press-conference would soon begin, and where the most unexpected terms for ending play might be announced. Yet the Kasparovs dithered, evidently awaiting instructions from somebody. The coaches were just about to leave without Garry when he appeared at our hotel room door and exclaimed "let's go!"

We reached the hall ten minutes before the start, to find it already full! Despite the lack of publicity and its sudden convocation, journalists had sniffed out with their professional sense that this press meeting would give them some rich material. Representatives of all the main news agencies were in the hall that day to observe this grandiose spectacle.

The sporting bosses' eyes bulged with surprise when they noticed Garry at the hall doorway. Krogius recovered his composure first and offered Garry a place in the front row of the stalls. Then, with his faculties fully restored, he pleaded with the challenger not to make any statements to the press. Garry, with his coaches around him, pushed his way through to the back rows of the main hall and was immediately besieged by journalists. Karpov, unaware of Kasparov's arrival, was at the time sitting in his car equipped with a car phone near the hotel and finishing discussions with the FIDE president on terms for ending the match. He was informed straight away that Kasparov had shown up in the hall, and that threw a spanner in the works of everything they had agreed. Campo, worried at this turn of events, rushed into the hall still not knowing on what terms he would stop the match. He appeared in the hall smiling, yet the video camera remorselessly recorded the confused state of the president as he looked from side to side.

The long, introductory part to the statement that the journalists heard from the president, who had shown up almost an hour late, consisted of a string of sentences with little coherence linking them. It seemed like a verbal screen behind which the president was feverishly sifting through options in his head to solve the problem. Finally, he made his choice and declared that he was ending the match with no result, and that the new match with the players (and with their approval!) would begin on 1 September with the score at 0:0. We got the impression that he had significantly reworked the final part of his announcement and had neglected to say something important. The reference to the players' approval was a poorly disguised proposal to Kasparov to accept the terms for ending the match.

The press-conference was stormy and unpredictable. Karpov showed up at its height, immediately occupying his familiar place at the head of the presidium. He stated that he was ready to play, only not that day, and after moving the microphone away he said to Campomanes quietly that the latter had announced something quite different to what they had agreed.

The confused president decided to ask Kasparov openly for his opinion, but here the most important information was spurted out by a representative of the Foreign Ministry, who was formally chairing the press-conference but who had actually been silent almost all the time. He suddenly objected to Campomanes: "But the decision has been taken!" Attention then switched to Kasparov, and Garry decided to push through to the podium. He spoke passionately and convincingly, demanding that the match continue without hindrance.

Against a background of an indescribable noise in the hall, a break was announced, as the wish expressed by both players in the hall to continue playing contradicted the president's claim that they agreed with him. The match officials went off to confer elsewhere. Karpov followed them, whereas Garry wasn't present during the first part of that meeting – he needed to calm down and take stock of the new situation. The passions raging in the hall were something new for him.

Forty minutes later, when Garry entered the room where the meeting was taking place, arguments were approaching their conclusion. Loyal Karpov ally and leading journalist Alexander Roshal witnessed and later reported on the discussion: "Karpov, the soldier loyal to higher bodies..." (well, his position made him more a colonel or a general than a soldier, but he still wouldn't ignore a party or government decision) "...was being implored 'Tolya, sign it... Tolya, sign it... Tolya, sign it... The match has to end. We've already told the leadership about the situation. And the leadership has already told us *The match is over!* Finished.'" And then the journalist himself said to his friend the world champion: "The decision has been taken. Oh, Tolya, Tolya... No harm will come to Campomanes [if their instruction is ignored] but it might come to you... Have you thought about that?"

Karpov signed his consent to end the match. Moreover, he then tasked his official representative at the match, Viktor Baturinsky, with presenting to Campomanes official proposals on organizing the match in September.

This task was carried out most promptly – that same 15 February evening! Later, Baturinsky would write in his memoirs: "I am morally responsible for failing to conquer Karpov's hesitations and convince him to continue the match." Karpov's aides, grandmasters Vaganian and Balashov, also tried in vain to convince him to gather his strength for one more punch.

Kasparov refused to sign the agreement, and, moreover, declared again to the press that he was ready to continue the match.

So the match was over. Journalists, arbiters and coaches headed home. Three days after that press-conference, Garry and I decided to test how much strength we had left and accepted the challenge from Journalists from the *Izvestiia* newspaper to play football with them in the sports hall. Quite unexpectedly, the authorities warned us that we were engaged in reprehensible behavior. Everything was done to ensure that not a word was written about Kasparov playing football in the newspapers and that no photos appeared, either. The young grandmaster charged along the arena like some elk in both halves of the game, delighting those spectators who had managed to get in. As we got ready to leave we could see Karpov on the TV screen, sitting motionless behind a table and quietly talking about... the unfair decision of the FIDE president, depriving him of victory in the match when he was two points ahead. This meant that Karpov had changed his mind, and a new twist in the backstage struggle was beginning.

Unexpectedly, both the FIDE president and the Minister of Sport enquired whether the players were ready to continue the match that just a few days earlier had been announced over without result. Evidently, the mysterious forces had changed their decision, and intrigue targeted at simpletons was beginning.

At this point, Garry was able to continue the battle, but Karpov had only just begun a cycle of intensive recuperation and was unable to restart a day later or even a week later. However, in giving consent to continue the match, Garry might have fallen into a simple trap. The match could now have resumed at an advantageous moment for Karpov. In fact, we had observed a number of ploys used to gain time during the final month of that match, and I'm sure there were others we didn't see. The time spent waiting for the battle to restart could have turned into torture for Garry, as it was possible to constantly postpone the resumption on the basis of quite absurd and at the same time carefully thought through reasons. He would have had no chances to win the match had it resumed under such circumstances.

Garry had, though, guessed the essence of this cunning plan and refused to discuss the matter of resuming the game. Karpov, on the other hand, seeing that Kasparov wouldn't agree to continue, made frenzied efforts to restart the match. This pseudo activity somewhat made him look all innocent in the eyes of our society. The public was tired of trying to figure out the ins and outs of the conflict and they reacted with indifference to Karpov retaining his title. Thus successfully closed the second act of the show approved from the mysterious "above". Garry had been told that it was impossible to leave the chess throne empty, and that the crown should remain on Karpov's head until the next match. Now that this is all history you can burst out laughing at the micromanagement sometimes demonstrated by our government, ignoring far more important matters for the country. Maybe that is why our ranking fell so low in standard of living compared with other countries?

Once February was behind us, we cleansed all this peculiar commotion surrounding the match that was now over from our minds. We had very little time to rest and prepare for the new battle, just half a year. We were again in time trouble.

Chapter 3. A Titanic Battle (Match 2, 1985)

Our preparation for the new match, this time with a limited number of games, began in early April. We had accorded ourselves only a month and a half to rest – including from each other. Each of us strived to shed the burden of mental tiredness as quickly as possible. The excitement of extreme battle had infected us and, even far from each other, we constantly replayed in our head episodes from the match, seeking out errors and new ideas. All three training sessions that we were to hold took place in our favorite Zagulba. Its wonderful sandy beach, bright sun and cool park alleys enabled Garry to shed his tiredness rapidly and visibly regain his strength.

Our coaching team was the same as before. Having built up match experience, we managed to carry out a huge amount of work in a short time period. We worked out the chess reasons for failures and periods of deterioration in Garry's play in the first match. We identified more precisely the areas in which he was stronger than his opponent and in which he was weaker. This allowed us to devise an effective strategy for the second match and meant that Garry, with the exception of his unfortunate start, was fully in control of the situation. Garry worked incessantly during our preparation, constantly generating new ideas.

He played a number of games in Europe in May. His short training matches with Hubner and Andersson proved to be very useful, but it wasn't this part of the young grandmaster's European tour that got under the skin of the chiefs of Soviet sport and nearly played a critical role in his future career. While in Germany, Garry gave a big interview to the magazine *Spiegel*, which had actually financed the German part of his trip. This was the first time that a Soviet sportsman had spoken so candidly about the problems of sport in our country to such an authoritative publication. "*Glasnost*" was still taking baby steps at the time, and a lot of what Garry said to the magazine was viewed as "reactionary" in Moscow and unacceptably outspoken. The most interesting thing, though, was that the State Sports Committee had as usual sent a KGB agent to accompany Garry on his trip rather than a coach, that agent had been given instructions with regard to the interview in the magazine, and his report on the trip was accepted without comments.

After flying to Belgrade from Hamburg, Garry, apart from his victory against Andersson, made a lot of noise in the Yugoslav press about the end to the limitless match with Karpov and, in particular, the role of both the FIDE president and the chief arbiter Svetozar Gligoric. The famous Yugoslav GM, whom Garry himself had asked to act as chief arbiter, was according to my charge unable to demonstrate his effectiveness as an arbiter and incapable of resisting the violation of the regulations at the end. Moreover, the chief arbiter, who was responsible for ensuring the rules were strictly obeyed, took part in lobbying to end play, which was itself a violation. From Belgrade, Garry also sent a message to FIDE, in which he outlined his understanding of the role of the president in ending the match. He did all this without obtaining permission from the Soviet Chess Federation, or, to be more precise, from those bodies that hid behind its name.

The challenger started to annoy the party bosses with his independence and stroppiness. "And what's he going to do if he becomes world champion?" they were thinking. So they decided to teach the young rebel a lesson.

At the very height of our preparation for the match clouds formed above the challenger's head. With less than two months to go before the start, Karpov suddenly announced to the press with delight that there would be no changes on the chess Olympus in 1985. Of course, he had every reason to count on winning the match, but such an unchallenged claim gave the impression that a very weighty "directive opinion" stood behind this sharp worsening of the Moscow leadership's attitude towards Garry. The date of the punishment soon became known – 9 August. A special session of the presidium of the Soviet Chess Federation was called to "analyze" the "anti-state" behavior of Kasparov abroad. He was even due to be censured for the interview in the "reactionary" magazine Spiegel, despite the fact that it had been sanctioned by the Sports Committee. Of course, two years later our leader Mikhail Gorbachev would host Spiegel's chief editor in the Kremlin and call the magazine a serious and authoritative publication.

The "analysis", or rather the shower of criticism to which Garry had been summoned, was a way of punishment for actions that were not to be found in the criminal code but which nevertheless required penalties, most often harsh ones. Usually, this was how people were punished for violating unwritten but strictly protected ideological norms set by the communist regime. The selected punishment was usually announced publicly – so that others would take note. Sometimes the very process of "analysis" was recounted, without even a hint of objectivity. However, the real "hearing", which would take place sometime before, in secret offices, in the absence of the accused, was never discussed. The sentence would actually be determined there, and the subsequent discussion with the wider audience was but an empty formality with an "edifying" message. The decision sent "from above" was usually lying on the chairman's table from the beginning, and all that remained was to add the words "punishment approved by the overwhelming majority" to the meeting minutes.

The fact that the meeting of the Soviet Chess Federation presidium was an extraordinary one and convened prior to the start of the match meant only one thing: the pre-determined punishment was disqualification. In saying that there would be no changes on the chess Olympus in 1985, Karpov knew what he was talking about.

Aliev was at the time on a lengthy foreign trip. Garry begged the leaders of Azerbaijan who were still in the country for support, but they proved helpless to cancel the decision to disqualify him. Just a few days before the presidium was due to meet Garry managed to gain a meeting with Alexander Yakovlev, who occupied a leading party position at the time. After examining the root cause of the problem, the latter pronounced: "The match has to go ahead." His words became a new party directive that had to be obeyed.

This was a horrible blow for Karpov and his protectors. The presidium meeting resembled an absurd and in places comic spectacle as though the actors had been assigned completely different roles just before they walked on the stage, without being given their lines, so they ended up improvising. People were forced to leave important matters and fly urgently to Moscow just so that they could be physically present when the young grandmaster was given a spoken(!) reprimand for the lack of tact in some of his statements. In truth, they had turned the mountain into a mole-hill.

The match began in Moscow, just as Campomanes had originally announced, on 1 September. To the seconds' delight, Gennady Rzaev was appointed head of the Azeri delegation. This was a man who did much to support our young talent when he took his first steps in Big Chess. He demonstrated titanic patience, self-control and the mastery of a diplomat to ensure that our creative team was able to function effectively and without hindrance, and to make sure that the coaches were always able to communicate with the challenger.

The match was of course a success, and I think it was the best of all the matches between the two Ks. It was remarkable for its high quality of games, rich content and intense struggle in each of them. The sole short draw, in game three, produced a theoretical novelty by Kasparov and Karpov's clever defense. There were ten or so games that made your head spin like the most intricate detective novels.

Karpov had already demonstrated at the start of the match that he had recovered his fighting strength, and not only. This would not have been enough to compete with his opponent who had managed to significantly gain in both ability and self-confidence. The champion was surprised at the sharp increase in the challenger's psychological fortitude, at the aggressive nature of his match strategy, and at the fundamental renewal of his opening repertoire.

From the very first game, Karpov had to endure a hail of theoretical novelties, as his chief second Zaitsev later admitted. These forced him to tackle difficult problems out of the opening. The first such surprise was an unpleasant shock. Garry for the first time deployed a system found in the fighting repertoires of at least four grandmasters aiding the champion. None of them could have expected the lad from Baku to dare to play a variation that they knew well, and Karpov turned out to be quite unprepared for such an opening. Studying that variation, Garry was convinced that the continuations considered by theory to be best, and which the experts had without doubt shown the champion, were quite inappropriate to his style of play. As if it wasn't enough that his heavy defeat in game one took him quite unawares, Karpov was tortured just about the entire match playing black in the Nimzo-Indian Defense, unable to find an antidote to Kasparov's setup.

Our creative team, in designing our match plan, correctly judged that, with so little time allocated to prepare for the match, work on openings, in particular, on preparing opening surprises, could play a decisive role. Karpov showed up at the match with his old baggage, and the start of play turned out to be punishment for him. In the second half of the match he often found himself fighting for equality even with the white pieces.

In truth, in drawing up the match strategy, adjusting it at the right time as the match progressed, and identifying the effectiveness of measures used to implement it, Garry together with his seconds proved to be a big step ahead of his opponent. It was only in analyzing adjourned positions that we failed to bridge the gap. Garry didn't want to assign anybody to take the lead in this particular analytical workstream. The speed of his thinking was as before significantly greater than ours, and nobody could keep up with his ideas. His southern temperament prevented our analysis from being an orderly and, more importantly, calm process. To a large extent due to this, Garry failed to carry through a second successive victory at the beginning. The second, wild game was adjourned in a position that everybody assessed to be discouraging for the champion. The coaches suggested two paths to victory. Garry came up with a third, which had to be a "brilliant" one, and expressed his displeasure whenever anybody tried to switch away from his line. The defect in his idea was found by chance an hour before resumption. Our mutual reproaches upset Garry and he drew quickly.

Our missed win pained us for a number of days, right until he lost game four. We were really disappointed as Garry simply ruined one of his best opening ideas. When he only needed one precise move to draw, he suddenly, just like in the star-crossed 27th game of the previous match, started to mark time and lost after coming under an attack. Karpov played the next game wonderfully, after which the challenger found himself in his familiar position of playing catch-up, but turned significantly... calmer. He still had to get used to the role of leader in such a contest.

Evidently, the world champion had counted on gaining success at the beginning of the match, before tiredness mounted and before his opponent reached peak form. Botvinnik believed that Garry had chances of winning the contest, but to do so he needed to stand equal at the start of the second half of the match. After his cold shower at the very beginning, Karpov played about eight games with maximum energy, trying, like in the first match, to break the young challenger. However, Garry had already managed to feel out his own strength and wasn't as helpless as he had been in the Hall of Columns. The opening problems with which he tormented Karpov forced the latter to expend much energy and nerves on figuring out solutions to the problems that he had been posed from the first moves. Karpov's decision to forego serious opening analysis in his preparation meant that his ambitions, amazing fighting qualities and most subtle understand of chess were nullified by his antediluvian opening weapons. It's perfectly possible that the reason for that was to be found in his protectors, who had rashly promised him that the match would not take place, thereby interfering with the rhythm of his prep. His pressing gradually softened – the great warrior sensed fatigue and frustration. This was especially apparent in game eleven. Tired of defending a difficult position as black he make a blunder that cost him the point.

Karpov lost any illusions he may have still harbored after the saga with Kasparov's gambit that I describe in my notes to the famous game 16 later in this book. His team had spent about ten days developing a refutation, but it ended in a dramatic, crushing defeat.

Kasparov had significantly toughened his character even during the month and a half since the second match started. He reacted far more calmly to regaining the lead. The tense struggle lasted through to the final, 24th game, due to Karpov's phenomenal battling qualities. Obviously he wasn't going to surrender his crown without a fight, yet such fierce resistance under a hail of tactics with the challenger waiting to punish his opponent for the slightest inaccuracy was expected by nobody.

In game nineteen Garry delivered the champion another huge psychological blow. He destroyed his opponent's defense in typical Karpovian style, brilliantly exploiting the hapless position of just one(!) black piece. It seemed that the champion had no chance of surviving after two nasty defeats as the match approached the finishing line. He had run out of weapons, yet he somehow remained on his feet and defended with desperation, trying to find a powerful counterpunch. In fact, Kasparov did much to help him here, losing his balance as the end drew ever near. Garry's state of mind during that tense period was typical of a person who had set themselves an ambitious target and was now on the verge of achieving it. His desire to win the match as quickly as possible unexpectedly transformed into fear of losing his cherished advantage.

Kasparov's overwhelming advantage in the openings, which was particularly apparent in the second half of the match and which enabled him to regularly begin battle in quite familiar and advantageous situations, left the champion hoping for a miracle. And it nearly happened. At the closing stage, Karpov only gained bearable positions out of the opening in one game, game 22, and was able to carry out unhurried maneuvering. The challenger, who needed to gain just one more point for victory, suddenly lost the thread of the game and in just two weak moves turned an equal position into a lost one. And after Garry was unable to win game 23, the fate of the chess crown went down to the last match.

A feature of Garry's character is that he is fully on top of his game and plays at full strength in situations when his back is against the wall. And now in this final, decisive game, he needed to avoid losing. Tomorrow would have been too late. On this occasion, his seconds managed to outsmart the other team. We guessed with great precision the opening variation and particular line that would happen in that game. This accorded Garry an additional shot of confidence that was so needed in the decisive duel. I described how we managed to guess the opening so well and how Garry won the crown in my commentary on the game later in the book.

The players fought 24 complicated and tense games in this fierce match. The reason for that was not only their chess and physical form, but also their psychological strength despite the constant heavy stress. Once again, our team had no professional psychologist, unfortunately, and we solved many problems relating to Garry's psychological strength and maintaining a healthy atmosphere within our creative team through trial and error, often expending time and energy in doing so. Our doctor was not a professional psychologist, and could only teach Garry how to apply autogenic training prior to and during each game. Yet the doctor was our psychological rock, as he constantly radiated kindness and calm in even the most difficult situations. The coaches were still united at the time, and we found it easy to maintain a calm creative atmosphere. I hope that this accorded our charge additional strength. During our daily hour-long walks with Garry we would avoid arguments, trying not to deprive our "client", as we called the lad among ourselves, of nervous energy.

Wishing to suppress his effusiveness, we pushed to ensure order and stability even in the tiniest details, especially on playing days. So we introduced a strict ritual that avoided unnecessary activity and improvisation. For example, we would always arrive at games with Garry with the exact same set of team members, and always in the same car. Moreover, the topic of conversation would always be agreed in advance. Nothing was to distract Garry from the upcoming battle. Before he exited the car we would slap him on the shoulder, and this ritual resembled ice-hockey players gathering around the goalkeeper before their game began. From then on, Garry would completely detach himself from us and belonged to the wooden army set up on the board.

On that decisive day, our team displayed neither panic nor excessive emotion before the game. This tense calm in anticipation of the battle of life and death probably had a beneficial impact on Garry, and he was silent and unusually collected. We left for the game bang on time, and we were mostly silent during that journey. On this occasion, Dorfman delivered the short pep-talk: "Garry, today you might become world champion shooting out of a trench. The system that will most probably appear on the board today is very reliable, and if you are careful you will manage to draw. But you are now really strong and can go into battle fearing nothing. And another request – please sit straight at the board, don't arch your back as though you're being hit. Everything will be OK!" Finally, we arrived. It was time to get out. Our final ritual send-off in the car. No emotion – everybody really calm and confident... Please give him strength, make sure he doesn't mess up!

This was the last match which I "sat through" together with Garry. Arriving with him to the game, I would make my way to the spectators hall, sit in the same place each time so that I could see my charge, and stay there to the end. During the match I never once visited the press-center where grandmasters and journalists gathered and which bubbled with life. The playing hall was my Olympus, where Garry was playing, and would transform into my Calvary when he suffered misfortune. At the time, I "sensed" him so much that I could accurately tell what he was thinking about, and whether or not he liked his position. For several years I was a particular kind of psychological support for the lad, increasing his confidence during the game. Looking at me, he could also tell whether or not I liked his position. In this match, so that there were no grounds for complaint, the chairs next to me were left free – nobody sat there. Even in the most complicated situations I retained my calm and tried to convey it to my charge. This was my main aim in sitting in the hall. After becoming world champion, Garry raised his self-opinion, and the natural striving of young people to obtain independence and shed the protection of adults was in his case no longer held back by any financial dependence. He started to find my influence a burden, and our mutual understanding quickly decreased. By the time of his match in Seville he would be accompanied to the games by people incapable of furnishing him any help, instead of by his coaches, and I only attended the clash of passions in the chess theater on three occasions, spending most of that match in the press-center.

The psychic Dadashev turned up at our residence several times during the 1985 match, but his work with Garry was a mystery to the coaches. I only spoke with him once, when I asked him to use his influence to grant Garry's mother confidence – we all badly needed that. A couple of years later, Dadashev gave an interview where he claimed that he had advised Garry on his match strategy and even what opening setup to play in the decisive 24th game.

Karpov always assigned great importance to psychological preparation as well. This work was carried out in his team at a far more serious level. Professor of psychology Vladimir Zukhar played a huge role in his 1978 victory over Korchnoi, perhaps even the decisive role. He regularly held long-lasting calming sessions, and in the last weeks of that match used hypnosis to treat the sharply weakened champion's insomnia. Zukhar expended so much energy and strength at that match that he spent the next year himself being treated by doctors in order to restore his ability to work. After that match ended Zukhar was forgotten – nobody was meant to know about the champion's frailties. "...We bid farewell to Zukhar straight after Baguio City and never saw him again..." Zaitsev was to write several years later. Then, at the 1981 match with Korchnoi in Merano, the huge Soviet delegation included a psychologist from the Institute of Space Medicine. However, he didn't have much work to do, as Korchnoi had clearly weakened and Karpov won easily. After that, at the 1984 match, specialists from the same institute ended up working intensively with their patient. In the last months of that match routine hypnosis proved to be insufficient. So they applied methods for astronaut rehabilitation, including strong medicines. Evidently, the doctors and patients were unhappy with each other. Moreover, the champion couldn't tell which of the doctors might have leaked information about the method of his recuperation.

He then found himself a new guru for the 1985 match in Odessa, where he held his training sessions. Grigory Rozhnovsky, who claimed to be a hypnotist and brought a group of assistants to the match, got particularly close to Karpov. The problem of lack of sleep evidently remained a painful one for Karpov, but the help of the hypnotist proved to be effective. Even after his heavy defeats the champion would turn up fresh for the next game.

In the last game, though, I was on the verge of a conflict with his team. Sitting in my usual seat, I suddenly noticed one of Rozhnovsky's assistants in the middle of the front row 30 minutes after the game began. His chair was just a few meters from the players' table and he was glaring constantly at Garry. He would only relax, leaning back on his chair, when Garry got up from the board. I watched this behaviour for half an hour, and once I had no doubt left in my mind I dashed to the foyer, found doctor Mikhail Gershanovich, who accompanied Karpov to all of his matches, and demanded that he immediately remove this assistant who was trying to disturb Garry. Mikhail Yakovlevich understood me straight away. By the time I returned to the playing hall, the assistant had disappeared and didn't come back.

Karpov's group constantly sported a second psychologist as well. Mikhail Novikov was responsible for maintaining the interpersonal relations required for a large team to work effectively. He was a top class specialist and we could only envy our opponents.

This was also the first match in which our coaching team was subject to pressure from various non-chess structures interested in Karpov retaining his title. This turned out to be just a dress-rehearsal for a widescale campaign to influence the coaches. The conflict caused by two of Kasparov's coaches belonging to the same club as Karpov was accepted by us calmly and with understanding. However, a true headhunt was organized to attempt to persuade Dorfman, who wasn't from Karpov's army club, involving a promise of a large sum of money and moving his family's apartment from Lvov to Moscow, to pass our chess prep to the Karpov camp. Dorfman immediately informed the head of our delegation and asked for protection. However, this "game" proved to be far from harmless, and as Kasparov enjoyed a huge advantage in opening prep, the insistent proposals combined with threats continued throughout the match, making us nervous and distracting us from our work. I am a long way from the thought that Karpov initiated this idea, and he probably didn't even know about it. However, his non-chess entourage included people capable of organizing this, believing that the end justified absolutely any means. Their actions were of a wider scale in the next match and, unfortunately, more effective.

The closing ceremony was remarkable for the fact that the very people tasked with doing everything in their power to carry out the directive and prevent Kasparov from winning had to officially congratulate the new champion and place the laurel wreath over his neck, given their officials roles

– Krogius and Sevastyanov, as well as the FIDE president. At the young champion's moment of triumph their faces resembled those at a funeral. Yet Kasparov noticed nothing and was as happy as a child. When we returned from the closing ceremony to the hotel, carefully carrying this cherished laurel wreath, the newly-baked 13th world champion demonstrated that he was still very young. He wandered from room to room shouting out with joy, just shouting! His shout contained his shedding of all the pain and stress that had tortured him on the path to the chess Olympus, as well as the triumph of the winner. Oh, that was some Victory!

The question immediately arose – for how long? Before the closing ceremony, Garry, in a state of euphoria, had been easily persuaded by the "responsible comrades" not to quarrel with Campomanes over a return match and not to reject it out of hand at the champion's traditional press-conference. "How can there be a return match with Karpov in such a state and his questionable financial operations?" Sports Minister Gramov had said to Kasparov at the time. Not a word was said about a return match throughout November.

At that time, the bosses were intrigued by the development of events in a strange story that suddenly appeared involving the disappearance of money belonging to Karpov (around one million Deutsche Marks). Before the last, decisive match game in Baguio City, Karpov's mood had been lifted after he signed a contract with a firm called NOVAG to advertise the Tolinka chess computer. Despite the multiple KGB agents accompanying him at the time in the city, that signing remained a secret from the Sports Committee. The strangest thing was that, after entrusting his German agent to receive the payment for the advert, Karpov completely forgot about the money and suddenly remembered about it seven years later, and only thanks to Campomanes! Although the court case in Hamburg ended with condemnation of his trusted representative, both "heroes" of this story suffered damage to their image.

At his first press-conference as champion, Garry unexpectedly announced that he would restart his work at the Botvinnik school, this time as an equal partner of his teacher, who after a break of eight years had decided to return to coaching children. Of course the creative dialogue between these two champions had continued during those eight years. Garry often visited his teacher to bare his soul, to tell him of his successes and to share his doubts. The teacher's advice gradually acquired a more general, even ritual character. This was perfectly natural, as the lad's chess ability was making huge progress, and his experience and self-confidence grew in tandem. It had seemed that Botvinnik's educational activities had ended, yet in 1986 the school gained a double-barreled name "Botvinnik – Kasparov", and all the young talents, as a rule on the verge of big success, were immediately drawn to it, sometimes from other schools. This was also perfectly natural: what young talent would refuse to study under such a powerful tandem? Just four sessions of this unique school were held, ones that gave a big impulse to already ambitious lads ripe for gaining serious titles. Great champions coached by these leading grandmasters appeared one after another – including Tiviakov, Akopian, Ulibin, Shirov and Alterman. However, the unique pedagogical alliance didn't last for long and ended in late 1987. Lessons at the school ceased forever.

Just a month after his coronation, Garry was in Holland, where he played a short and brilliant match against Jan Timman. The score itself could not be called brilliant (+4 -2 =0) – but the brilliancy was in the beauty and richness of ideas invested by both players in each of the six mind-boggling duels. The match had a huge effect of popularizing chess in Europe. Thousands of fans came to watch the wonderful play of the young champion, with significant coverage in the press and on TV. Chess in Europe was becoming a social phenomenon. Businessmen were increasingly taking an interest in it.

Having concluded that the sports bosses really didn't plan a new match between him and Karpov, and that he would be champion for at least two years, Garry built ambitious plans to take part in chess and public life. However, he sobered up quickly, at the end of December, as soon as he returned from Holland. That same Gramov, gloomily looking at the champion, told him that the return match should be played in the near future, and that Karpov had fully legitimate rights to demand it. Two presidents were immediately quoted in the press – that of FIDE and of our federation. Their key arguments were strikingly similar: a refusal by Kasparov to play a return match would automatically deprive him of his crown.

The new champion's peaceful life had ended just as it was beginning. It was time to get back to training.

Chapter 4. Games Behind the Scenes (Match 3, 1986)

So how did the return match become a legitimate reality? Well, it turned out that a day before the second match began Garry signed an obligation to play a return match against Karpov in 1986. That's correct – the ancient right to a return match had been resurrected only for Karpov and would disappear with him! The experienced functionaries had ensured that Garry had no means of avoiding it.

Once he became world champion, Garry attempted to restore fairness, suggesting either to write into the rules that such a right would exist for all subsequent champions, or else to abolish it once and for all. However, our chess federation didn't support him. Eventually, a compromise was reached: Karpov would get his return match, but not in February as our federation president demanded. Rather, in July or August. In the history of world championship matches, there had never been less than a year between them. If for no other reason than out of respect for the winner, he would be accorded time not only to rest but also to enjoy his glory for a little while.

It was strange to watch our federation president, who had so recently been touchingly concerned about the health of the players in the limitless match, now insist on a resumption of battle at the earliest. There were no longer any conversations about their health. However, the reasons for which some people were attempting to reduce the break until the next match to a minimum soon emerged.

The postponement of the match came in very handy for Garry, as in February he urgently flew off to distant Novosibirsk, where one of his coaches, grandmaster Timoshchenko, both lived and was carrying out military service in the rank of major. He had suddenly become the target of some persecution, as a result of which the army leadership deprived him of the right to travel abroad. That would have prevented Gennady from attending the upcoming match. He only managed to be "rehabilitated" a month later, after a lot of fuss.

That same February, Sevastyanov and Karpov unexpectedly visited Lvov, where another Kasparov second, grandmaster Dorfman, lived. They came to see not so much large audiences, as much as the local leadership. Perhaps it was a coincidence, but after they left the processing of our colleague's foreign travel documents was halted. Garry had to appeal for help to the leadership of the country's trade unions for this "accidental" problem to be resolved.

Our third coach, Vladimirov, was left alone – though he was also carrying out military service, with the rank of a warrant officer. He lived in Almaty, but continued to travel freely around the country, sometimes for personal reasons and without obtaining the required documents. This was quite a risky enterprise for conscripts, and the rest of us were surprised at how he got away with it. I think that at some point in January our opponents finally managed to identify a weakness in the coaching team working with Garry. Vladimirov's personal travels across the country were hardly unnoticed for long. Evidently, he was told that he was on the hook and could be severely punished at any time as a conscript voluntarily going missing for long periods from his garrison.

The training base in Zagulba became home to our team for three months from March. Garry took in a tour of Europe, during which he crushed English grandmaster Tony Miles in a short match, while we continued without him.

In the middle of our prep, we discovered by chance that one of our coaches was secretly copying down certain sections of our joint analysis. Instead of immediately asking him to explain the reason for such a stark violation, which risked our coaching team being wound up, we decided to pretend that nothing was happening, to say nothing about it to Kasparov, and to fly to London with the current team, instead taking measures to prevent the leakage of information. A professional should have taken the decisive role in this decision, which is what we considered Litvinov to be. We had to change our work program, reducing joint analysis to a minimum.

So now there was a deep internal fracture in our training team. An unpleasant one but not of course the first dispute. Our until recently closely-knit group was falling apart. Our creativity had begun to plummet compared with its peak in 1983-85. We suddenly noticed that we were all different – in age, temperament and even ambitions. In the past we had been united by a single goal, shared with Kasparov and towards whose achievement we expended time and efforts. We then considered Garry a member of our team and supported his campaign for justice in the chess world, while trying to maintain a spirit of equality and fairness in relations among us. We were additionally united by the large volume of work we were carrying out.

The further Garry ascended Mount Olympus the more he distanced himself from his team of soul mates. To some extent this was all to be expected – his successes had raised his public status, and many new interesting projects appeared feeding his self-image that not only demanded a lot of his time previously spent on chess, but which also seriously exaggerated his evaluation of his own importance in society.

For a long time, the best hours were when we would talk with Garry but sensed that although he was a top chess player he remained for us not a challenger, not a world champion, but just Garry, to whom we could say anything, knowing that he would listen attentively and with a positive attitude. Gradually, such hours became fewer and further between. Now, as we approached him, his thoughts would be elsewhere, even focused on quite mundane matters. Any phone call would allow his mother to enter the room where we were carrying out our coaching, whereupon she would interrupt us and take Garry out of the room for yet another "important" conversation with the caller. The airs of a boss were increasingly heard in his voice. On the basis of somebody else's rather ill-considered advice he started to act early on as an employer. "We are a single team, so we should act as I see fit," he suddenly came out with at the end of the first match. Then, too, during one of his numerous interviews, he referred to us all as "staffers".

I think that if a creative alliance is built on the basis of voluntary acceptance of a specific form of interpersonal relations, then any cardinal change to that form of interaction will lead to the collapse of the said alliance. Well, we had put together a team of equally creative individuals, and when that equality began to imperceptibly but inexorably erode, the alliance started to collapse. The ambitions of each member suddenly made themselves felt, and mutual trust was disturbed. Some people were unhappy, offended, while our enemies remained wide awake. It was summer 1986...

Before we left for the match in London our group suffered another shock. Up to then, I had always performed the role of chief second at the matches, with Dorfman as deputy chief. I always highlighted that our coaches were equal. This was right if not for any other reason than the fact that the real role of seconds had long been taken away by the Kasparovs, who would take decisions about time-outs, changes to our timetable and so on. Well, somebody managed to whet Timoshchenko's ambitions, and he suddenly demanded to be made chief second for the upcoming match. I immediately suggested I would give way to him, but Garry messed things up, saying that he would not tolerate any dissent in the army. As a result, Gennady flew to London angry at everybody and everything. He lived separately from the team and only came to our sessions when Garry specially asked him. He completely refused to stay in the team in the second half of the match and after returning from London flew straight to Novosibirsk.

The pre-match frictions of our fragile coaching team didn't end on the air carrier's steps. After we flew into London, we learnt that Adorjan was also there, specially to aid Garry. After the first match, only Garry had maintained contact with him, but when it came to the Hungarian working with us in

London the champion decided to display diplomatic skills that were absent during the conflict with Timoshchenko: he asked the coaches to take the final decision. Adorjan flew home to Hungary the next day.

The English organized the match splendidly. The opening ceremony was an unusually grand occasion. Prime Minister Thatcher welcomed the participants. English chess fans filled the playing hall and foyer to overflowing, standing in long queues for the tickets. For the first time we saw such diverse and effective use of computers for projecting the games, work in the press-center and entertainment of spectators in the foyer.

In my view, this was the best match that Kasparov ever played. As we later found out, he fought his opponent in particularly challenging conditions, but was so strong that nothing could break him. Garry's play had become even more universal than in the second match. He was all for devising and beautifully executing subtle positional plans, and took decisions at the board with significantly more confidence. Some weakening of his calculation abilities was compensated for by his evidently improved evaluation of the position, which was down to the large number of positions and analyses etched in his memory.

His opponent had managed to learn the sorry lessons from the previous matches and appeared in the unusual role of chess player of mystery and capable pupil of Kasparov. He was particularly successful in the middle game, not afraid to head for sharp complications and often sacrificing a pawn for the initiative. However, what surprised Garry most of all was that Karpov for the first time went willingly for the sharpest and most principled continuations in the opening, consistently proving to be on top of the latest achievements of chess theory and avoiding all of our novelties.

Instead of enjoying help from ten or so grandmasters like in his previous matches, Karpov created a new group consisting of GMs Zaitsev, Makarychev, and Lerner and experienced masters Podgaets and Ubilava. He also made use of advice from grandmasters Salov and Beliavsky. However, to reach – I would say leap to – the level of opening preparation that the ex-champion demonstrated in this match, would have required a lengthy effort by a more powerful team or else some extra special measures.

Judging by the way the Moscow bosses suddenly rushed with starting this match, extra special measures were prepared at the very start of the year and enabled Karpov to build an unusually aggressive strategy for himself – a typical Kasparov one, in fact – as any other strategy in the "Kasparov-like" opening setups that arose in almost every game would have been inapplicable.

The beginning of the match was controlled by the new world champion. In Garry's first two white games he completely destroyed Karpov's greatest remaining trump card that we knew about – his superiority in being able to weave subtle fibers of positional play. In those games Karpov was outplayed in "Karpovian style" by Kasparov's gradual buildup of tiny positional advantages right out of the opening. Garry believed that with this blow he had driven his opponent into a corner.

The point to note here is that preparation for a match usually ends with a battle strategy being set. The player and his seconds, after evaluating the output from chess prep as well as physical and psychological shape and similar factors, estimate the approximate balance of strength over the expected match duration, and select the moments when a decisive storm will be launched together with the time and order of introducing opening novelties intended to change the direction of the match. It's particularly important here to assess the strengths and weaknesses of one's play with maximum objectivity and precision, to compare them with those of the opponent, and on that basis to determine in which areas you are stronger, again taking not only pure chess aspects into account.

Before the match, we believed that Karpov could count on success in play built on subtle and unhurried positional maneuvering together with his ability to deflect tactical blows. After the fourth game, in which he was crushed, we got the impression that the only asset he still possessed was the ability to resist – which was insufficient given that he needed to win the match. However, strange things began in game five...[3]

The fifth game led me to the worst possible assumption: that leaked information had become a component of Karpov's strategy. That evening, Karpov chose a very complicated and dangerous variation of the Grunfeld Defense. Garry sharply diverged to a little explored continuation which was to be crowned with a novelty that I had found. I thought it up once we were in London, just seven days before that game. I showed it to Garry and the other coaches sitting with us. He examined it for ten minutes, said something like "yeah, interesting...", and then we all forgot about it, as we were more worried about other opening problems. I watched with amazement and horror as our opponent rapidly approached "my" position, as though they had planned in advance. I hoped that Garry had forgotten about that idea, as we hadn't analyzed it seriously, but, alas, his memory was excellent.

---

[3] According to Kasparov's book *Garry Kasparov on Garry Kasparov: Part II* Kasparov first got the impression during game 4 that Karpov was being fed his prep (publisher's note)

Garry would later write: "...Karpov found a refutation of my idea after about 20 minutes. This put me on my guard – Karpov could not have prepared so scrupulously for my 'new' opening, the Grunfeld Defense, before the match. While if this problem was new for him, his thinking at the board about this highly complex line should have taken up far more time. So perhaps this was home prep that he'd come up with in London? Yet at the start Karpov had other, more urgent problems, for example in the Nimzo-Indian Defense, where he never managed to equalize. It's hard to figure out how his team managed to prepared such a complicated variation with an important improvement in less than a week, all the more so in a sideline rather than a main line. They must have been psychic!" Could it have been the case that during our express analysis an invisible "Karpov" sat beside us, and then polished the line at home, finding holes in it?

From this game on, Karpov began to hit Garry's opening repertoire painfully, in its pressure points. The champion, failing to understand the reason for this, came to view his opponent as a high-class psychic, got upset and started to worry. Our biggest ace – the huge advantage in the opening which Garry enjoyed in the second match – had suddenly and mysteriously disappeared, even though we had increased the number of novelties and setups specially prepared for the match. This was an extremely unpleasant blow. Garry suffered enormously and twisted himself in a knot trying to figure out what was going on, gradually coming to an awful but logical conclusion. I asked Litvinov to do something, anything, to end the leaks, but nothing changed. To this day, his passivity in the matter remains a mystery.

If it hadn't been for Garry's huge advantage in chess ability, which enabled him to outplay his opponent in complicated middlegames and thereby cancel out Karpov's opening omniscience, the match could have ended in disaster. Garry would later write: "...Mental puzzles tortured me in London after almost every game. Sometimes it was the astoundingly perfect copy of our narrowly focused analytical investigations, even including repeating at the board our analysis together with mistakes later found in it(!) – including those that proved disastrous for my opponent repeating them, as happened in game four – and sometimes it was the inexplicable way Karpov guessed what I was going to play next... I first raised my suspicion that information had been leaked after game seven. After game twelve I stated that the information was most probably being passed on from somebody in my camp..." After his win in the tense eighth game Garry regained the lead, and our struggles in London ended relatively favorably. Several days later, we flew to Leningrad, where the remainder of the match was to be held.

"I calmed down somewhat in Leningrad," Kasparov continued in his memoirs. "I realized that I played better than Karpov, and planned to increase my advantage. I managed to do this as early as game 14, although Karpov again easily and rapidly found his feet in what was a new opening position for him. Therefore, my happiness at winning was again mixed with a sense of alarm."

Several days before game 16, Garry discovered a wonderful combinational idea in an opening line that Karpov always played. He asked Vladimirov and Dorfman to perfect his analysis, and they demonstrated that white's attack was very dangerous even though he was a piece down. Prior to starting the game, Garry warned his mother that he would sacrifice a knight and she shouldn't worry about it. "However, instead of stepping on a mine, my opponent thought for a short while and then chose a different path, which theory correctly considers to be second-rate. I really got the impression that he did this without enthusiasm. I felt that this was a replacement for the main, fighting variation. A replacement prepared in a hurry, literally just before leaving for the game. I found my way better than my opponent in huge complications. I squeezed the fight out of his pieces and now stood three points ahead in the match. Against a background of everybody else's euphoria nobody took seriously my perplexity and alarm: 'What's going on? Karpov again guessed my opening!' That was exactly when Vladimirov first muttered that he'd had enough of the 'spy mania' and would leave our team after the match."

The following events were full of drama. The apparently broken Karpov, playing in his familiar aggressive style, won three games in a row and equalized the score. All the questions we asked ourselves and which eventually forced us to decide on 'surgery' centered on the odd 18th game.

This is what Igor Akimov wrote about it. Akimov was a friend of Karpov, and he boasted that he spent with the challenger all of the latter's time when he wasn't playing or analyzing chess: "...it was after 2 a.m. and he was still sitting looking at the position... I'm sitting opposite Karpov. I like the white pieces, but not his position at all.

'Where is this position from, Tolya?'

'This will be the position tomorrow...Oh, what do I mean tomorrow? It's today already! But I don't yet sense this position. I move the pieces around, but it all seems to belong to somebody else. I don't feel anything natural here... It's a typical Kasparov position.'

'So why will you play it?'

'Nothing is what it seems, you know. Kasparov has familiarized himself with this position, crafted it at home. He knows its potential and pitfalls. He isn't afraid of it and will go for it... See my queen there? I move it here on move ten, and that immediately changes the situation. This move has never been played before..."'"

That is a lot to admit in just a small extract! So many inconvenient questions that it poses to Karpov! The night before the game, the player is torturing himself, trying to find acceptable ways to play a bad position which he doesn't like yet which will appear on the board in the playing hall in ten or so hours' time of his own free will. Karpov knows all this! How could he have known with such certainty after two crushing wins with the Spanish Opening in his last two white games that Kasparov would suddenly "switch hands" and opt for 1.d4 ? OK, let's give him the benefit of the doubt and assume that he guessed correctly. And then he made the second amazing guess in a row, that, despite his clear winning of the opening battles at the start of the match with the Nimzo-Indian, Kasparov would suddenly reject that fearsome opening and go for a Queen's Indian. OK, let's also give Karpov the benefit of the doubt and assume that he amazingly guessed correctly again, like a genius. Bravo! But how could he have guessed, too, that Kasparov wouldn't go for his favorite line 4.a3 that he knew so well and instead choose a subvariation that he had never played in his life? Moreover, how would Karpov have known that Kasparov had "familiarized himself with this position" (and that really was the case – we had written down several pages of analysis)? Further, how did Karpov know that the modest queen advance on move ten would be a surprise for his opponent? Surely he hadn't read our pages of notes where this unenterprising move wasn't analyzed? Yet even if he had read them, surely it would have been a big risk to count on changing the course of play by opting for a third-rate move against an expert in this particular opening, and the world champion at that?

I will stick my neck out and say that Karpov's deeply psychological trick had the aim of again demonstrating to his opponent that he knew "everything" in order to further unbalance Garry's fragile state of mind. As was meant to happen, Kasparov easily solved the chess puzzle posed to him and gained a huge, perhaps even decisive advantage. However, he became so nervous during his opponent's time trouble that he adjourned in a position where he now had to fight for a draw.

We analyzed the game all night. Karpov had three possible continuations. In the first, the most dangerous one for Garry, after a long search we managed to find a good defensive plan giving us immense chances of a draw. We found a definite draw in the second most dangerous line. We didn't spend much time analyzing the third one, which Karpov surprisingly picked. It was so obviously harmless that we limited ourselves to noting down a short, purely illustrative variation, but which contained a mistake... on the very first move! We found a simple way to draw, with just two moves, but only after the game. Garry, of course, was forced to try this unfortunate line at the board. Yet how could we understand Karpov's decision to choose an obviously weak continuation counting on his opponent making the only possible blunder, which we could have avoided had he spent five minutes thinking about it at the board? What was this? A new flash of his genius guess-work? An amazing congruence of our analysis, including blunders? Or further proof of his "omniscience"?

Our team meeting late that evening after such an awful second session was held in a state of alarm. When we started to think about possible ways that information had been leaked – and almost nobody doubted that it had been – questions only arose in respect of the behavior of one of the coaches. Later, people from Karpov's inner circle were to say that until the very start of the second session he didn't know which of three(!) continuations to select. Our colleague deflected the questions with difficulty and, most importantly of all, very nervously. However, there was no direct evidence and our logical deductions could have been mistaken. For the last time, we decided to increase vigilance and made do with the slogan: "Guys, let's live in harmony and not make each other nervous."

By the way, Karpov's agreement to house his team in a building just a few hundred meters from us was highly suspicious. In both previous matches and in London, and in the following match in Seville, the residences of the two Ks were located as far away from each other as possible. And that was totally logical. Given the huge and lengthy nervous tension, even a chance meeting during a stroll could have provoked a mass of negative emotions. The place where we were to stay in Leningrad was identified before the match began, and Karpov, with support provided by the city government, would have found no difficulty in gaining somewhere to stay far from our team. As soon as we flew into Leningrad, we learned that our opponents were housed in the most inconvenient part of Kamenny Islands, yet very near us. Their building was located by a film studio infested with rats and those buildings were adjoined to a cancer hospital. Moreover, their building housed other guests. This was a strange choice, contrary to Karpov's nature, which was used to ceding no ground to the opposition.

After we decided not to leave the building for several days in order to avoid mutual suspicions, and having set up monitoring of all phone calls and ensured that the coaches would all work separately – natural measures taken in this extreme situation that had suddenly arisen – it was once again our colleague Vladimirov who announced that he would not fulfill these requirements. One has to admit that even an inexperienced "spy" would have realized that this action was ill-considered and an act of self-exposure. Garry convinced him to put up with several days of our state of alarm, but he again openly violated our rules prior to game 19. And again, Karpov demonstrated remarkable knowledge of our new and complicated opening line, which we had prepared long before but kept deep in reserve. He played the game aggressively and wonderfully, but given his poor memory he could only have played out the opening if he knew what was going to be on the board that evening.

"Karpov already knew how to break through the Grunfeld Defense, and it again collapsed," Akimov wrote. This appears to be an innocent sentence, but is in fact excessive frankness of a close friend of Karpov with no grasp of chess subtleties. Never again would Karpov apply the super-aggressive lines of the Grunfeld Defense, neither against Kasparov nor against anybody else, that delivered him such astounding success in this match. So where did his deep knowledge and fantastic foresight disappear?

Our next meeting was stormy and extremely frank. The main topic of conversation consisted of the assumption which had been kept from Kasparov at the start of the match but to which he gradually arrived on his own. The coaches again confirmed their readiness to work in a regime that would avoid any suspicion, and again only one was categorically opposed to the idea. Moreover, he tried his best to retain a phone in his room. Maybe he had a nervous breakdown at the end of the match, but with such a large quantity of unpleasant "coincidences" befalling us we had no alternative but to ask him to leave the residence. Early in the morning of game 20 our chauffeur drove him to the airport, only for us to be told at midday that there would be no game – our opponent had taken a time out!

According to Akimov: "Karpov woke up in a bad mood [after three wins in a row! – A.N.]. He had a headache... [maybe he hadn't slept properly, got overly worried about something, or there had been some incident in his building – A.N.]... Two of the team's leaders walked into his bedroom. They had never before entered it so early [did this really happen? – A.N.] Everybody knew and understood everything already, except for me, a novice in this matter[!]... Five minutes later somebody went to tell the arbiters that Karpov was taking his last time-out."

Well actually, nobody understood anything! The absurdity of such a decision by this greatly experienced fighter was plain to see. He was giving his collapsing opponent a three-day break! Claims that he had difficulties in the openings seem ridiculous, but maybe Karpov was right. He really did have problems. For the first time he had to come on stage knowing that we were working to completely change our opening repertoire, but this time not knowing which specific opening position would appear on the board.

Our Doctor Gasanov, helped by Klara Kasparova, had to work hard to pull Garry out of his trance. In those three days the seconds put together a new robust weapon for him that could be used in the remaining five games. However, there proved to be no need for it!

"I'd rather not write about the remaining games..." Akimov lamented, and not for nothing. People carefully following play got the impression that after this absurd time-out the last five games were played by a rather unskilled Karpov double. He demonstrated nothing – not a trace of aggression in his play, amazing foresight, speed or confidence in his decisions.

I think there really was a channel leaking valuable information, well packaged and ready for immediate use, and that it ceased to exist after that tragic nineteenth game's second session. But what role was played in that story by our colleague who suddenly left us isn't clear to me to this day. I cannot rule out that his highly-strung state, the nature of which we didn't understand, was maintained by somebody else artificially and was used to hide the work of another, main informer, who may have got frightened at the possibility of being unmasked and hence lay low, with the organizers of this venture not knowing what would happen if the investigation continued. Well, we didn't have time for any investigations, and none of us wanted to play detective at that moment. In any event, had Karpov been clean, he would have been absolutely required to maintain the nature of his play that had suddenly brought him huge dividends as the finishing line approached, both to win the match and to save his reputation.

However, something else happened during Karpov's absurd time-out. We heard later that the challenger had even managed to make a blitz visit to Moscow. I think that some event occurred in those days that made him lose interest in the match's outcome.

It seemed during those last five games that a seriously scared person sat opposite Garry. Scared so much that he wasn't much interested in what was taking place on the board. Kasparov was never in any danger of losing during those games, while the epiphany that he experienced after time-trouble was over in game 22 allowing him to find a pretty path to victory proved to be a just present from Caissa for his bravery and resilience. The world champion had no trouble drawing the last two games, as his opponent was capable of doing nothing more than holding the fort.

It's a shame that this match, ten of whose games from the first 19 could justifiably be treated as works of art, was blackened by quite un-chess-like play drummed up by people supporting Karpov and trying to ensure that he won at any price.

The Leningrad authorities did much to demonstrate that they needed "their" Tolya to win. Towards the end of the match, when the outcome suddenly came into question, the fans' passions transformed into shouts such as "Tolya, kill him!" and the match turned into some sort of political battle with a nationalist underbelly. The closing ceremony was neither solemn nor fun. The artistic part of the program, whose icing on the cake was meant to be dancers performing a fragment of game 19 won by Karpov, was naturally cancelled, and the rest was totally prosaic.

Both players had resorted to the use of psychics in this tense battle. Dadashev flew in for game 22 to help Garry, while before the start of the match Karpov went to visit the famous Evgenia Dzhuna several times to energize himself. At their last parting she presented him with an amulet containing her picture, which he was meant to wear the entire match without taking it off. Well, don't rush to judge these great fighters for that. This endless chain of battles for the chess crown, year in year out, sucked all reserve energy and nerves out of them, and usual methods of recuperation worked far from always.

Immediately after the match, both grandmasters travelled to the Olympiad in Dubai, where the Soviet team was about to withstand fierce competition from the US and English teams. Our grandmasters had to fight hard for their gold medals, but they did so spectacularly. The world champion defeated Poland's Wlodzimierz Schmidt in the final round and delivered the team victory after all the other games in that round had ended. The two Ks quickly transformed from irreconcilable rivals into team-mates forging out victory together, and I almost found myself feeling sorry at the extent to which their endless battle for the chess crown had crippled their relations.

This was the first time that I acted as a coach for Garry at an Olympiad. Our team's chief coach Efim Geller said this of my work: "Nikitin made a huge contribution to managing the team. Even in the most difficult of times his confidence and coolness supported me well..."

Garry, although he won the competition among board one players, found it hard going, as he spent all time when not playing on organizing opposition to Campomanes's reelection among delegates of the upcoming FIDE congress. However, he failed to achieve his goal. The Soviet delegate at the congress had been given a directive to support Campo, and that was that. Nevertheless, at the Olympiad the world champion managed to encourage the grandmasters into creating a sort of trade union for chess professionals.

Soon, the Grandmasters Association was officially registered in Brussels, led by Kasparov and Belgian businessman and big chess fan Bessel Kok.

Garry ended the year winning a strong tournament in Brussels. That was his first official individual competition in three years that wasn't a match against Karpov. Getting used to tournament battle again, the need to face a new opponent each day with his own style of play and opening repertoire, required intense preparation, and he needed to work exceptionally hard. Prior to the last round, Kasparov was ahead of second-placed Korchnoi by 2.5 points! He also reached a new rating record at the end of the tournament – 2750 ! This was a happy end to a tough and nerve-racking year.

Grand plans to create a chess community based on the principle of fairness were hatching in Garry's mind. Yet he had to face new tournaments... and a new match with Karpov.

Chapter 5. Ambitions and Nerves (Match 4, 1987)

In the days when Botvinnik and Petrosian were champions chess remained a prestigious, "royal" game, and world champions were respected. However, they didn't play any remarkable role in public life. When they became champions, they were mature, formed personalities, aware of their weight and place in society. There were almost no chess professionals in the western world playing for a living, and only 20-30 grandmasters from the USSR and Eastern Bloc countries were financed by the state. This enabled them to remain at the top of the list of the strongest chess players in the world. It hence demonstrated the "superiority" of the socialist way of life in those countries. However, even those grandmasters could not publicly call themselves professionals. Formally they ranked as undergraduate students, post-graduate students, military personnel or sports instructors.

Bobby Fischer's storming of Mount Olympus in 1972 was accompanied by an unprecedented chess boom. For the first time, chess was on the radar screens of many politicians, forcing its way to the front pages of leading newspapers, and even gained the attention of businessmen. Fischer could easily have become an important public and even political figure on the back of his remarkable popularity. However, he, just like his legendary fellow-countryman Paul Morphy, suddenly walked away from chess after attaining global recognition. The mystery surrounding his peculiar reclusion managed for several years to retain the heightened public interest in this wise but, as it turned out, harsh game capable of breaking the character and even sanity of grandmasters. However, the public demanded new heroes, and they appeared very quickly.

It turned out that these clever gardeners, cultivating a decent harvest in the chess garden, were the young but since childhood very pragmatic Karpov, and his amazingly capable "pupil" Kasparov. Karpov worked in the garden methodically and without excess noise, collecting the crop, maintaining the garden in a good state and gradually widening it. He counted on farming this paradise for a long time to come, as he was protected from trouble by experienced stewards and aides who knew their jobs well. However, peace in the garden was unexpectedly disturbed by the young and very noisy Southerner, who forced the head gardener to squeeze up and make room for him, and suggested to his team that they find alternative employment. Thanks to Kasparov's efforts, the chess garden transformed radically. New buildings were constructed, trees were planted, and journalists and TV cameramen ran up and down the paths. The quiet garden gradually turned into a public park filled with fairground rides and little shops. It brought more income, but a lot of it had nothing to do with gardening. Actually, with every year the new chief gardener cared less and less about that, and everything that was going on came to resemble the plot of Anton Chekhov's *Cherry Garden*.

Garry started to expend all of his youthful energy on popularizing chess and gradually transforming it from a social phenomenon into a profitable industry. The champion's activity in this area began as soon as the match in Seville ended. He said: "Behind all of my organizational and commercial projects you will find the nature of a practical dreamer. I want to promote chess using all tools available to me – games, books, new forms of competition, and I'm ready to experiment, even taking part in chess forums meant as entertainment... "

So he began his experiments, playing in 1987 a commercial match with Short on the stage of the London Hippodrome. Both players and organizers were mostly happy with the results of this show. However, the world champion's participation turned out to be a badly thought through venture. The six-game match was played over just two days, as it was a rapid event with 25 minutes per player instead of the classic 2.5 hours for 40 moves. This was a great advert that sparked huge interest in rapid chess. There were even conversations about creating the title of rapid grandmaster and introducing separate ratings and so on. The FIDE President unleashed a burst of activity to organize a rapid world championship cycle. Campo, still shunned by Kasparov at the time, wanted to use the new title of rapid champion to devalue the title of classical, "slow" world champion. As a result, over the next two years Garry had to make a massive effort to dampen the wave of excitement around attempts to legitimize the equal significance of fun types of chess that were perfectly appropriate for fan competitions, and classical chess competitions that required talent and years of hard work to gain success.

After seeing off Short, Garry flew to Brussels where he and Kok continued to develop the GMA, and then to Germany, where he gave a clock simul against a team of masters – one of the best in the Bundesliga. His first attempt against them with clocks, in December 1985, was a bit of a calamity. Garry, the best simul player in the world, lost in an exhibition (3.5:4.5) for the only time that I can recall. In 1987 he won the return match convincingly. Today his simuls are much more successful and he regularly scores 70% or more, even against national teams reaching the top ten at Olympiads.

He spent the whole of March in his home city of Baku, first coaching children at the Botvinnik – Kasparov school, and then playing simuls for the lads at the Pioneers Palace tournament.

After that, it was back to Brussels, where he gained first place in an international tournament ahead of Karpov, Korchnoi, Tal and Timman. This serious tournament ended with a grand blitz competition that the organizers even called the world championship. He won that convincingly, too, two points ahead of Timman and 4.5 points above Karpov. There is no doubt that his natural wonderful calculation ability, strengthened by his immensely rapid thought process, was responsible for ensuring his first place among the older generation of blitzers. However, the young grandmasters Short, Ivanchuk and Anand compete with him increasingly successfully with every year that passes.

Garry began to prepare for his next match against Karpov at the end of May after he returned home with his mother from Barcelona, where he was awarded his fourth chess Oscar. His coaches met up with him in a cozy building in the Azerbaijan mountains. The building's grounds, allocated for vacations of VIPs, encompassed a tennis court, a basketball court, a tarmac running track and a swimming pool which never had any water in it. Garry enthusiastically ran 20-30 minutes every day round the track. I tried to compete with him at running a number of times but never lasted more than ten minutes. This wasn't to do with the difference in our ages or Garry's speed, or even because we were running in the mountains, where breathing was far more difficult than in the valley. No, Garry, in order to beef up his resilience and patience, ran at noon, when the burning sun softened the tarmac. And he ran at that time every day!

Our team of seconds changed significantly. We were joined by Zurab Azmaiparashvili, a young and hardworking Georgian master with an unusual playing signature. Working with Garry was very useful to him and he became a grandmaster a couple of years later. Zurab really helped Garry to master a new opening to be deployed in his match – the English.

Grandmaster Sergei Dolmatov also agreed to help his recent rival in junior tournaments. He had sharply improved his level of play and had won the reputation of a skillful analyst, having learned this craft from Dvoretsky. Sergei's influence was immense at the match in Seville, as a result of which it was Karpov rather than Garry who found himself disadvantaged in analyzing adjourned positions.

Garry worked hard at our training sessions, around 5-6 hours per day. We coaches worked much longer hours, as there was a lot of dirty preparatory work to be done.

An interesting surprise was prepared for us at the second training session, held in Zagulba. We later learned that a person by the name of Feldman who was close to the Karpov camp flew in and attempted to convince Kasparov that the ex-world champion had been lacking in gratitude towards him and, hence, that he (Feldman) wanted to get his own back. It turned out that it was Feldman who had attempted to turn Dorfman in Moscow in 1985, offering him a hundred thousand rubles and the opportunity to move with his family to Moscow in return to coming to work for Karpov. Among other information, our guest told Kasparov that during the Leningrad match the source of prep leaks was not the coach that everybody had suspected, but quite a different person. This turn-coat's trip to Zagulba was mostly kept a secret from us coaches, though he was shown to us at tea after lunch one day. I figured out that this was a peculiar investigative experiment to see if we recognized him – the home-baked psychology professors Viktor Litvinov and Klara Kasparova stared at us inquisitively.

Garry became increasingly nervy as the match approached. During the year since the last match he had managed to enjoy the taste and other delights of the champion's glory, made lots of predictions, built a ton of plans, and got infected by the fear of losing his crown. The champion recounted with increasing frequency that defending his title would be far more challenging than winning it, and that the energy that had driven him upwards was no longer there... However, when in another interview Garry stated that he would organize his opponent a first-class funeral, this hackneyed method of frightening opponents so loved by boxing pros simply underscored his lack of confidence.

Karpov, meanwhile, combined his preparation with resolving in a German court the problems concerning the money due to him from advertising computers. On the eve of the match he claimed that he had no doubt of victory. The psychological battle began.

The match was held in the ancient and unusually picturesque Spanish city of Seville. The Lope de Vega opera theater hosted the match. When, five days before the beginning, we flew into Seville and went to examine the playing hall, our first impression was a mixture of delight at the amazing spectator hall and horror at the foyer and players' rest rooms, which resembled pigsties. The theater was in the midst of a refit. However, they promised us that the works were sticking to the timetable. Indeed, the last workman left the theater half an hour before the opening ceremony. Only a strong smell of paint in the players' rest rooms reminded us of the refit. It was gone after a few days, though.

Before the start, Kasparov presented his autobiographical book *Child of Change*, written by an English journalist. The book turned out to be a pretty poor one. Moreover, it was hardly wise to try and time its publication to coincide with the start of the match. However, the laws of commerce dictate certain decisions.

Just like before the match with Korchnoi in 1983, Garry's bravado started to slip a few days before we began. The day of the first game he was in a very tense and defensive state of mind. His psychological disturbance became clear after the tragic second game, when he deployed the English Opening for the first time. Garry went for a well-known line, hoping to try a new idea discovered in Zagulba that changed the position's evaluation in white's favor. Karpov intuitively sensed a trap, and, after thinking a little, pulled from the depth of his memory a counter-idea which, as later transpired, he had analyzed about twelve years earlier. The effect was breathtaking. Garry spent an incredible 83(!) minutes on deciding whether to capture a dangerous pawn. He seemed to be in shock. Once the game was over, he was unable either to show us cohesive variations or to explain coherently on what he had spent so much time. It was hard for him to count on success after such a "snooze", and he was severely punished.

During a five-hour game, chess players have perfected the stereotypical alternation between heavy pressure (when thinking what move to make) and, relatively speaking, a rest mode (during their opponent's move). A grandmaster's body is used to this work regime, and any sharp deviations from it impinge on the quality of their work. Almost an hour and a half of intense thinking while bearing nervous tension, worries and doubt, provoked a depressive, faltering state in Garry that lasted the rest of the game and led to him forgetting to press his clock shortly before time control, when he just sat at the board in a detached pose. In accordance with the rules, nobody could tell him of his misstep. Garry only snapped out of it when the arbiter was required to come to the board and stand next to the table, ready to declare the game lost on time a couple of minutes later. The champion's loss in this game was the logical conclusion of the factors involved. The most important of these was that his opponent noted his awful psychological state, which encouraged Karpov at the start of the battle.

Had Karpov not created himself problems in the English Opening we would have had a tougher time, as it took ages for Garry to recover. He was constantly criticizing himself, which merely drained his strength. The analysis of each game played, carried out by the player together with his seconds, sometimes leads to evaluations which are the complete opposite of those provided by experts in the press-center. Naturally, the players' seconds do not seek arguments in the press-center to demonstrate the absolute truth. So we spent the whole subsequent year racking our brains to try and figure out why, despite winning game two, Karpov would never again repeat his successful idea. He began to use less reliable setups, and playing with the black pieces became real torture for him, while the English Opening unexpectedly turned into a golden-egged goose for Garry. Had the champion not been in such a poor psychological state he could have won more white games in the first half of the match.

In game five Karpov applied a new plan devised by his second, Igor Zaitsev, in the main line of the Grunfeld Defense. This surprise became Karpov's key opening weapon for some time, causing our team's coaches all sorts of torment. We found the purpose of the idea for white quite quickly and came up with original methods of creating counterplay. However, the champion, who seemed to find threats in every white move, demanded (the time when he simply asked for something had long gone) deep analysis of all acceptable continuations. As we were now deprived of the opportunity to spend long periods of time with him, couldn't speak with him man-to-man and couldn't calm him man-to-man, all that remained for us was to attempt to restore his confidence with long analysis, which he sometimes even forgot to review.

Karpov's first outing with Zaitsev's idea in game five might have been its last one, had Garry steered the game, which he played pretty well, to victory. However, once again it was his long thinking (64 minutes on a single move!), torturous indecision and an overestimate of his opponent's threats that led to sudden confusion during a time scramble and a series of suicidal moves.

Our delegation was split into two parts: the other coaches, doctor and official delegation head stayed in a hotel in the center of the city. The other half – Garry with his mother, Litvinov and I – lived in a villa with a swimming pool and a little English courtyard in a suburb of Seville. By the way, Karpov wanted to stay in the opposite part of town, and not near us as was the case in Leningrad. I asked our official head more than once to change the set of people staying in the villa, at least temporarily, to exclude Garry's mother. That would have enabled us to change the course of the match. However, my request would be followed by a consultation with Litvinov and the reply that this was impossible.

In the second half of the match, Garry, who enjoyed a minimal lead, was willing to draw the rest of the games. He wasn't afraid of Karpov, who was playing more weakly than he had done in the past. No, the champion was afraid of himself, of mistakes that he might make, and, most importantly of all, he was panicking at the prospect of losing his crown. He had made too many plans as world champion – in public life, in the business world and even in politics. Were he to become an ex-champion, some of his plans would collapse and many new "VIP" friends would stop meeting with him.

Before us was now a new Kasparov, believing in Kabbalah numerology and all sorts of superstitions. Prior to game 16, instead of serious preparation, he attempted to convince both himself and us just as seriously that he always plays game 16 wonderfully. As a result, instead of a wonderful game, he lost his way and Karpov levelled the score. Constant nervous tension led him to forget his opening analysis. He couldn't remember the precise paths devised by his seconds, and in game 21 he even offered a draw in a position where he had a material advantage without compensation for his opponent.

Before the second session of game 17 we were just a step from tragedy. The adjourned position was assessed by everybody as totally drawn. Garry spent the entire evening criticizing his opponent for ruining the forthcoming day by forcing him to focus on the resumption. All of our attempts to begin serious analysis of the adjourned position were met by his laughter. So we decided to begin analysis the next morning and the other seconds left for their hotel. That morning, our brief analysis was stopped at the champion's insistence "for pointlessness", and we began to discuss how to ensure a draw in the game after that.

Midday came but there was no phone call with a draw offer. This meant that the resumption would happen, and the annoyed champion went to bed, as he always did on a playing day. The coaches, split into two pairs, went for a walk to wonder calmly what had prompted Karpov to continue the battle. The adjourned position was spinning in the heads of all of us, and we walked in silence, trying to find some crafty Karpovian move. Well, the epiphany hit all of us at the same time, and both pairs, though located far from each other, sharply changed direction and rushed back to the villa. We met by the gates and, looking at each other, realized that we were all thinking about the same thing. After moving the pieces around the board in the analysis room, we realized that our worst fears were true. There was only an hour and a half left before the resumption, and we couldn't find any immediate refutation of our opponent's plan. Meanwhile, the recently awoken champion was heartily eating his traditional steak in the canteen, staring gloomily ahead as usual. Noting our faces he concluded that the coaches had again failed to understand something and looked up at us with a piece of bread in his hand.

Analysis at crazy speed began just seconds later. It was headed not by the champion – he was working on it separately with Dorfman – but Dolmatov. In just over an hour we found an elaborate path to a draw. Garry even arrived at the match 15 minutes late, and Karpov, fortunately, thought that this was some protest at having to play an unnecessary resumption. It turned out that he had only decided to continue play to deprive Garry of energy before the next game. After playing four moves he offered a draw...

While the champion left for the game with his constant psychological "support group" – his mother and Litvinov – his coaches had remained at the villa and continued to move the pieces around out of habit. With calm reigning we quickly found another spectacular and clear path to a draw and waited impatiently for the live TV broadcast of the session to begin. Karpov's very first move demonstrated that our worries were unjustified. After the players quickly shook hands Garry, breaking his rule of leaving the stage immediately, started to demonstrate something to Karpov on the board. After returning full of beans and happy from the session he told us: "Those lines struck me so much that had Karpov left immediately I would have shown them to the chief arbiter. I couldn't help asking my opponent why he didn't move his rook as soon as we stopped the clocks. He looked on with amazement as I moved the pieces around and his face gradually turned pale..." The next morning we were told that Karpov had taken a time out...

Again, I have to acknowledge the wonderful fighting qualities and psychological control of the ex-world champion. Karpov went to fight any position, sometimes taking big risks. He realized that the only way to win was to create conditions that would provoke Kasparov into a psychological collapse. It was tough for him. I think that sometimes he was even afraid, as his guns sometimes misfired – then he would grab a grenade and a rifle with a bayonet and charge forward. He would slip but keep going.

The two final games were the culmination of the nervous tension, prior to which the players had equal points. In advance of game 23 we easily figured out which opening line Karpov would choose – he would avoid the painful Grunfeld Defense in which he had no serious weapon left and instead opt for the English. After a day of intense work we found a path to equality. And before Garry left for the game we thought we had convinced him not to try anything sharp.

After a peaceful opening, when black only needed to play a couple of moves to achieve equality, he suddenly charged forward with his pawns. Such a turn of events required from Garry decisiveness and inventiveness, but, after starting this "war", he abruptly stopped a couple of moves later, as though recalling our behest to play calmly. Well, pawns don't move backwards, and Karpov gained a considerable advantage. After that chances got even again, but the champion made a poor final move before time control and the game was adjourned in a dangerous position for him.

Although we coaches agreed with this assessment, we didn't believe that Garry risked losing. In order to beef up his advantage, Karpov needed to write down a far from obvious sealed move after a nasty time scramble, whereas another more natural move that appeared to be just as dangerous and strong would have allowed black to create sufficient activity for equality in an unexpected and original way. The morning newspapers provided us with the necessary information, reporting that the ex-champion had spent just three minutes on his sealed move. So he had gone for the obvious and less strong move and we were unconcerned about the outcome of the second session. But mistakenly so...

Karpov had indeed been tempted by the obvious continuation. The second session followed our analysis and appeared to be heading inexorably to a draw. The only cause for concern was the long time spent thinking by both players, who with every move increasingly approached time trouble. Then, when the players had only about five minutes each to make time control, they burst into a series of lightning-speed moves begun by our charge. After that, the clocks stopped and the players disappeared from the stage in a flash. The TV screen switched off. I sat there understanding nothing. Then I phoned the press-center but there, too, nobody knew how the game ended. The champion soon arrived back, looking pale and crushed. In time trouble he had opted for a mistaken combination and blundered a rook away. I silently showed him notes from our analysis, where this losing combination was recorded together with an alternative path to a draw from a position of strength. It was like a scene shot in slow motion.

In order to shake the numbed champion out of his state of total indifference I suggested to Litvinov that the three of us travel for the first time to the other coaches' hotel. So we arrived there and painted a nonchalant smile on our faces as though we were happy that everything would finally be over the next day. We then bumped into one of Karpov's aides by the lift. What good luck! In just a few minutes, Karpov and his circle would learn that Garry had gone to that hotel as though nothing had happened. We then spent a couple of hours trying to convince him (and ourselves) that all was not lost, distracting ourselves from dark thoughts as well as we could. It was long after midnight when we returned to the villa and Garry, totally exhausted, fell asleep immediately.

In my opinion, the scenario for game 24 that we devised was one of the greatest achievements of our coaching team. Garry listened obediently, as he didn't seem to have any strength left for arguing. His remaining energy was needed for the evening, where everything would be decided. He needed a win to retain his champion's title. No other champion had achieved such a feat in living memory.

We decided to make the game as tight and long as possible. To this end, Garry was told to avoid a sharp battle. With each move he had to pose his opponent a small (and only small!) problem. About an hour and a half before the start we finally agreed on an appropriate opening, one which Kasparov had never before played, and in which no crisis could occur earlier than at move 30 if the game progressed normally. We concluded that our only chance of winning the game (with neither player having any energy left) was to head for a nearly equal position and keep it in that position for as long as possible. Then, the opponent, who would have been expecting mad pressure from the very start of the game, would unexpectedly find himself in a situation with no evident threats but no obvious path to equality either. This, we believed, would leave Karpov feeling uncomfortable, and increasingly so the more the uncertainty lasted. Were our strategy to succeed, the consequence of such discomfort would be time trouble and mistakes made by the player on the defensive. Naturally, these exhausted players were bound to make mistakes, and we could only hope that Karpov would make bigger ones.

That day, our entire team went to the playing hall to support Garry. We sat in a place where he could always see us to feel our moral support. The game progressed exactly according to our scenario. We could see Karpov literally torturing himself to find clear equality. Garry managed to create a position where his opponent had to wait patiently for gradual equality, but Karpov was too impatient. As a result, his position worsened with every move, and he ran catastrophically short of time. When Garry decided that he'd achieved his aim he relaxed and carried out a "spectacular" maneuver with his queen, that might have cost him everything he had gained so far. However, Karpov was by then so used to being on the losing side that in terrible time trouble he was unable to react correctly. He had just seconds remaining and needed to make his last moves. At the very end of the game Garry again relaxed his bind, and the game was adjourned in a position where his extra pawn gave him great winning chances but not a guaranteed win.

For the last, decisive time, our analytical work proved to be of far higher quality than that of the opposite team. We managed to identify all resources and subtleties of the position. Karpov and his seconds came to the session assessing his position too pessimistically. Garry realized this, noting that the ex-champion's lucky mascot and main pillar of support, his young wife Natalia, was absent from the hall. Karpov resisted feebly, played poor moves and lost quickly. This was the loudest ovation that the theater, overflowing with spectators, had heard since the greatest opera singers had performed on its stage!

What a difference from the second match, when Karpov, then the world champion and needing a win with white with the score also 11:12, managed to lose the game and hence the match 11:13.

So, the fourth K vs K match had ended in a draw. It was unusually nervy and had exhausted everybody with its tension, which sometimes even arose when we least expected it. Games from this match were painful for me to recall for a long time to come, just like touching raw nerves, as there had been so many mistakes in them – sometimes, quite strange ones. During this standoff (here this word is more apt than "battle" or "duel") psychology dominated chess creativity for the first time.

By the way, this was the first time that Garry played a title match without professional psychological help. Even the faithful doctor Gasanov was left at home. The champion decided to place himself in the hands of the psychological mastery of his mother and Litvinov. Alas, events proved yet again that common sense, life experience and the greatest of intentions cannot replace professional know-how in extreme situations.

Karpov, meanwhile, had delivered us another surprise in this match. After his failure in the previous match he lost faith in Dzhuna and found support in Dadashev. Yes, he was being supported by that psychic psychologist who had aided Garry in the previous matches. Such a switch of teams by a trainer is a hard blow for a sportsman, and indeed a step that forever darkens the reputation of the defector. The transfer of a psychologist to the enemy camp is nothing short of treason. After all, for a psychologist to provide real help to a patient the latter has to open up to them fully, recounting all their weaknesses in order to help the expert identify new reserves of character and mental balance. A psychologist for a sportsman relying on them is like a priest listening to a confession. And there is no greater crime than retelling somebody's confession or using what they said to harm them. Evidently, Dadashev considered his transfer from Kasparov to Karpov to be nothing more than replacing his patient. As Dadashev would say later, he gave Karpov three pieces of advice. Karpov followed two of them to the letter, but ignored the third and failed to win the match for that reason.

The game of chess enjoys lots of definitions: sport, science and art, a model of life and the wise game. Well, at the risk of repeating myself I will say that at the highest level chess is a cruel game. Caissa, that jealous protectress of chess, cannot abide rivals and refuses to share her favorites with anybody. Protecting grandmasters, she demands in return full, selfless devotion to serving the art of chess. She may exact cruel revenge on anybody who betrays her. In his youth, Garry dared to treat her without due respect. Before this match, he was regularly distracted from the activity in which he really was strong by all sorts of pleasant and "prestigious" but in essence secondary matters and responsibilities. He managed to become the president (oh, how Kasparov loved this word) of an international association of grandmasters and even of a Moscow computer club. In so doing, he got caught up in his own Afghanistan – a long and ultimately unwinnable war with FIDE and its president. The confines of the chess world had long cramped his active and vain nature, and Garry followed Karpov's example in getting involved in the computer business as well as public and charity work.

This time, Caissa nobly forgave her favorite, leading him just for a second towards disaster. She forgave him for his amazing and beautiful talent and also for withstanding the trial – stuck in a catastrophic situation at the end of the match he found the strength within himself to alter the course of history in an incredible way.

The match was over and we rushed home. This attractive villa had been like a golden cage for me for 75 days. The famous tower of gold, the ever cool halls of Alcazar Palace, that fortress of Seville's ancient rulers, the magnificent pillars of one of the world's greatest cathedrals – I only managed to see these sights from the window of the bus taking us to the airport...

Chapter 6. Storms Instead of Calm (1988-1990)

It was only after winning his last game in Seville that Garry finally became a "full" and yet three-times world champion. Now, his royal rights would extend over three whole years. Nevertheless, his life didn't get any quieter – and the king was himself to blame for this. He decided not only to play frequently in tournaments but also to introduce his own *perestroika* to the chess kingdom. With the headiness and inexperience of youth he attempted to reform the activity of the Soviet Chess Federation, trying to counter its weight by creating a powerful chess federation in the trade unions and reviving the union of Soviet grandmasters.

Well, he didn't get very far in this endeavor, but expended much energy and made himself a ton of enemies, especially among the sporting bosses. They found the champion's innovations to be alien, remembering wistfully the quiet old days. When Garry extended the sphere of his *perestroika* activities and sharply notched up his struggle for the recognition of professional sport in the USSR, he became the State Sports Committee's enemy number one.

Actually, adult sport had essentially been professional for many years. Sportsmen belonging to various national teams spent most of their time taking part in competitions or preparing for them at special training sessions paid for by the state. It was sport that comprised their lives when they were young and then a profession that enabled them to pay their way.

Officially, all our sportsmen were classed as "amateurs". This enabled them to compete at the Olympic games when professionals were banned from taking part. At competitions abroad they would only perform as members of our sporting delegations, sent by the State Sports Committee or its junior bodies. Sportsmen were unable to travel to competitions as individuals. As a result, everything that the sportsmen earned abroad was taken from them by the "boss" who had sent them – that very State Sports Committee. In exchange, the sportsmen were paid a stipend in rubles akin to a good worker's salary. Actually, some of them got paid partially in hard currency – in accordance with the principle of divide and rule prevalent in sport.

One big difference, though, was that a worker could eventually retire on a pension. A sportsman, after his time in the team was up, would find himself on the threshold of a new life far from sport, and tragedies began here. They had no savings, but they had to feed their families somehow. They were devoid of professional qualifications, no longer had the sporting chiefs looking out for them, and had no life coach who would tell them what to do today and what to do tomorrow. They kept their memories of delighted fans, but now that delight was addressed to new heroes, and nobody noticed you anymore. You were an "ex" something, but not like everybody else, because you were now 30 something and were not qualified for any profession, while the distance learning degree you held, all the more so from some physical education establishment, was nothing more than an empty sheet of paper. You didn't know how to do anything, whereas your old classmates who had looked at you enviously when you returned from far-off countries were qualified professionals who stood firmly on their two feet. In those days, nobody gave any thought to the social adaptation of sportsmen to ordinary life.

There were of course exceptions, which were often created artificially. Famous champions of the past sometimes became sports bosses, and some even managed to obtain research degrees. Their lucky fortune was usually brought up in order to counter the "nasty claims" that our former sporting heroes' lives had come undone. In the same breath, those making the argument would point to the supposed "criminal lives" of American black professional boxers and highlight "fatal stories" from the West.

When launching the battle for the rights of sportsmen, Garry hardly expected the sporting prison named the "State Sports Committee" to collapse just three years later, and that athletes would cease to depend on the charity of the poor man's Komsomol and party functionaries.

Garry was madly busy on the international front. In his first champion's year he completed the project that he had begun at the Dubai Olympiad. Together with Belgian banker Kok and several western grandmasters he finished setting up the GMA and made a huge effort to organize the World Cup, a robust set of competitions for chess professionals. The young world champion's fantastic energy and massive popularity together with the Belgian businessman's great organizational ability and financial resources led to six major tournaments being held in 1988-89 in which 25 of the world's strongest grandmasters took part. The first "tournament" world champion was determined based on each player's three best performances. Kasparov won the series.

In fact, victory in the second tournament, a point ahead of his eternal opponent, was enough for him to win that title. The other grandmasters ended up far behind in the series. They were capable of putting up resistance to the two Ks at best in a single tournament, but certainly not in the entire cycle.

The competition between these two leading players didn't quieten down at all in this three-year period. Rather, it led to the renaissance in Karpov's play and ambitions, which was quite unexpected by many. He played in a number of international tournaments and raised his rating to its highest ever level of 2755! The two Ks competed against each other in five tournaments in this period. Garry was the outright winner in three of them, while they shared first place in the other two. Their rivalry was relentless and fierce throughout.

As a coach, I was glad that their rivalry had continued, as I was worried that during his three "champion's" years Garry, occupied with both public work and his business ventures, would reduce his playing level. To avoid this happening, I had to invent a whole series of new goals for the young man at the top of the chess world that would stimulate him forwards.

A person needs a goal in life, and really several, otherwise their existence on Earth transforms into nothing but a biological process. The main goal of a talented person must be a challenging one, demanding constant effort – only that way will they make full use of their talent. Some of our ex-champions had a very short reign at the top, because after reaching it they simply began to enjoy life and the glory and were unable to prepare themselves to defend the crown that they had won with such difficulty. Being world champion is a profession in its own right, and a very difficult one at that.

The World Cup's two-year cycle saved the young champion's chess career. It proved easy to convince him that the title of world tournament champion wouldn't cause any harm. This ensured that Garry took the World Cup and chess prep seriously. However, a year later I needed to raise his motivation further, convincing him to chase the fantastic 2800 barrier – this was like a nine-meter long jump.

Garry needed these new goals, given victory in the overall World Cup was basically assured so early. He had time until mid-1990 to reach the new rating target, after which he had to end tournament play in order to prepare for his new match with Karpov. This way I hoped to maintain his fine sporting form until the match.

Actually, I found it hard to believe that Garry would manage to reach 2800 in such a short time. His weak points were evident to me as his coach more than to anybody else. Yet something unbelievable happened – with all his chess and non-chess weak points, with his head focused on a mass of problems, dozens of big projects and hundreds of small matters, while still joking about his poor health and total lack of energy, he touched the 2800 level at the end of 1989!

I aided Kasparov at a grandmasters tournament held in November 1989 in the Dutch city of Tilburg. I enjoyed seeing the proof that our many years of collaboration to improve his play, together with Garry's maturity into a full adult, bore wonderful fruit. Free from the need to meet some critical goal he played at ease, confidently and even with aplomb. Yet his aplomb was anything but bravado – rather, it was a natural reflection of the confidence of a true champion in his superiority over his opponents, whose weaknesses he knew well and all of which he could use against them – given that his play had become so diverse and perfected.

His early achievement of his rating target didn't stop him. Moreover, his enemies in FIDE, in charge of calculating the Elo numbers, had taken measures to ensure that his rating didn't rise above 2800. So Garry played his tournaments in 1990 attempting to exceed this record. He won the super tournament in Linares, which certainly made him richer, but it was his victory in a non-commercial match against Lev Psakhis that gained him another five rating points and hence a rise above this level that for other grandmasters at the time was quite unimaginable.

Garry's rival also had his own, rather interesting motivation, which impacted him quite effectively and was intended to be long-lasting. Karpov had long been used to considering himself as person number one – which is a totally required aspect of a champion's nature. After he lost his title of world champion the role of number two – be it in the rating list or World Cup – didn't interest or stimulate him in the slightest. Two stimuli forced him to work at chess: the desire to win back his title, and, more realistically, the desire to set a record that Kasparov would find extremely hard to match, and probably never would.

Karpov intended to reach a hundred and fifty tournament victories (included shared first places). He had started to keep count around ten years earlier, when the number of his tournament victories grew rapidly. One would have thought that the count would have slowed in the period of his matches against Garry. Yet not at all! He started to win rapid tournaments and even team tournaments. Karpov reached a hundred victories and didn't stop there. He then made a huge effort to get to a hundred and fifty, but victories proved to be increasingly difficult...

Kasparov's chess achievements delight fans, who gain great pleasure from his games. Moreover, Garry's victories are like stars in the sky that young players use to find their way, comparing their early career with his achievements.

Garry managed for some time to protect his champion's title from attacks by the sports bosses, who refused to recognize in the champion an equal partner with his own independent views on sporting issues in our country. They quickly realized that he would never become "their" soldier and they used every opportunity they could find to harm and even humiliate the best chess player on the planet.

The 55th USSR championship was held in 1988 in Moscow. All the strongest Soviet players took part. This time, Kasparov was unable to steal a lead on his eternal shadow, and these "Chuckle Brothers" shared the top two spots in the table. However, the match between the two top players, which was stipulated in the tournament rules, was never held, even though at the closing ceremony a draw was held to kick off that match. Karpov simply changed his mind and during the day when the first game was meant to be held he went for a walk in far-away Leningrad. Meanwhile, none other than Botvinnik defended him in Moscow, in his role as chief arbiter of the tournament. Well, just like Gligoric in 1985, he proved that a world-class grandmaster could not always act as a strong and independent arbiter capable of resisting various situations that life threw at him.

The State Sports Committee ostentatiously took Karpov's side in the matter of whether a playoff should be held to decide the USSR champion. It's amazing how events repeat themselves, even farcical ones. A press conference was convoked in the playing hall on the day that the first game was supposed to take place. The role of Campo, who had cancelled the 1984-85 match, was to my great regret played by Botvinnik, who informed journalists that the match would not take place due to... the players' irreconcilable differences! Kasparov, who was never to learn what these supposed differences were, again sat in the hall, but this time didn't utter a word. After that, collaboration between the Teacher and his pupil ended. Garry was pained at this parting of ways, but his sense of justice, which that year still governed the champion's actions, left him with no choice.

While we were in Tilburg, when I began a conversation that it was time to start preparing for the title match due the following year, Garry, after a moment's thought, replied: "Let's wait until I return from Baku. A couple of months won't make any difference, all the more so as I'll end up playing Karpov." I knew straight away why he was reluctant to make plans for the following year.

In the Azerbaijan capital Baku, where his mother and closest relatives were anxiously waiting for his return, the atmosphere was tense. When Garry flew to his home city at the beginning of January 1990 after a long period of foreign travel he found himself right in the cauldron of an interracial conflict between the Turkic (Azeri) and Armenian populations of the republic. For seventy years these two historically enemy nations had lived in Azerbaijan, obeying the laws of peaceful co-existence, and the state had diligently watched out for anything that would destabilize the situation. *Perestroika*, declared in our country in 1985, soon escaped the control of its initiators and provoked furious resistance from the numerous and powerful members of the bureaucratic party class fostered by our system for seventy odd years of Soviet power. Functionaries worried about losing their previous power decided to act according to the principle "the worse for the public, the better for us". Sabotage and confusion took hold in the country, the economy collapsed and all the ills of our society created by but hidden within our social system suddenly slid to the surface.

Still before arriving in Baku, Garry gave an analytical prediction of how events would pan out in this conflict, offering his own solution to the problem. The analysis and forecast proffered by the world champion proved to be deep and subtle, but neither Baku nor Moscow listened to his proposals. The country's leadership at the time had its own plan and its own goals in the heating conflict.

Garry arrived in Baku when the flames of the conflict were already engulfing the public. Armenian apartments were ransacked, their inhabitants attacked and sometimes murdered. Shocked at the reality of the events, he sat at home, saw people miraculously escape the enraged crowds and listened to horrific reports from the injured. Leaving his apartment block behind, he and his mother moved to his training base located forty km from Baku. His relatives and friends soon descended on it, as well as Shakarov with his family. The majority of them had come to take refuge, chased out of their homes by the mad crowds – exhausted and without their belongings, which had been stolen from them. Their number grew relentlessly...10 then... 20... 25... 30... Soon Zagulba itself was no longer safe. The security detail allocated by the authorities to protect the world champion consisted of just two guards, armed with pistols.

The situation became desperate when telephone communications were broken and the world champion found himself cut off not just from Baku, but from the Soviet capital. A decision was then taken in Moscow to arrange an operation that would extract Garry and the people with him from the trap they had found themselves in. There was no chance that they could fly out to Moscow by a usual flight – the roads leading to the airport were now patrolled by Azeri militants looking for Armenians to attack, and anyway the airport had no aircraft left. Many people and organizations took part in the operation to save Kasparov, and although they were working off the cuff they managed to coordinate their actions perfectly. Head of the Soviet Sports Trade Union Boris Rogatin obtained the consent of the government to send a special aircraft to Baku, while Chairman of the Soviet Chess Federation Vladimir Popov, who was also a minister in the government of the Russian Soviet Federative Socialist Republic, arranged a special telephone line to Zagulba and transformed his office into the operation's command center for a couple of days. The Chess Players Union found the means to finance the operation, while Garry's business colleagues insured the aircraft crew's risks and paid to receive the refugees in Moscow.

Once all of the details had been agreed to a strict timetable an empty airplane flew off from Moscow one sunny January day. As dusk descended on the city in its usual rapid fashion (the calculation was exact!) the airplane landed at the furthest part of the airfield. Then it froze as the wait began. At that very moment, a bus and two passenger cars drove up to the aircraft along a remote, half-forgotten road. The poor soon-to-be refugees sat in these vehicles squashed against each other. How they managed to avoid being seen by the Azeri patrols was a professional secret of competent persons who had assured Moscow of the safety of the Kasparov party on the road to the airport. It took no more than ten minutes for everybody to clamber into the airplane – there was no need to load luggage into the hold. They were escaping from Baku with almost no belongings.

The night before the escape, Garry had persuaded his friends in the KGB to enable him to bid farewell to the home that he was now leaving forever. This was risky, even reckless (his apartment block was in the city center), but perfectly understandable. A remarkable chess player who had delivered glory to Azerbaijan with his victories was now saying his goodbyes to the land of his birth.

The aircraft flew in to Moscow late at night. This group of people, overwhelmed with grief, descended on the snowy ground. Their faces bore no joy at being saved – rather, their eyes had adopted a constant expression asking: "Why me?" Some were so exhausted that they needed to be helped down the trap. Several of them were lightly dressed, wearing the same home clothes in which they had escaped their apartments. I came to meet these people, who had arrived in a totally alien environment for them. Officially, our "lucky" country had no refugees. And although the operation to save the champion had been precisely executed and ended in success, its outcome wanted you to weep from hurt and shame. All of these unfortunate people were united by the fact that they no longer had a home country, a Motherland, that was capable of protecting them. What an awful fate!

Garry's massive innate energy, his inquisitive mind, excellent analytical skills that he applied not only to chess, artistic nature and ability to capture the audience's attention made him a visible figure on the scene of public life. As a rule, an active role in public life serves as a trampoline to a political career. Even before he returned that time to Baku, using his fantastic calculation and analytical abilities honed at the chess board, together with his huge historical knowledge accumulated in his glue-like memory, Garry attempted to analyze the events taking place in the country. Functionaries of various ranks, right up to the country's top leadership, were familiar with his brave, youthfully radical and yet interesting and carefully thought through ideas and assessment of the political events.

After returning from Baku, Garry, taking on a grave demeanor, dived into action, attempting to gain the attention of people, in particular in the government, to the problems of hot spots in our country, whose number kept growing. He gave interviews, read lectures, criticized, argued, and offered his solutions. He held long conversations with Yakovlev and even with Mikhail Gorbachev. However, Garry quickly figured out that high-level politics in our country were subject to rules with which he was unfamiliar.

Time passed and everything got back to normal. After the last Armenian families had left the territory of Azerbaijan on which they had up until then lived, the slaughter ended, although the enmity of two peoples who had until then lived peacefully side by side certainly didn't end. The leadership of Azerbaijan called for Russians and Jews who had also left the country urgently in fear for their lives in those tragic January days to return home. However, no such appeal was addressed to the hundreds of thousands of robbed and humiliated Armenians, blown by an evil wind from their birthplace and devoid of everything they had once owned. Searching for the reasons for the tragic situation in which his country found itself and a way out of the quagmire, Garry joined the opposition to communism. The logical consequence of the transformation of his political outlook was his resignation from the Communist Party in May 1990. I never discussed with him the reasons that had prompted him to join that organization back in 1983. I knew his views at the time – views that were perfectly critical of many communist dogmas. However, life in a system built on lies and his desire to fulfil his huge talent forced him to be calculating in his more critical decisions. Joining the Party was a necessary step forced on him. "I was twenty years old and I really wanted to become world champion," he wrote. "I was told that in the environment of the time a Party membership card was a necessary key to the door to the chess Mount Olympia. If I declined then the only way to get a match against Karpov was to emigrate." Having equalized his status with Karpov's in terms of Party membership, he gained the right to appeal to the Party leadership that ran the country. This deprived his rival of an important trump card in the behind-the-scenes battle accompanying their matches.

Life was tough for the refugees. There were tens of thousands of people in a similar situation in Moscow. Those who had managed to emigrate from the USSR were considered the luckiest, but those who had managed to rent at great cost an apartment in Moscow or another city were also glad. However, that was only a small percentage of the total. Garry had it relatively easier. His young wife Maria already lived in Moscow, so he already had somewhere to live. However, her small two-room apartment in a five-floor prefab didn't even have enough room for Klara Kasparova, and the world champion was forced to rent more apartments in Moscow for his relatives. Shakarov's family was helped at first by his fellow coaches who had worked with Garry during the match in Seville.

The Baku tragedy, worsened by the government's inaction and lack of desire to find an effective way to resolve the problems, hardened Garry, and chased back inside him his kindness and responsiveness. He turned into a stern and even cynical fighter. His firmness and even callousness became felt with increasing frequency in his relations with people. This didn't frighten his enemies, but disheartened his friends. Garry's authoritarianism in making decisions grew sharply and we witnessed an obsessive desire to be at the head of all and everything no matter what the cost.

This time, Garry began to prepare for the next match without me. I had seen the Kasparovs taking over planning and running his prep, and in this situation the coaching experience that I had built up was of no use. Our collaboration was at an end. I chose not to wait to find out the role that the Kasparovs had assigned me in the match and decided to leave the game. Instead, I went to work on implementing other plans of mine and making use of my coaching experience from those years. We separated at a time that was far from the toughest one in his chess career, and more compliant candidates were found to replace me. Garry had plenty of choice and he went for Grandmaster Makarychev, who had been actively helping none other than Karpov not so long ago.

Seventeen years of close collaboration with Garry – this was a big chunk of my life, full not only of roller-coaster emotions but of intense joy in the days of my pupil's greatest successes: three times he donned the world champion's laurel wreath alongside me. *At the beginning of my career as a coach I promised to do my utmost, using all my strength, knowledge and experience, to bring up a challenger capable of replacing Karpov on the throne. I am proud that I kept my promise and achieved my aim.*

Garry and me with Timoshchenko (left) and Vladimirov (right), Vilnius, 1984

The chief arbiter examining a chair. Match vs. Karpov, Moscow, 1984

Garry sees everything from above. Match vs. Karpov, Moscow, 1985

Garry in Irkutsk, 1986

Analysis without looking at the board, Zagulba, 1986

Together against Portisch, Tilburg, 1986

The three fierce Ks smiling together, Brussels, 1987

Before the final resumption. "So where is the win, guys?", Seville, 1987

Garry and Botvinnik, before their parting, Moscow, 1988

Garry in Majorca, with pupils including Vladimir Kramnik and Sergey Rublevsky, 1989

The champion's new suite, Moscow, 1990

Chapter 7. Select Games (1982-1989)

Game 1

The Yugoslav city of Bugojno hosted a grandmaster tournament that proved to be the scene of one of Kasparov's most stunning performances. He achieved a number of combinational victories, though by that time we were all used to those. For me, a win that on the surface looked quite simple was a real phenomenon. Above all, it was a victory over himself. Up until Bugojno he had only managed a single draw versus the ex-world champion. Two fierce attacks by Garry had crashed against the armor of fantastically skilled defense.

Several months before the Yugoslav tournament, another ex-world champion, Boris Spassky, my childhood friend, had flown into Moscow. The three of us spent several evenings engaged in long conversations that were most useful for Garry. In one of them, the lad complained that he found it impossible to break the defenses of Iron Tigran. Boris, who had of course played two world title matches with Petrosian and had studied his play thoroughly, gave a quite surprising reply: "Tiger, however paradoxical it sounds, possesses fantastic tactical vision that against the background of his immensely subtle understanding of positions and supernatural sense of danger nobody notices. Try not to sacrifice anything, and in general, don't play directly against him. He'll always find a defense, no matter how improbably, against concrete threats. His Achilles heel is defense in a slightly worse position, especially when he has no counterplay. Even then, you have to positionally squeeze him gently, without rushing and without making any sudden movements."

The careful reader might note that the recipe for beating the great defender contained components that were quite alien to the playing style of the young and temperamental grandmaster. I had no doubt that two or three years later Garry would learn to play in that style, too. However, when it came to chess improvement he preferred leaps to measured walking. Half a year after our conversations with Spassky the lad once again met the cunning Tiger in battle. Well, take a look at how he digested the lessons of the former matador.

G. KASPAROV – T. PETROSIAN

Bugojno. International tournament. 15.05.1982
Bogo-Indian Defense. [E11]

1.d4 ♘f6 2.c4 e6 3.♘f3 ♗b4+
In the language of professionals, this check is a demonstration of a peaceful frame of mind. Petrosian

clearly didn't want to repeat their recent clash in the sharp 3...b6 4.a3 ♗b7 5.♘c3 d5 6.cxd5 ♘xd5 system, which he only won after a massive effort.

4.♗d2 ♕e7 5.g3 ♗xd2+ 6.♕xd2 0-0 7.♗g2 d5 8.0-0 dxc4 9.♘a3 c5

A hard-to-spot inaccuracy dictated by black's confidence that the boredom being created on the board was not Kasparov's cup of tea and that a peace treaty was around the corner. It was more accurate to advance this pawn after the initial 9...♖d8 10.♕c2.

10.dxc5 ♕xc5 11.♖ac1 ♘c6 12.♘xc4 ♕e7 13.♘fe5 ♘xe5 14.♘xe5

The exchange of knights actually deepens black's difficulties in developing his queenside. It was only his absence of pawn weaknesses and the young man from Baku's volatile chess temperament that gave Petrosian hope that the threat would pass, even if more slowly than he would have liked.

14...♘d5 15.♖fd1 ♘b6 16.♕a5!

A wonderful queen maneuver paralyzing black's queenside. It suddenly transpires that the black knight's transfer has been a complete waste of time, as he cannot even pressure white in the center. So instead he needs to make the last possible useful move.

16...g6

The previously planned 16...f6 weakens the seventh rank, and this sharply strengthens the effect of the

white pieces' invasion along the c-file – 17.♘c4 ♘xc4 18.♖xc4 b6 19.♕c3 ♗a6 20.♖c7 ♖ad8! 21.♖xe7 (21. ♖xd8 ♕xd8 22.♗f1 ♖f7) and then 21...♖xd1+ 22.♗f1 ♗xe2 23.♕c7! ♖xf1+ 24.♔g2 ♗d3 25.♖xg7+ ♔h8 26.♖g4 with a win.

17.♖d3!

An excellent move, stamping out the attempt at a further exchange – 17...♖d8? 18.♕c5! while preparing to gain the c7 square for the white pieces.

17...♘d5 18.e4! ♘b6

He needs to go back, as 18...♕b4? 19.♖xd5!, 18...♘b4? 19.♖c7, and 18...b6 19.♕d2 ♘b4 20.♖d6! are equally unappealing. Petrosian again hopes to chase the white knight from the center.

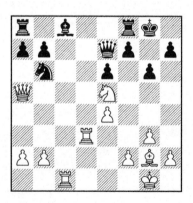

19.♗f1!

Just a year earlier Garry could not have come up with such a move – his level wasn't there yet. It's rare when a piece returning to its starting square decides the game. Now, Petrosian's sole hope of saving the game by breaking out with 19...

f6 20.♘c4 ♘xc4 21.♖xc4 b6 would turn out to be suicide – 22.♕c3 ♗a6 23.♖c7, and all because the crafty bishop now protects the rook, while the reply 23...♕c7 is no longer available.

Black has no useful moves left, though he can avoid an immediate loss. Perhaps he should have given up a pawn with 19...f6 20.♘c4 ♗d7! 21.♘xb6 axb6 22.♕xb6 ♗c6, although after the obvious 23.a3 it would not be hard for white to convert his material advantage into a full point. Petrosian decides to grit his teeth and wait for a miracle to happen.

19...♖e8 20.♖dd1! ♖f8 21.a3!

Now even the pawn sac 21...f6 22.♘c4 ♗d7 23.♘xb6 axb6 24.♕xb6 ♗c6 fails to slow the chain of events, as 25.♗b5 opens all the doors to black's house.

21...♔g7 22.b3!

Again black cannot get out at the cost of a pawn – 22...f6 23.♘c4 ♗d7 24.♘xb6 axb6, this time due to 25.♕b4!

22...♔g8 23.a4!

White's last three modest pawn moves, like an ancient form of Spanish torture, have prevented black's king from moving – 23...♔g7 24.♖c5! f6 25.♘c4 ♘xc4 26.♖xc4 b6 27.♕c3. Petrosian, disappointed, attempts to exchange a rook pair. However, his king on the eighth rank means that even hoping for a miracle is a waste of time.

23...♖d8? 24.♕c5!

Now black immediately loses with 24...♕e8? 25.♘g4!, although the "better" 24...♕xc5 25.♖xd8+ ♕f8 26.♖xf8+ ♔xf8 leads to a position after 27.♖c7 where resistance is pointless. Therefore, **black resigned**.

I don't recall Petrosian ever losing to anybody else in such style. After analyzing this masterpiece of positional skill, I came to the conclusion that there was nothing more I could teach Garry about chess. He had demonstrated that he knew how to do absolutely anything. My function now could only be to help him prepare for competitions and give advice of an experienced master.

Game 2

Introduction to the training games contained in this book
(by Dorian Rogozenco)

Kasparov played training games against his coaches and other players which have never been published. In this book twenty such games have been published for the first time, ten versus Timoshchenko and another ten versus Vladimirov. These games, evidently all played in Azerbaijan based on what Nikitin and Kasparov wrote in their memoirs, can be split into five sets as follows.

A. July 1982
– One game against Timoshchenko on 13.07.1982.
– The time control was likely 1 hour and 30 minutes for 36 moves and then half an hour until the end of the game (such a time control was quite usual then).
– Goal: check a concrete opening variation in the Sicilian for black (the Scheveningen Variation, Keres Attack).
– Game result: the record of the game stops after 35 moves, with no result. In the final position Kasparov was better.

B. August 1982
– Six games against Vladimirov over 16-22.08.1982.
– The time control was 2 hour 30 minutes for 40 moves, then unclear (maybe adjourned, maybe one hour more. Anyway only one game lasted more than 40 moves, and that was just 42 moves).
– Kasparov had white four times and black twice.
From the opening point of view the main goals were:
– Trying variations with black against the King's Indian Fianchetto.
– Trying the Catalan with white.
– Match result 3-3.

C. January 1983
– Four games against Vladimirov over 23-26.01.1983.
– The time control was 2 hour 30 minutes for 40 moves, then unclear (no game lasted more than 40 moves).
– In all four games Kasparov had white.
– Goal: trying new ideas for white against the Queen's Gambit (no more testing of the Catalan as in the previous match) and the Slav.
– Match result: Kasparov won 4-0.

D. February 1983

D1. Two classical games against Timoshchenko over 3-4.02.1983

– The time control was 2 hour 30 minutes for 40 moves, then unclear (no game lasted more than 40 moves).

– Kasparov was black in both games.

– Goal: prepare the Tarrasch with black for the upcoming Candidates match vs. Beliavsky.

– Result: Kasparov won 1.5-0.5.

D2. Four rapid games against Timoshchenko on 5.02.1983

– The time control was 15 minutes each for the whole game.

– In all four games Kasparov had black.

– Goal: practice a specific variation of the Sicilian for black.

– Result: Kasparov won 3.5-0.5.

E. July 1983

– Three games against Timoshchenko, 7-10.07.1983.

This mini-match (and especially the last game on 10.07.1983) was played under big pressure due to political problems surrounding the candidates match against Korchnoi. On 12.07 Kasparov was already in Moscow, meeting Campomanes and negotiating the conditions of the match with many influential political figures from the Soviet Union.

– The time control: I suspect that the time control in this match was not the same in all games. In the first game the time control was 2 hours and 30 minutes for the first 40 moves. Then the game was adjourned in a winning position for Kasparov (and didn't resume). The second and third games most likely were played with a time control of 2 hours for 40 moves.

– Kasparov had white in one game and black in two games.

– The goal was to practice the Tarrasch with black and Queen's Gambit with both colors.

– The result was most likely 3-0 in Kasparov's favor.

The scoresheets of all 20 games in Kasparov's handwriting are found in Appendix 5 to this book. The time recording and especially the fact that many moves are circled is very interesting. Note that the approach to time recording of Kasparov (and hence the commentator) in the first training game is to show the time remaining, and then he shows the accumulated time used in the other games where time is recorded at all.

G. TIMOSHCHENKO – G. KASPAROV
Training game. 13.07.1982
Sicilian Defense. [B81]
Commentary by Dorian Rogozenco

1.e4 c5 2.♘f3 e6 3.d4 cxd4 4.♘xd4 ♘f6 5.♘c3 d6 6.g4

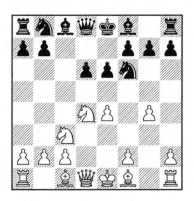

6...e5!? [1.29]

This move was very rare at the time. Black used to meet the Keres Attack almost exclusively with 6... h6, 6...♘c6 or 6...a6. By advancing the e-pawn Kasparov tries to solve black's opening problems immediately. Nowadays 6...e5 has become a viable option for black. In the present game Kasparov successfully employs a novelty and achieves a good position. Nevertheless, later he never played this line again (and generally tried to avoid the Keres Attack). One more curious fact: in the book *Sicilian Defense* written by Kasparov together with Nikitin in 1984 the move 6...e5 is only briefly mentioned as deserving serious attention. One of the two short variations in that book follows the main line from the present game, but without mentioning Kasparov's novelty! See below the comments on black's move 13.

7.♗b5+ [1.25]

Another big line is 7.♘f5 h5 and despite analysis supported by strong computers even today it is not clear if white can achieve a real advantage in this messy variation.

7...♗d7 [1.28] **8.♗xd7+** [1.24] **♕xd7 9.♘f5** [1.23] **h5 10.♗g5** [0.54]

The main move these days is 10.gxh5 and after 10...♘xh5 the spectacular continuation 11.♗h6 has become white's most popular choice in modern practice. However, black's compensation after 11...g6 (but not 11...gxh6? 12.♕xh5 with a large advantage for white) 12.♗xf8 gxf5 13.♗xd6 ♘c6 is very close to enough for equality.

10...♘h7 [1.26]

10...♘xg4? 11.h3 ♘f6 12.♗xf6 gxf6 13.♘d5 shows the strategic danger for black in such a pawn structure.

11.♗d2 [0.37]

Keeps the e3 square available for the knight.

In case of 11.♗e3 hxg4 12.♕xg4 (12.♘d5 g6 is better, with a double-edged position in which black's chances are no worse) 12...g6 13.♞h6 ♛xg4 14.♞xg4 f5 white is in trouble.

The only way to fight for an opening advantage in this line is the sharp 11.f4.

11...hxg4 [1.23] **12.♛xg4** [0.35] **g6 13.♞e3** [0.34]

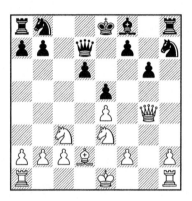

13...♛xg4! [1.22]

Kasparov's strong novelty changes the evaluation of the line. It turns out that the apparently active knight on g4 will in fact be misplaced (because of ...f7-f5 ideas), while the bishop on f8 is still needed to protect the pawn on d6.

In the previous game with this variation the Israeli Grandmaster Jacob Murey had played the logical-looking move 13...♝h6, but after 14.0-0-0 black has no time to exchange queens on g4 due to problems with the pawn on d6. In their book dated 1984 on the Scheveningen Variation of the Sicilian Defense Kasparov and Nikitin wrote about this position: "White keeps his positional advantage, but we think that black's

play can be improved". It certainly can, as Kasparov knew very well because of the present training game already played by him in 1982. The strong 13...♛xg4 was introduced to practice for the first time one year later by the Soviet Master Jakob Meister (now he is a GM living in Berlin). At the top level it was first played only in 1994, by Judit Polgar.

14.♞xg4 ♞d7

Played instantly. All this had almost certainly been analyzed by Kasparov before the game, because black had spent less than 10 minutes up to this point. Also, he plays the next part very quickly, which means that even the upcoming exchange sacrifice must have been known by Kasparov. Truly amazing preparation! In later practice black players also scored fine with 14...♞c6. Therefore, the entire variation starting with 11.♝d2 is considered harmless nowadays.

15.♞b5 [0.29]

This ambitious move will allow black great activity soon. On the other hand, it must be said that it would have been very difficult to realize over the board that after winning material it would be white who had to fight for a draw.

15.f3 f5 16.♞f2= (16.♞e3 ♞g5 17.♚e2 f4 18.♞ed5 ♚f7 followed by ♞e6 is better for black).

15...♜c8! [1.20] **16.♞xa7** [0.28] **♜xc2** [1.20] **17.♞e3** [0.21]

Or 17.♝c3 ♞c5 18.♚d1 (18. f3 ♞g5 wins quickly for black. Suddenly his rooks coordinate perfectly) 18...♖xc3 19.bxc3 ♘xe4 with great compensation for the exchange.

17...♖xb2 [1.19] **18.♗c3** [0.20] **18...♖b6 19.♘d5**

White wins the exchange, but after the next move he will lose the pawn on e4 and will be struggling to survive.

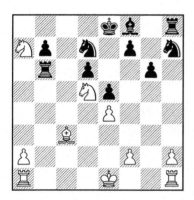

19...♘g5 20.♘xb6 [0.15] **♘xb6** [1.18] **21.♖b1** [0.10]

The best move: white needs quick activity before black develops the kingside.

21...♘a4 [1.13] **22.♗d2** [0.06] **22...♘xe4** [1.11] **23.♖xb7** [0.05]

Judging by the scoresheet at this moment white had only 5 minutes left (not clear whether it was until the end of the game, or until a certain number of moves), while black had spent less than 20 minutes up until now and had more than one hour left. So given that this was a training game for Kasparov, his opponent Timoshchenko received one additional hour on the clock at this moment.

23...♘ac5 24.♖b8+ [0.53] **♔d7** [1.10] **25.♗e3** [0.51] **♔c7** [1.08] **26.♖b1** [0.31]

The only serious mistake in the game, explained most likely by tiredness. It is very difficult to solve complicated problems for two hours continuously, while your opponent is playing very strongly and quickly.

26.♖e8 was correct, after which black should objectively take a draw by repetition with 26...♔b6 (the attempt to play for a win with 26...♔b7 27.♘b5 ♘e6 threatening ♘f6 is not enough, since after 28.a4 ♘f6 29.♘xd6+ ♔c7 30.♖xe6 fxe6 31.♘f7 white obviously doesn't risk anything) 27.♘c8+ ♔c7 28.♘a7 ♔b7=.

26...d5 [1.06] **27.♘b5+** [0.28]

After 27.f3 black has 27...♘g3! 28.♖g1 ♘f5 with a large advantage.

27...♔c6 [1.04] **28.0-0!** [0.24]

The best decision: Timoshchenko sacrifices the knight for his opponent's powerful central pawns. 28.♔e2 d4 29.♗d2 ♖h3 is hopeless for white.

28...d4 [1.02] **29.♘xd4+ exd4 30.♗xd4 ♖h5** [1.00] **31.♖fc1** [0.20]

Black will soon win the h-pawn and remain with two knights for the rook. It is however unclear if this material advantage is enough for victory due to the limited material left on the board, the active white rooks and the passed a-pawn.

31...♗d6 [0.47] **32.a4** [0.16] **♗xh2+** [0.44] **33.♔g2 ♗f4 34.♖c2** [0.15] **♖g5+** [0.43] **35.♔h1 ♖d5** [0.37]

On the scoresheet the game ends at this moment without a result. In the final position white must continue either 36.♖b4, or 36.♗xc5 ♘xc5 37.a5, in both cases with good chances of achieving a draw.

Game 3

G. KASPAROV – E. VLADIMIROV
Training game. 16.08.1982
Queen's Indian Defense [E12]
Commentary by Dorian Rogozenco

1.d4 [0] **♘f6** [0] **2.c4 e6** [01] **3.♘f3 b6** [02] **4.a3** [02]

The Petrosian Variation of the Queen's Indian brought Kasparov many important victories. Quite strangely nevertheless: after 1982 he used it only occasionally.

4...d5 [03]

A relatively rare, but absolutely playable variation. These days most grandmasters prefer 4...♗b7 5.♘c3 d5 6.cxd5 ♘xd5.

5.♘c3 [03] **♗e7** [04]

By continuing 5...♗b7 black had the opportunity here to transpose to the main line mentioned above. Therefore, if white wants to avoid it, it makes sense to take on d5 on the previous move.

6.cxd5 [15]

The strongest move, which was played by Kasparov after 12 minutes of thinking. This exchange on d5 is nowadays the main reason why black players prefer 4... ♗b7. The point is that taking back with the knight on d5 allows white the immediate advance e2-e4 and that's why it would be less logical for black here than after 4...♗b7 (when after ♘f6xd5 white cannot play e2-e4 immediately due to the loss of the e4-pawn).

6...exd5

6...♘xd5 7.e4 ♘xc3 8.bxc3±

7.g3 0-0 [6] **8.♗g2 ♗b7** [7] **9.0-0** [18]

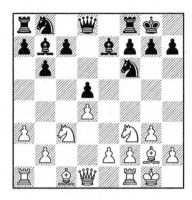

A typical position, which can arise via different move orders. Black's plan is to play c7-c5 quickly, when a standard middlegame with a hanging pawns structure usually arises. It is generally white who can claim some pressure in such structures, but objectively the position is very close to equal and it's a matter of taste which side to prefer. Some grandmasters have no problem playing it with either color.

9...c5 [09]

The main alternative is to postpone this advance a little bit and start with 9...♘bd7. In the blitz match Kasparov-Kramnik (2001) Kramnik played 9...♘a6 twice here and then brought the knight to c7, once after c7-c5 and once after c7-c6. Both those blitz games ended in a draw.

10.dxc5 [27]

White decides to clarify the pawn structure immediately.

The main alternative 10.♗f4 happened in one of Karpov's games almost 30 years after the present

encounter: 10...♘bd7 11.♘e5 ♖e8 12.♖c1 h6 13.e3 ♘f8 14.g4?! ♗d6 15.h3 ♖c8 16.♗g3 ♘e6 with an advantage for black in A. Wirig – A. Karpov, Germany 2011.

10...bxc5 11.♘e5!?

Much later Anand treated this position differently: 11.♘h4 ♕d7 12.♗g5 d4 13.♗xf6 ♗xf6 14.♘e4 ♗e7 15.♕b3 ♗c6 16.♕c2 ♘a6 17.♘f3 ♗d5 18.♘ed2 when black is at least no worse here, so a draw was agreed in the rapid game V. Anand – P. Nikolic, Monte Carlo 2000. Kasparov's knight jump in a central direction is more concrete and probably stronger, though with precise play black can keep equality in the game as well.

11...♘a6 [13] **12.♗f4** [34] **♘c7** [15] **13.♕a4** [36] **♗d6** [20]

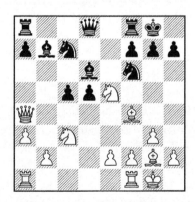

14.♖fd1 [56]

After a long think Kasparov most likely came to the conclusion that this move, which is connected to a piece sacrifice, must be white's best practical chance to fight for an advantage. The point is that in the upcoming complications it is easier for black to go wrong.

The forcing line 14.♘d7 ♘xd7 (14...♗xf4 is answered by 15.♘xc5) 15.♗xd6 ♘b6 16.♗xc7 ♕xc7 (16...♘xa4 17.♗xd8 ♘xc3 18.bxc3 ♖axd8 19.♖fd1±) is closer to equality than to an advantage for white. The active 17.♕g4 is answered by 17...f5!

A very interesting option in the diagram position is 14.♖ad1 with a similar idea as in the game. Now if black plays the line 14...g5 15.♗xg5 ♗xe5 16.♕h4 ♕d6 17.f4 ♗xc3 18.bxc3 ♘d7 19.♗e7 ♕e6 20.♗xf8 ♘xf8 the rook is better placed on f1 (from where it supports the f-pawn) than on a1.

14...g5 [37]

Vladimirov accepts the challenge and enters the complications. This is objectively the strongest continuation, since the alternative 14...♖e8 leads to better chances for white after 15.♘d7 ♘xd7 (15...♗xf4 16.♘xc5!) 16.♗xd6 ♘b6 17.♗xc7 ♕xc7 (17...♘xa4 18.♗xd8 ♘xc3 19.bxc3 ♖axd8 20.♖ab1 followed by e3 or c4 is worse for black) 18.♕g4±.

15.♗xg5 [67] **15...♗xe5 16.♕h4 ♘e6?** [46]

Black could maintain the balance in the position with 16...♕d6! 17.f4 ♗xc3 18.bxc3 ♘d7 19.♗e7 (19.e4 f6 20.♗h6 ♖f7 21.c4 ♔h8 22.exd5 ♖g8 23.♖e1 ♖e7∓) 19...♕e6 20.♗xf8 ♕e3+ 21.♔h1 ♘xf8=.

17.♗xd5! [78]

Now in order to avoid losing back the piece and ending up with a

hopeless position, black must give up the queen for two more pieces.

17...♘xd5 [67]

In order to keep his light-squared bishop alive Vladimirov rejects the objectively stronger alternative 17...♗xd5 18.♘xd5 ♕xd5 19.♖xd5 ♘xd5, where black has a rook and two knights for the queen. Anyway white keeps much better prospects here as well: 20.♖d1 ♘b6 (or 20...♘dc7 21.♖d7 ♗xb2 22.f4) 21.a4±.

18.♗xd8 ♖axd8 [68]

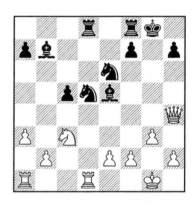

In this complicated position, where white has a queen and two pawns for his opponent's three minor pieces, white actually has a large advantage. However, it is difficult to accept that there is no direct win. Instead of searching for a quick victory white must combine attacking ideas on the kingside with central activity (doubling rooks on the d-file, or placing the rooks on d1 and c1 in order to win the c5 pawn). The strongest continuation is 19.♘e4! ♗g7 (after 19...f5 20.♘g5 ♘xg5 21.♕xg5+ ♔h8 22.♖ac1 ♖c8

23.♕d2! followed by ♕a5 black's position falls apart; also 19...♔h8 20.f4 ♗d4+ 21.♖xd4 cxd4 22.f5 ♘g7 23.♘g5 h5 24.♘xf7+ wins by force.) 20.♖d2 and black is in big trouble. A few variations are: 20...f5 (20... h6 21.♖ad1 f5 22.♘c3 ♘d4 23.♘a4 ♘b3 24.♖d3+−) 21.♘g5 ♘xg5 22.♕xg5 ♔h8 23.♖ad1 ♖d6 24.e3 a5. What else? Black is totally paralyzed. 25.♕h5 ♗c6 (25...a4 26.♕f3 ♖fd8 27.♕xf5+−) 26.♕e2 a4 27.♕c4+−.

However, Kasparov had a different plan.

19.♘xd5 [82] **♗xd5** [70]

19...♖xd5 20.♖xd5 ♗xd5 21.♕h5 f5 22.♖d1+−

20.f4 [83]

Too impulsive. The march of the f-pawn doesn't reach its goal, while losing the b2-pawn and weakening his own king proves important. Now black has more chances to hold the balance.

After 20.♕g4+ ♗g7 (20...♔h8 21.♕f5 ♗xb2 22.♖ab1 ♘g7 23.♕c2 ♗f6 24.♕xc5 ♘e6 25.♕xa7 with a large advantage is worse) 21.e3 it is not easy for black to defend. Any active move can quickly backfire, for example 21...f5 22.♕e2 ♘g5 runs into 23.♖xd5 ♖xd5 24.♕c4 ♖fd8 25.♖d1 ♘f3+ 26.♔g2 ♘e5 27.♕xd5+ ♖xd5 28.♖xd5 with a winning endgame for white.

20...♗xb2! [81]

20...♗d4+ 21.♖xd4! ♘xd4 is weaker (if 21...cxd4 22.f5 ♘g7 23.♖d1 white wins the important pawn and his task is much easier)

and 22.♕g5+ ♔h8 23.♕f6+ ♔g8 24.♔f2 with an advantage.

21.f5 [88] **♘g7** [82] **22.♖ab1** [90] **♗d4+** [83] **23.♖xd4**

Practically forced. 23.♔f1 ♘xf5 24.♕g5+ ♘g7 25.e3 f6∓ was certainly not the idea behind the march of the f-pawn.

23...cxd4 24.f6? [91]

As already mentioned, bringing the pawn to f6 doesn't bring the desired result. The black knight gets the e6 square and protects the important pawn on d4 (and the g7 square). Now black is clearly better thanks to his material advantage.

24.♖b4 d3! 25.exd3 f6 is equal, but 24.♖d1 ♗c4 25.♖xd4 ♖xd4 26.♕xd4 ♗xe2 27.♔f2 ♗b5 28.g4 was a good try to keep some pressure on black, who cannot easily coordinate his forces. It must still be a draw, though.

24...♘e6   25.♖f1   ♗b3 [91] **26.♖f5** [100]

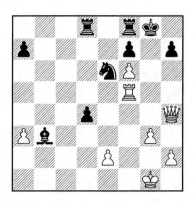

Bringing the rook to the kingside was the idea started six moves ago by Kasparov. With the two strongest pieces in attack and the pawn on f6 it does look very dangerous for black, but it turns out that white cannot create any serious threats, because the h7 pawn will be protected by the bishop from the b1-h7 diagonal, while the king on h8 will feel very safe (if necessary the rook will come to g8). However, it is understandable that Vladimirov was happy to exchange one pair of rooks, after which black can't risk anything at all.

26...♖d5? [95]

The problem after the exchange of rooks is that black also considerably reduces his own winning chances. Black's plan to play for victory in this position is to weaken white's king with d4-d3 and then create a combined attack with his pieces. In the long run he must be winning in that case, but with just one rook on the board he won't be able to do that, especially after Kasparov's next two moves.

26...♗c2 27.♖a5 ♖d7 would have kept more winning chances. For instance after 28.♕h6 ♖b8 29.♖g5+ ♗g6 30.h4? d3 31.exd3 ♖xd3 32.h5 ♖b2 black wins.

27.g4!? [114] **a5** [97]

Black could still prevent white's idea and retain winning chances with 27...♖fd8 28.♖h5 ♗c2.

28.♖h5!! [125]

Played after another 11 minutes of thinking. The plan of doubling the pawns on the h-file is brilliant, as explained below.

28...♖xh5 [98] **29.gxh5!**

30.♕g3+ and 31.♕xb3 is the threat now.

29...a4 30.h6 [126]

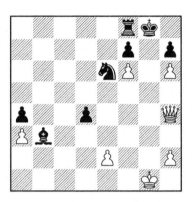

This position is a draw, because the black king is caged in (there is no possibility to play ...h7-h6 and ♔h7), the rook must always control the back rank or stay on the g-file and black doesn't have the g6 square for his bishop or knight in order to close the g-file, due to the fact that white can always push the second pawn to h5. In the next part of the game black tries to coordinate his pieces against the white king, which, as mentioned before, is not enough to create serious threats.

30...♔h8 [100] **31.♕e4 ♖d8** [114] **32.h4** [130]

32.♔f2 d3 (or 32...♗c4 33.♕c6) is an easy draw after 33.exd3 ♗c2 (33...♘c5 34.♕e7) 34.♕g2 ♖xd3 (if 34...♗xd3 35.♕c6 black loses the a4-pawn) 35.♕c6 ♖d2+ 36.♔e1 ♖d1+ 37.♔f2 ♖d2+ 38.♔g3 ♖d3+ 39.♔f2=.

32...d3 [116] **33.exd3 ♘c5 34.♕e7** [134] **♖g8+** [117] **35.♔f2 ♘xd3+ 36.♔e3 ♖g3+** [119] **37.♔d4** [141] **♘f4** [122] **38.♕e4** [143]

38.♕e8+ ♖g8 39.♕e7 is again somewhat easier, avoiding the unnecessary king journey into black's camp: 39...♘g6 (or 39...♗e6 40.♕a7) 40.♕e4 ♖d8+ 41.♔c3=.

38...♘e6+ [126] **39.♔e5** [144] ♖g8

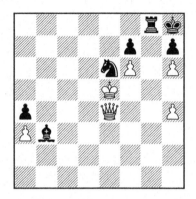

40.♔d6?? [145]

This careless move played quickly by Kasparov is a blunder, allowing black to create a mating net.

With the king on e5 white must be a little careful, but it's not at all problematic. A move like 40.♕b7 would have kept the position equal. For instance 40...♘f8 41.♔d4 ♖g4+ 42.♔e3 ♔g8 43.♕f3 ♖xh4 44.♕g2+ ♘g6 45.♕a8+ ♘f8 46.♕g2+ with a draw via repetition.

40...♖d8+ [127] **41.♔e7** [147]

41.♔c6   ♗d5+−+;   41.♔e5 ♖d5+−+

41...♖d7+! **42.♔e8**

42.♔xd7 ♘c5+−+

42...♗d5

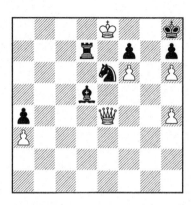

There is no result on the scoresheet, but Kasparov most certainly resigned. After 43.♕xa4 ♖c7 white loses the queen due to the threat ♗c6 mate.

White resigned.

This must have been a bitter loss for Kasparov, who played very creatively and blundered unnecessarily in an equal position. But such a punishment for excessive victory drive without having objective reasons can often have (much bigger) positive effects. Self-confidence should not be confused with over-optimism. As Nikitin wrote elsewhere in this book, the match's "...unexpected result (3:3) proved to be great medicine for his big head before the upcoming interzonal tournament."

1982	16.08						
Game No.	1	2	3	4	5	6	Score
Kasparov	0						0
Vladimirov	1						1

Game 4

E. VLADIMIROV – G. KASPAROV
Training game. 17.08.1982
King's Indian Defense [E69]
Commentary by Dorian Rogozenco

1.d4 [01] **♘f6** [01] **2.c4 g6** [03]
3.♘f3 [02] **♗g7 4.g3** [03] **0-0** [05]
5.♗g2 d6

The King's Indian Defense was the beloved opening of the young Kasparov. He played it very often until 1983, then rather occasionally until 1989, after which he returned to the KID by making it again one of his main weapons against 1.d4.

6.0-0 [04] **♘bd7 7.♘c3** [05] **e5**
8.e4 [06]

Black has many possibilities to meet the ultra-solid Fianchetto System. The plan with ...♘bd7 and ...e5 is the most classical way.

8...c6 9.h3 [07] **♕a5** [06]

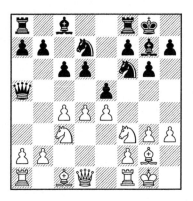

The main purpose of the queen sortie to a5 is to keep an eye on the knight on c3 and thus prevent white from playing b2-b3. This is important

when the c4 pawn gets attacked later by the knight (from b6 or e5) and/or by the queen from b4. The present game was a test for this variation and although Kasparov succeeded in carrying out one of the main ideas behind 9...♕a5 and even won the game, he must not have been entirely happy with the resulting positions after the opening and never played this variation in his practice again.

10.♗e3 [09]

One of the strongest continuations for white.

10...exd4 [11] **11.♘xd4 ♘b6** [13].
The main idea behind 9...♕a5. White must make some concessions now, because the natural move b2-b3 would leave the knight on c3 unprotected.

12.♕d3 [12] **♕a6** [14]

Pinning the c4 pawn. 12...♕b4 is pointless now because of 13.b3±.

13.b3 d5 [15]

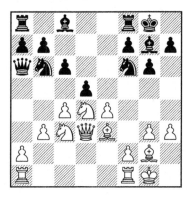

Kasparov has achieved the main goal for such a structure: he has managed to execute the d6-d5 break without losing a pawn or allowing the reply e4-e5. In the diagram position it looks like black has already successfully solved all his opening problems and can be optimistic about the future, but as we'll see, things are more complicated than they appear.

14.exd5 [14]

14.e5 is simply bad in view of 14...dxc4 15.bxc4 ♘fd7 and white loses a pawn.

14...♘fxd5 [50]

Played after 35 minutes of thinking. Due to the fact that 14...cxd5 doesn't work well, white will now keep the pawn chain a2-b3-c4 intact, leaving the black queen misplaced on a6. Another problem for black remains his undeveloped queenside and the difficulty in finding a good square for his c8 bishop.

I suppose that around here Kasparov started to feel unhappy about the whole opening line, because it turns out that black is unable to create dynamic pressure against his opponent's position.

14...cxd5 is bad in view of 15.♘cb5! dxc4 16.bxc4 and white's active minor pieces secure him a large advantage everywhere: 16...♗d7 (16...♕a4 17.♖fc1 ♗d7 18.♕b3±) 17.a4! (this is even stronger than 17.♘c7 ♕xc4 18.♕xc4 ♘xc4 19.♘xa8 ♖xa8 20.♖ab1±) 17...♖ac8

18.♖fc1 ♖fd8 19.a5 ♘a8 20.♕b3±. Perhaps black should agree to a slightly inferior position after 14...♘bxd5 15.♗d2.

15.♗d2 [22] **♖d8** [74]

This move took Kasparov almost another 25 minutes. The alternatives don't entirely solve black's problems either: 15...♘xc3 16.♗xc3 ♘d5 17.♗b2 ♗d7 18.♖ad1±; or 15...♘c7 16.♕e4 ♘e6 17.♘de2±.

16.♕e4 [28] **♘c7** [114]

This somewhat sad retreat means that black has lost the opening battle. Kasparov thought here for another 40 minutes, making it altogether almost two hours for the first 16 moves (!). But the alternatives are worse: 16...♘xc3 17.♗xc3 ♗f5 18.♕f4!±; or 16...♘b4 17.♗e3 ♗xd4 18.♗xd4 ♗f5 19.♕h4 ♖xd4 20.♕xd4 ♘c2 21.♕d2 ♘xa1 22.g4! ♗e6 23.♘e4 ♘d7 24.♖xa1±.

17.♗e3 [38]

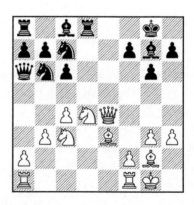

White has a small but stable advantage: his pieces are well centralized, while most of his opponent's pieces are awkwardly placed on the queenside. Black has little choice but to try to improve his pieces and hope to simplify the position.

17...♕a5 [115] **18.♖ac1** [51] **♘e6** [126] **19.♖fd1** [54]

Up to this point Vladimirov had played simple and strong chess, but here he unnecessarily allows black to develop the light-squared bishop conveniently. 19.♘de2 ♗d7 (19...♘c5 20.♕e7±) 20.♖fd1 was better.

19...♘xd4

Of course! Black uses the opportunity to exchange the knights and complete development very quickly.

20.♗xd4 ♗f5 [128] **21.♕f4** [57] **♖xd4** [128] **22.♖xd4 c5!?**

Kasparov's feeling in the approaching time-trouble will prove to be right: black complicates matters again, because the normal continuation 22...♗xd4 23.♕xd4 leads to a stable advantage for white due to black's weakened dark squares on the kingside. With accurate play black certainly must be able to hold the position and achieve a draw, but this is not a simple task. For instance, the most natural move 23...♖e8 is no good in view of 24.g4! ♗e6 (24...♗c8? loses on the spot due to 25.♘e4 ♘d7 26.♘d6) 25.♘e4 ♘d7 26.♖d1 and white has strong pressure against the opponent's position.

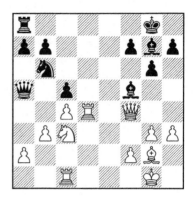

23.b4 [66]

The only move, otherwise white just loses material.

23...cxb4 [131]

23...♕xb4 deserved consideration as well, with some compensation for the exchange after 24.♘d5 ♘xd5 25.♖xd5 ♖e8 (25...♗e6 26.♖d3 followed by ♖b3 is worse).

24.♘d5 [67]

This most natural continuation leads to an equal position and was played very quickly by Vladimirov. The computer shows that white can achieve an advantage by jumping in a different direction: 24.♘b5! It is not easy to figure out that after 24...♗xd4 25.♘xd4 black is in fact in trouble due the power of the c-pawn, which will advance very quickly after the pawn on b7 falls. Instead of taking the exchange on d4 black can try to keep things complicated by taking 24...♕xa2, although after 25.♗xb7 white is better.

24...♘xd5 [132] **25.cxd5** [75]

25.♖xd5 ♕xa2 also secures black sufficient counterplay thanks to the passed b-pawn.

25...♗xd4 [137] **26.♕xd4 ♖c8** [140] **27.♖xc8+** [76] **♗xc8 28.d6** [77] **♗e6**

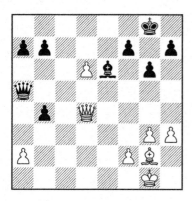

After a series of logical moves black is a pawn up, but white has a strong passer on d6 and a powerful queen on d4. Also the weakness of the a2 pawn is compensated by the weak dark squares around the black king. The position is equal.

29.h4 [86]

29.d7? doesn't work in view of 29...♕d8 and white loses his main trump card.

Also 29.♗xb7? would be a big mistake not because of 29...♗xh3?? 30.d7+−, but due to 29...♕b6! 30.♕xb6 (30.♕e4 ♕xd6 is hopeless for white) 30...axb6 and black is winning: 31.♗d5 (31.h4 ♔f8−+) 31...♗xh3 32.f3 ♗d7 33.♔f2 ♔f8 34.♔e3 ♔e8 35.♔d4 (35.f4 ♗e6−+) 35...g5 36.g4 (36.♔e5 h5 37.♔f6 h4−+) 36...h6! (36...f5? 37.gxf5 ♗xf5 38.♗e4 ♗e6 39.♗xh7 ♗xa2 40.♗e4 is a draw. A possible continuation is 40...♗g8 41.♔e5 b3 42.♔f6 b2 43.♗b1 ♔d7 44.♔xg5 ♔xd6 45.f4

♔c5 46.f5 ♔d4 47.f6 ♔e3 48.♔g6 ♔d2 49.f7 ♗xf7+ 50.♔xf7 ♔c1 51.♗h7 b1=♕ 52.♗xb1 ♔xb1 53.♔e6 and white is right on time. There was no way for black to gain a tempo) 37.♔e5 ♗b5 38.♔f6 (or 38.f4 gxf4 39.♔xf4 ♔d7 40.♔e5 f6+ 41.♔xf6 ♔xd6 42.♗g8 ♗d7−+) 38...♔d7 39.♗xf7 ♔xd6 40.♔g7 ♔e5 41.♔xh6 ♔f4 42.♗d5 ♗d3 43.♔h5 b5 44.♔h6 ♗c4−+.

29...♕b6 [144]

29...h5 30.♗xb7=.

30.♕e5 [88]

The endgame 30.♕xb6 axb6 31.♗d5 ♔f8 (or 31...♗c8 32.♔f1 ♔f8 33.♔e2 ♔e8 34.♔d3 ♔d7 35.♔c4=) 32.♗xe6 fxe6 is a draw, but it requires a lot of precise calculation and there is no need for it. Keeping the dominating queen is good enough.

30...a6 [145]

In case of 30...h5 the quickest way to force a draw is to open the position of the opponent's king with 31.g4 hxg4 (31...♗xg4 allows 32.♕e8+ ♔g7 33.d7 winning the bishop) 32.h5 and perpetual check soon.

31.h5 [90]

Threatening h5-h6.

31...♕b5 [146] **32.♗d5** [91]

A spectacular move, resuming the threat of the further advance of the h-pawn. 32.♕d4 gxh5 (32...♕xh5? 33.d7+−) 33.♕d2 is also enough for equality.

32...h6

The only move.

33.hxg6 ♗xd5

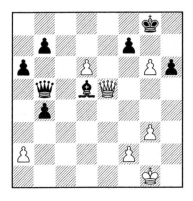

34.♕e7?? [94]

A typical mistake in one's opponent's time trouble! Having half an hour for seven moves Vladimirov made this move quickly, most likely influenced by the fact that Kasparov had only four minutes left. As a result, white misses his opponent's reply.

34.gxf7+ is a draw by perpetual check: 34...♔xf7   (34...♗xf7?? 35.♕xb5 axb5 36.d7+−) 35.♕f5+ (or 35.♕e7+ ♔g6 36.d7 ♕d3 37.♕e8+ ♔f5 38.♕h5+ ♔e6 39.♕e8+=) 35... ♔g7 36.d7 ♕c6 (the only move to

draw) 37.♕g4+ ♔h7. The black king obviously cannot step on the d8-h4 diagonal allowing white to queen the d-pawn with check. So it's a draw by repetition after 38.♕f5+.

34...♕c5! [147]

Everything else is lost for black, but this multipurpose move wins the game! Black pins the d6-pawn and combines attack with defence. White is helpless.

35.gxf7+ [98] **♗xf7**

Now white cannot advance the pawn and the only check is on d8, which will blockade the pawn. This important detail is decisive for the outcome.

36.♕d8+ ♔g7 37.d7 [99] **♗d5** [148]

Now the e7 square is protected by the queen and white has no good checks.

38.♕c8 [104] **♕d4**

Again there are no checks. After 39.♕c1 ♗c6 Vladimirov loses the d-pawn, so **white resigned.**

1982	16.08	17.08					
Game No.	1	2	3	4	5	6	Score
Kasparov	0	1					1
Vladimirov	1	0					1

Game 5

E. VLADIMIROV – G. KASPAROV
Training game. 19.08.1982
King's Indian Defense [E60]
Commentary by Dorian Rogozenco

1.d4 ♘f6 [03] **2.c4 g6** [05] **3.♘f3** [02] **♗g7 4.g3** [03] **c5 5.♗g2** [04]

5.d5 leads to the Benoni Fianchetto, which is not to everyone's taste among players who deploy the Fianchetto against the King's Indian.

5...♕a5+ [06]

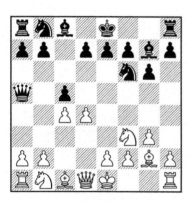

A very rare move those days, played only a few times before 1982. Judging by the time recorded on the scoresheet Vladimirov was unaware of it, while Kasparov had analyzed it before the game and was now probably testing to see how it works against an unprepared opponent.

6.♗d2 [10]

Later this variation with the check on a5 was played only once by Kasparov, in the SWIFT Blitz Championship in 1987 against Karpov. In that game black quickly achieved an advantage after 6.♕d2 ♘c6 7.d5?! ♘e4 8.♕xa5 ♘xa5 9.♘a3 ♘d6 10.♘d2 ♖b8 11.e3 a6 12.♖b1 b5.

The most critical move in the diagram position is 6.♘c3, which Kasparov himself played as white in the rapid "Man + Computer" match against Topalov 16 years later. That game continued 6...♘e4 7.♕d3 cxd4 8.♘xd4 ♘c5 9.♕d1 ♘c6 10.e3 ♘e6 11.0-0 ♕c5 12.♘db5 a6 13.♘a4 ♕xc4 14.♘bc3 ♖b8 15.♘b6 ♕c5 16.♘cd5. White achieved overwhelming compensation for the sacrificed pawn, G. Kasparov – V. Topalov, Leon 1998.

6...♕b6 [06] **7.♘c3** [24]

7.dxc5   ♕xc5   (7...♕xb2? 8.♗c3+–) 8.♕b3 ♘e4 9.♗e3 ♕a5+ 10.♘bd2 ♘c6=.

7...cxd4 8.♘a4 [28] **♕d6** [12]

The principled reply, keeping the pawn on d4 protected. After other retreats white is better.

9.♗f4 [39]

In case of 9.0-0 ♘c6 white's compensation for the sacrificed pawn is enough only to keep the balance. The game V. Filippov – Y. Shulman, Minsk 1996 continued 10.c5 and now after 10...♕b8! 11.e3 (11.b4 b5!

12.cxb6 axb6∓) 11...dxe3 12.♗xe3 0-0 the chances for both sides are about equal.

9...♕b4+ [14]

Black doesn't really have a choice, since 9...♕a6 10.♘xd4 delivers a clear advantage for white (and 10...♕xc4?? is not possible in view of 11.♖c1+−).

10.♗d2 [51] **♕d6** [19] **11.♗f4** [64]

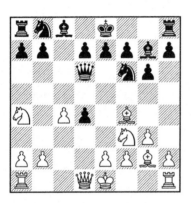

11...♕b4+ [20]

Draw agreed with repetition coming up.

The line 4...c5 followed by 5...♕a5+ has a certain surprise value, but this game showed one of its (relative) drawbacks: if white wants to achieve a draw, then objectively black can't deviate, otherwise he will end up worse. On the other hand, white has a few options to try playing for an advantage, so possibly this is why Kasparov never included this variation in his opening repertoire.

1982	16.08	17.08	19.08				
Game No.	1	2	3	4	5	6	Score
Kasparov	0	1	0.5				1.5
Vladimirov	1	0	0.5				1.5

Game 6

G. KASPAROV – E. VLADIMIROV
Training game. 20.08.1982
Catalan Opening [E04]
Commentary by Dorian Rogozenco

1.d4 [01] **♘f6** [01] **2.c4 e6 3.g3** [02]

One of the main goals of his first training match against Vladimirov was to test the Catalan, which Kasparov had never played before and which later became an important part of his opening repertoire.

3...d5 [02] **4.♗g2** [03] **dxc4** [03] **5.♘f3 c5** [04] **6.0-0** [05] **♘c6**

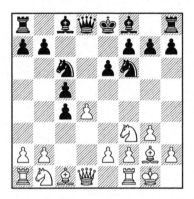

This line is also nowadays one of the main weapons for black players against the Catalan. In the diagram position white has a choice between several options, but even modern theory doesn't have an answer as to what the best continuation is.

7.♕a4 [10]

These days many top players try to prove an edge in the endgame after 7.dxc5 ♕xd1 8.♖xd1 ♗xc5 9.♘bd2 c3 10.bxc3, where modern theory only starts. Kasparov always preferred more complicated play. His famous victory over the supercomputer Deep Blue continued 7.♘e5 ♗d7 8.♘a3 cxd4 9.♘axc4 ♗c5 10.♕b3 0-0 11.♕xb7 ♘xe5 12.♘xe5 ♖b8 13.♕f3 ♗d6 14.♘c6 ♗xc6 15.♕xc6 e5 16.♖b1 ♖b6 17.♕a4 ♕b8 18.♗g5 ♗e7 19.b4 ♗xb4 20.♗xf6 gxf6 21.♕d7 ♕c8 22.♕xa7 ♖b8 23.♕a4 ♗c3 24.♖xb8 ♕xb8 25.♗e4 and white converted his positional advantage after very long resistance by the machine, G.

Kasparov – Deep Blue, Philadelphia 1996.

7...♗d7 [06] **8.♕xc4** [21]

Played after 11 minutes of thinking. Two days later Kasparov would try 8.dxc5.

8...b5 [07]

The theoretically important variation 8...cxd4 9.♘xd4 ♖c8 10.♘c3 ♘xd4 11.♕xd4 ♗c5 12.♕h4 was suffering a crisis in the late seventies and black players had started to switch more and more to 8...b5, which became the main continuation.

9.♕d3 [22]

Taking the pawn with 9.♕xb5 is bad in view of 9...♘xd4 10.♕d3 ♗b5.

9...♖c8 [11] **10.dxc5** [25] **♗xc5** [19] **11.a3** [26]

Kasparov tries a little-known line. The main continuation is 11.♘c3.

11...h6 [27]

Possibly Kasparov's choice of 11.a3 was inspired by the game M. Najdorf – R. Sanguineti, Buenos Aires 1965, which continued 11...0-0 12.b4 ♗e7 13.♘c3 a6 14.♗b2 a5 15.♘xb5 axb4 16.♘d6 ♖b8 17.♘g5 h6 18.♗xf6 hxg5 19.♗xe7 ♘xe7 20.axb4 ♗b5 21.♘xb5 ♕xd3 22.exd3 ♖xb5 23.♖fb1 ♘f5 24.♖a5 ♖fb8 25.♖xb5 ♖xb5 26.♗c6 ♖b6 27.♗a4 ♘d4 28.♔f1 and white finally won this endgame a pawn up. On the other hand, black could equalize by playing 13...a5 right away, without spending time on the move a7-a6.

Together with 11...0-0, the straightforward 11...b4 (preventing the opponent from playing b2-b4) should also be enough for equality, while 11...h6 is hardly a necessary move at this moment.

12.b4 [28] ♗e7 [28] **13.♘c3** [35] **a6** [31]

With the king in the center black must protect the pawn, because both 13...a5 14.♘xb5 axb4 15.♘d6+ and 13...0-0 14.♘xb5 are clearly better for white.

14.♖d1 [41] **0-0** [35] **15.e4** [42] ♕c7 [37]

15...e5 16.♘d5±

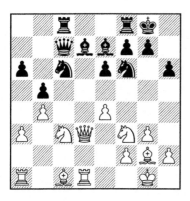

16.♕e2!? [78]

After 36 minutes of thinking Kasparov sacrifices a pawn for the initiative. The quiet continuation 16.♗b2 ♖fd8 17.♕e2 leads to an equal position.

16...♘xb4 [43]

Typically for his approach in the match Vladimirov accepts the challenge. It is very likely that in case of 16...♖fd8 Kasparov was ready to sac a pawn in a different way: 17.e5 ♘xe5 18.♘xe5 ♕xc3 19.♗b2 although objectively black is doing fine here as well.

17.♗b2 [82]

The alternative 17.axb4 ♕xc3 18.♗b2 allows white to win back the pawn after 18...♕c7 19.♖xa6, which is equal, but Kasparov had different plans for his c3 knight.

17...♘c6 [45] **18.e5** [90] ♘d5 [63]

18...♘h7 19.♘e4 ♖fd8 20.♘d6 ♗xd6 21.exd6 with compensation for white is worse thanks to the strong bishop on b2.

19.♖xd5 [92]

The computer is skeptical about this second sacrifice, too, but taking with the rook on d5 is the best practical chance to put black under pressure. It is not surprising that it took Kasparov only two minutes.

19...exd5 20.♘xd5 ♕d8 [70]

The engine has no fear and takes the queen away from the kingside with 20...♕a7!, claiming an advantage for black. The point is that after 21.♘f6+ gxf6 (21...♔h8 22.♕e4 gxf6 23.♕f4 wins for white) 22.exf6 black has 22...♗c5! (everything else loses) 23.♕d2 ♗xf2+. This little detail is decisive: white has sacrificed too much material and cannot allow himself to exchange queens. After 24.♔h1 ♗e3 (but not 24...♕e3 25.♕xd7 and unclear) black is winning. All this means that white should find something else on move 21. For instance, he can try to improve the position of the second knight with 21.♘d2 and then to e4, hoping to launch an attack later on.

21.♖d1! [93]

With the queen on d8 the situation changes dramatically: it turns out that she is misplaced there, because black doesn't have the desired blockading move ♗d7-e6. Without blockading the e-pawn black will always have to reckon with the advance e5-e6, opening the long diagonal for the dark-squared bishop.

21...♖e8 [72]

With this logical move black fights against both ideas e5-e6 and ♘d5-f6. Further, he wants to bring his bishop into defence by placing it on f8.

In case of the computer's preference 21...♗c5 white also has enough compensation by continuing 22.♖d3!? This prepares ♕d2 with pressure on the d-file and keeps an eye on the h6 pawn (which involves the ideas ♘f6+ and, after ...gxf6, ♕d2xh6). Let's continue with black's best defence according to my computer (asmFish at depths starting from 40): 22...♖e8 23.♕d2 ♕a5 24.♗c3 ♕xa3 25.e6! (opening the long diagonal) 25...♖xe6 (25... ♗xe6 loses in view of 26.♗xg7 with

the double threat ♖xa3 and ♕xh6) 26.♗f1 ♕a4 27.♘f4 ♘b8 28.♘xe6 ♗xe6 29.♖d8+ ♗f8 30.♖xc8 ♗xc8 31.♗xg7. Here the computer's evaluation at depth 52 is 0.00.

22.♘f4! [100]

White wants to advance the e-pawn, therefore black makes a move according to his plan.

22...♗f8 [84]

This natural retreat turns out to be a mistake. The only way to keep the balance was 22...♕c7 23.e6 ♗xe6 (23...fxe6 24.♗xg7 ♔xg7 25.♕e4+−) 24.♘xe6 and now the most precise is 24...♗f8 25.♗h3 ♖xe6 (25...fxe6 26.♗xe6+ ♔h8 27.♕e3 is again bad for black) 26.♗xe6 ♕e7 27.♗xf7+ ♕xf7 with equality.

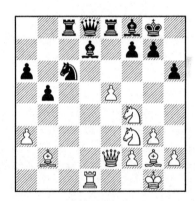

23.♗h3 [102]

It is hard to believe that this active move throws away white's advantage. Instead Kasparov could win with the incredible 23.e6! fxe6 (23...♖xe6 24.♘xe6 fxe6 25.♗h3+−) 24.♘h4!! And it turns out that black is defenseless against the attack on the b1-h7 diagonal. White's plan is ♗e4 followed in most cases by ♕d3 (or other maneuvers, such as for instance ♗e4-b1 and ♕d3, or ♕h5-g6). There is no acceptable way for black to protect the weakened light squares around the king. Let's have a deeper look: 24...♖c7 25.♗e4 ♘e7 26.♕d3 (even stronger than 26.♘xe6 ♗xe6 27.♖xd8 ♖xd8 when black can still struggle on) 26...♘f5 27.♗e5 ♖a7 28.♘hg6 ♕c8 29.g4+−. Instead of 24...♖c7 other moves don't help either: 24...♘e7 25.♘xe6+−; 24...♘b8 25.♗e4 ♖c4 26.♘hg6 (not 26.♗b1? ♖xf4) 26...♕g5 27.♘e5 ♖xe4 28.♕xe4 ♗c8 29.♕a8 ♘d7 30.♕c6 ♘f6 31.♘fg6+−; or 24...♕c7 25.♗e4 ♘b8 (25...♘e7 26.♕g4 ♘f5 27.♘h5+−) 26.♕d3 ♖c4 27.♗h7+ ♔f7 28.♕f3 with mate soon.

23...♖c7 24.♕e4 [108]

24.e6 doesn't have a devastating effect anymore. The rook on c7 is helpful, while the bishop on h3 cannot exploit the weaknesses of the light squares in black's camp. For instance: 24...fxe6 25.♕e4 (25.♘h4 ♕g5 (with the idea ...♗c8) 26.♖xd7 ♖xd7 27.♗xe6+ ♖xe6 28.♕xe6+ ♖f7 29.♕xc6 ♖xf4 30.♘f3 ♕g4 31.♕d5+= and white's compensation is enough only for a draw) 25...e5 26.♘xe5 ♘xe5 27.♗e6+ ♖xe6 28.♘xe6 ♕e7 29.♘xc7 ♗g4 30.♕d5+ ♔h8 31.♖c1 (31.♕xe5 ♕xe5 32.♗xe5 ♗xd1 33.♗b2 ♔h7 34.♘xa6 g5 is also a draw) 31...♘f3+ 32.♔g2 ♘e1+ 33.♔g1 (33.♔f1?? ♕e2+ 34.♔g1 ♗h3-+) 33...♘f3+ 34.♔g2=.

24...♕c8

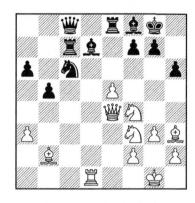

Black has successfully protected everything. Now the bishop on h3 is attacked and white has nothing on the kingside. In order to win back the sacrificed material white is forced to simplify the position, which leads to equality.

25.♗xd7 [117] **♖xd7 26.♖c1 ♖c7** [108] **27.♘d5** [118] **♖ee7 28.♘xe7+** [130] **♘xe7** [111] **29.♖xc7 ♕xc7 30.e6** [131] **♕d6** [112] **31.exf7+** [137] **♔xf7**

With little material white cannot exploit the slightly exposed position of the opponent's king.

32.♘e5+ ♔g8 [113] **33.♕g4** [138] **♕d2** [115] **34.♕e6+** [139] **♔h7** [118] **35.♘d7** [140]

After 35....♘g6 36.♘xf8+ ♘xf8 the position is equal, so a draw was agreed.

Draw agreed

A very entertaining game, which ended somewhat disappointingly for Kasparov. From the opening point of view white didn't achieve much, because first of all the move 11...h6 is not obligatory and secondly after white's positional pawn sacrifice black was objectively fine.

In the sixth game of this mini-match Kasparov was to try to fight for an opening advantage in a different way.

1982	16.08	17.08	19.08	20.08			
Game No.	1	2	3	4	5	6	Score
Kasparov	0	1	0.5	0.5			2
Vladimirov	1	0	0.5	0.5			2

Game 7

G. KASPAROV – E. VLADIMIROV
Training game. 21.08.1982
Catalan Opening [E04]
Commentary by Dorian Rogozenco

1.d4 ♘f6 2.c4 e6 3.g3 d5 4.♗g2 dxc4 5.♘f3 ♘bd7

This move, which is occasionally deployed by even very strong players, never became mainstream in Catalan theory. However, it was a very wise choice to have it tested in the present training game, because one year later Korchnoi with black would try to surprise Kasparov with this system in their 9th game of the candidates semifinal match.

6.0-0 ♖b8 7.a4 b6

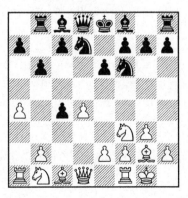

8.♘fd2

This is white's best continuation. 8.♘bd2 ♗a6 9.♕c2 c3 10.bxc3 ♗xe2 11.♖e1 ♗a6 with an unclear position happened in the recent blitz game S. Vidit – M. Carlsen, Kolkata 2019.

8...♗b7

8...e5 9.♘xc4! exd4 10.♕xd4 ♗c5 11.♕d3 0-0 12.♘c3 ♗b7 13.♗xb7 ♖xb7 14.♕f3 ♕a8 15.♗f4 a6 16.e4 led to white's initiative and later to a very important victory in the above-mentioned game G. Kasparov – V. Korchnoi, London 1983.

9.♗xb7 ♖xb7 10.♘xc4 ♗e7 11.♘c3 c5

11...0-0 12.e4±; 11...♘d5 12.e4 ♘xc3 13.bxc3±.

12.d5 exd5 13.♘xd5 0-0

Black has no time to exchange on d5 (and thus to avoid creating white a passed d-pawn, as in the game) due to the hanging position

of the rook on b7: 13...♞xd5?
14.♕xd5 ♕c8 (14...♖c7 15.♗f4+−)
15.♗g5! winning because of 15...
♗xg5 16.♞d6+.

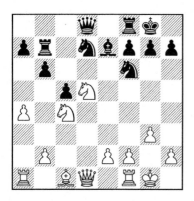

14.e4!

A small tactical trick, using the
fact that black cannot take on e4.
Black will not be able to tolerate his
opponent's strong centralized knight
for long and will be forced to create
white a strong passed pawn.

14...♞b8

14...♞xe4? 15.♞xe7+ ♕xe7
16.♖e1+−; 14...♞xd5 15.exd5 ♖e8
16.♗f4±.

15.♕f3! ♖d7

After 15...♞xd5 16.exd5 ♖d7
white continues 17.♗f4! preparing
to place the rooks on d1 and e1.
Black cannot take on d5: 17...♖xd5?
18.♗xb8 ♖d4 19.♞e5 ♕xb8 20.♞c6
winning the exchange.

16.♞e5

Here 16.♗f4 runs into 16...♞xe4
17.♕xe4 ♖xd5 18.♗xb8 ♖d4 and
black remains a pawn up.

16...♖d6 17.♖d1 ♞xd5 18.exd5 ♗f6

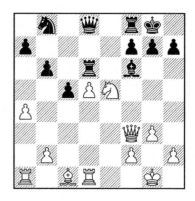

19.♗f4

Allowing the exchange of the
knight is not a trivial decision.
19.♞c4 ♖d7 20.♗f4 is obviously
a good alternative, but Kasparov's
choice is probably even stronger,
because after the exchange of his
knight white's position will still
contain enough resources to make
progress and increase the advantage.
It is important that without his
bishop black will have neither
stability nor counterplay (based on
placing the bishop on d4) and will
suffer due to a lack of space.

19...♗xe5

19...♖e8 runs into 20.♞c6 ♞xc6
21.dxc6+−.

20.♗xe5 ♖g6

A good practical choice, preparing
to blockade the pawn on d7 with
the knight. In case of 20...♖d7
21.a5 black won't be able to hold
the position in the long run: 21...b5
(after other moves white's advantage
is bigger: 21...bxa5 22.♗c3±; 21...
♖e8 22.axb6 axb6 23.♗f4 with the
idea 24.♖a8) 22.♕g4!? (or 22.b3±)
22...f5 23.♕f3±.

21.♖a3 ♘d7 22.♗f4 ♕f6

An inaccuracy, allowing white to take control over the e-file. 22... ♖e8± was necessary.

23.♖e3!+− h6

23...♕xb2 24.♖e7 ♘f6 (24...♘b8 25.♗xb8 ♖xb8 26.♕xf7+; 24...♖d8 25.♗c7+−) 25.d6 h5 26.d7+−.

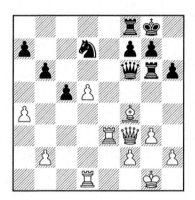

24.d6

This move is accompanied with a "?!" sign on the scoresheet. It does indeed offer black the e6 square for the knight in the future, but it is hard to believe that such a natural move can be wrong. Concrete analysis shows that white is still winning after 24.d6 and it was not the advance of the d-pawn that spoiled white's advantage later on.

Improving the position with something like 24.b3 ♖d8 25.♔g2 ♘f8 26.♕e4 leaves black without any hope for counterplay and is another way to convert the advantage, which is much bigger than it seems on the diagram. The problem is not only black's passivity or misplaced rook on g6, but simply the lack of useful

moves: 26...a6 (26...♘d7 27.♗c7 ♖c8 28.d6+−; 26...h5 27.h4+−) 27.♗c7 ♖d7 28.d6 ♘e6 29.♖f3 ♕g5 30.♕c6+−.

24...♕f5

24...♕xb2 25.♖e7 ♖d8 26.♕b7 ♘f8 27.♕c7 ♖a8 28.d7+−.

25.♖e7

The first mistake. It was right to start with the move 25.♕b7! and white's queen alone will cause big damage, preventing black from consolidating. The following variations show that white wins everywhere: 25...♖d8 (25...♕xf4 26.♕xd7+−; 25...♘f6 26.d7! ♘xd7 27.♗d6+−) 26.♕xa7! ♕xf4 (26...♘f8 27.♕xb6+−) 27.♕c7 ♕f6 28.♖e7+−.

25...♖d8 26.♕b7

This second mistake allows black to equalize. Although the queen move looks logical and strong, in this position it does not work concretely. 26.♖d5 ♕b1+ 27.♔g2 keeps a large advantage, e.g. 27...♕xb2 (27...♘f6 28.d7+−) 28.♖f5+−. White is also much better after the quiet 26.♔g2 and black cannot transfer his knight to e6: 26...♘f8 27.♖d5 ♕f6 28.♕e4 ♕xb2 (or 28...♘e6 29.♗e5 ♕g5 30.h4 ♕g4 31.♕xg4 ♖xg4 32.d7+−) 29.♖e8+−.

26...♘f8!

With a series of precise moves Vladimirov succeeds in escaping. Now the bishop on f4 is hanging and in contrast to the variation starting with 25.♕b7 here white cannot take on a7 and then regain the piece with ♕c7.

27.♕c7

27.♗e5 ♖e6!=

27...♖c8

27...♖a8 would be a mistake because of 28.d7 protecting the bishop.

28.♕xa7 ♕xf4 29.d7 ♘xd7 30.♕xd7 ♖f8 31.♖e8 ♖xe8 32.♕xe8+ ♔h7 33.♖d8 ♖g5

The position has simplified and is totally equal now, because white's attack on the 8th rank brings nothing. White's next two impulsive moves are probably explained by the fact that both players must have mentally agreed to a draw.

34.h4

A last try, setting a small trap. 34.♕c6=; 34.♔g2=

34...♕xh4

Avoiding 34...♖g4?? 35.h5+−

35.♖d7

Here the players agreed to a draw, although white still had to fight for it after 35...♕xa4 36.♕xf7 ♕a1+ (36...♕c6 37.♖d8) 37.♔g2 ♕xb2 38.♖d8 ♕e5 39.♕g8+ ♔g6. Therefore, instead of 35.♖d7, 35.♕g8+ ♔g6 36.♖d6+ f6 37.♕e8+ ♔h7 38.♖d8 was more accurate, which would soon end in perpetual check.

Draw agreed

1982	16.08	17.08	19.08	20.08	21.08		
Game No.	1	2	3	4	5	6	Score
Kasparov	0	1	0.5	0.5	0.5		2.5
Vladimirov	1	0	0.5	0.5	0.5		2.5

Game 8

G. KASPAROV – E. VLADIMIROV
Training game. 22.08.1982
Catalan Opening [E04]
Commentary by Dorian Rogozenco

1.d4 ♘f6 2.c4 e6 3.g3 d5 4.♗g2 dxc4 5.♘f3 c5 6.0-0 ♘c6 7.♕a4 ♗d7 8.dxc5

Kasparov deviates from the third game of the mini-match, which continued 8.♕xc4 b5.

8...♗xc5 9.♕xc4 ♗e7 10.♘c3 0-0

This position was very little explored in 1982 and judging by the scoresheet it took Kasparov 50 minutes for the next three moves. It must be said that even today the variation with 8.dxc5 is not particularly popular among white players, because the diagram position is very close to equality. Nevertheless, there are some strategic ideas for white. Ideally he would like to gain more space with the advance e4-e5, which (after e2-e4) is often prevented by black with ...e6-e5. In the resulting positions with the blockaded pawns on e4 and e5 white can hope for some advantage thanks to the fact that due to the better control of the d5 square (supported by the fianchettoed bishop) he has better chances of jumping with the knight to d5 than black has of getting his knight to d4.

Meanwhile, white has a concrete problem to solve: where to retreat the queen after black places the rook on c8.

11.♖d1

Another option, to retreat the queen to e2 at once, is advocated these days by Eljanov and Gelfand. 11.e4 ♖c8 12.♕e2 e5 13.♖d1 ♕a5 14.♘d5 ♗g4 15.h3 ♗xf3 16.♗xf3 ♘xd5 17.♖xd5 ♕c7 18.♗e3 was slightly better for white in B. Gelfand – S. Lu, Khanty-Mansiysk 2019.

11...♖c8 12.e4 e5 13.♕b3

By attacking the b7 pawn white provokes the opponent's knight to leave the center.

13...♘a5 14.♕c2 ♕c7 15.♕e2 ♗g4 16.h3 ♗xf3 17.♗xf3

By the odd-looking queen maneuver ♕c4-b3-c2-e2 Kasparov has in fact achieved something: the opponent's knight and queen are misplaced and white has the bishop pair. Now white can combine the ideas of ♗g5xf6 followed by ♘d5, or the immediate ♘d5.

17...h6

17...♘c6 18.♗e3 ♘d4 19.♗xd4 exd4 is interesting here, with the idea 20.♖xd4 ♗c5! and after the rook's retreat black has 21...♕xg3+. Instead of 20.♖xd4 white must fight for an advantage with 20.♘b5.

18.♗e3

After 18.♘d5 ♘xd5 19.♖xd5 (19.exd5 ♘c4 20.b3 ♘d6 looks closer to equality) 19...♘c6 20.♗e3 we have an amazing transposition to the above-mentioned game Gelfand – Lu (albeit here with the black pawn on h6 instead of h7). Possibly this was too little for Kasparov, who makes a logical developing move, after which white will additionally have ♘c3-b5 ideas.

18...♗c5

A positionally sound move, which has a tactical drawback. Difficult to say why Vladimirov didn't play 18...♘c4 and black has little to fear.

19.♘b5!

Suddenly the knight jumps in a different direction and it turns out that black loses a pawn.

19...♕e7

White's point was that 19...♕b6 is met by 20.b4! This was probably missed by Vladimirov when he played 18...♗c5. After 20.b4! the only chance to survive is offered by the queen sacrifice 20...♗xe3 21.bxa5 ♗xf2+ 22.♔g2 ♕c5 23.♖ac1 ♕xc1 24.♖xc1 ♖xc1 25.♔xf2 ♖fc8, although in the long run white should be able to convert his material advantage after 26.♘a3 ♖1c3 27.♕b2.

20.♘xa7 ♖cd8

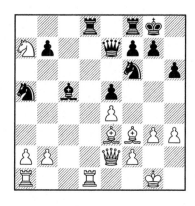

21.♘b5?

Kasparov returns the favor and misses his opponent's counterplay in a relatively simple position. 21.♖xd8 ♖xd8 22.♖c1, or 21.b3 would have left white a healthy pawn up.

**21...♗xe3   22.♕xe3   ♕b4!
23.♕e2 ♘c4**

There is no way for white to keep the extra pawn. Now the game ends quickly.

**24.♘c3 ♘xb2 25.♖xd8 ♖xd8
26.♖b1**

After 26...♕xc3 27.♖xb2 ♖d7 28.♔g2 there is little left to fight for.

Draw agreed

1982	16.08	17.08	19.08	20.08	21.08	22.08	
Game No.	1	2	3	4	5	6	Score
Kasparov	0	1	0.5	0.5	0.5	0.5	3
Vladimirov	1	0	0.5	0.5	0.5	0.5	3

Game 9

All games between Garry Kasparov and Viktor Korchnoi witnessed uncompromising battle. And this duel was their most furious. It went down in the history of chess olympiads alongside the historical game between Fisher and Spassky in 1970.

Actually, this game was not meant to take place. Before the match against the Swiss, our team enjoyed a solid lead in the tournament and it was Kasparov's turn to rest, having already played seven rounds in a row. Such a rule was strictly adhered to in such benign circumstances. However, the morning of the match Karpov unexpectedly requested to be excused his game. So Korchnoi and Kasparov found themselves playing each other for the first time in six years, but this time in a proper game and not a simul.

V. KORCHNOI – G. KASPAROV
Lucerne. 25th Chess Olympiad. 09.11.1982
Modern Benoni. [A64]

Although the organizers decided to show this game on almost all the TV monitors set up throughout the huge playing hall, it was impossible for anybody to squeeze through to the table even before the game began. The photographers only had one thing on their mind... the way the players would greet one another. The instruction from on high to chess players not to shake hands with Korchnoi was still in force. Viktor didn't want to put the young man in an awkward situation and dashed to the table only once his clock was started, while Garry sat staring at the motionless chessmen and seemed to notice nobody. Instead of any greetings Korchnoi quickly stretched his hands to the pawn and made his first move. The absurd ban had not been violated...

1.d4 ♘f6 2.c4 g6 3.g3 ♗g7 4.♗g2 c5 5.d5 d6 6.♘c3 0-0 7.♘f3 e6 8.0-0 exd5 9.cxd5 a6 10.a4 ♖e8 11.♘d2 ♘bd7 12.h3 ♖b8 13.♘c4

All this was theory built from a multitude of games using the moves

that had gained the best reputation. Grandmasters usually play through such moves quickly, thinking only about which well-trodden path they should follow today. An important role in such a choice could be played by considerations unrelated to the actual lines.

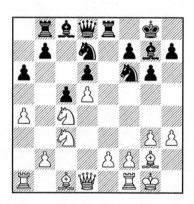

13...♘e5(16)

A different knight route is considered more solid: 13...♘b6, promising a relatively quiet flow of events. Kasparov instead chooses a strategically risky continuation, which does however force both sides to begin a battle based on concrete calculation. His hesitation when selecting the move was purely down to his decision on what move best supported his team's goals.

14.♘a3 ♘h5

The risky setup applied by Kasparov was given the thumbs up after being analyzed a dozen Yugoslav *Informants* later (chess players used this unit to measure time) in a slightly modernized edition – 14...♗d7!? 15.f4 ♘h5 16.fxe5 ♗xe5. However, when this game was played erratic fashion only favored this extravagant knight jump.

15.e4 ♖f8(20)

And this move was still theory, with a lot of games behind it. At the time the debate was which black move would complicate play the most – 15...♖f8 or 15...f5. Now that the weaknesses of both lines have been identified, the move 15...♗d7 is today considered more playable, transforming the knight on e5 into a kamikaze unit. We analyzed this line in Moscow after the game, and Kasparov's personal opening encyclopedia, unavailable to the public, still contains the analysis demonstrating the superiority of the new idea.

Its practical use was prevented first by the battle for the chess crown and then Garry's new rule not to play strategically risky setups. I don't want to publish this analysis (what if it becomes needed!), but it will wait for its hour of glory

without complaint and quietly grow old. A little bit of time passes and once handy discoveries become archive material, useful perhaps only for memoirs and academic articles. Chess analysis has the same fate as a chess player. It either gains fame at the right time or else disappears into oblivion, having failed to find the path to glory.

16.♔h2 f5(15)

Garry remembered that half a move later (17.f4) the last well-known path ended with Jan Timman's evaluation of the position as "unclear". Now he was left with a chess skeleton of a completely fresh game that nobody had probably analyzed seriously and which may turn out to be a dead end. He attempted to compare the variations and decide which was better – the already well-known 16...f5 or the intuitive 16...♗d7 17.f4 b5! to be followed by 18.fxe5 ♘xg3! 19.♔xg3 ♗xe5+ 20.♔f3 b4. The lines both seemed equally acceptable and equally dangerous, but he decided in the end to trust Timman. Although the latter had given the position only a cursory assessment, he had nevertheless done so during home analysis.

Several hours of independent analysis in Baku convinced Garry that he should trust his intuition more – the line beginning with 16...♗d7 turned out to be more promising.

17.f4 b5

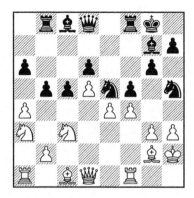

18.axb5

Many grandmasters would have made this move without much thought. Korchnoi, though, spent 12 minutes considering the consequences of losing control over the b5 square and the enhanced role of the bishop on d7.

18...axb5 19.♘axb5

For several moves in a row starting from this point, both players should have begun their thinking over the next move with an evaluation of the consequences of the impudent black knight's capture. However, if Kasparov had no choice in the matter, as the knight's retreat would have been tantamount to admitting his opening strategy had failed, hence he had no choice but to throw ever more wood on the burning fire of battle, Korchnoi faced a far more psychologically challenging situation. The abundance of normal continuations at his disposal and his fear of being short changed if he captured the knight before time placed white at times in the position of Buridan's ass. Having realized that

Garry wouldn't remove his knight from the center, Korchnoi decided to focus on strengthening his position. A real battle of nerves now began.

19...fxe4

A week before the Olympiad, Garry received the latest issue of *Informant* and managed to take a look at all the games it contained without setting up the pieces – necessary work for a chess pro. There he read up the game Alburt-Olafsson where white won after 20.♘a7 e3 21.♛e2, but the invisible analyst hidden inside Kasparov's head noted that 20...♗d7 was a more interesting continuation and stored it in a drawer in his memory. So that lad had come to this position with some analytical material in his brain. I very much doubt that his opponent knew more than that.

20.♗xe4

After more than 30 minutes of thought Korchnoi took a simple and wise decision – not to rush things. According to his understanding, the extra pawn and threat of capturing the knight would soon bring a turning point in the battle in white's favor.

20...♗d7 (37)

Black had to move the struggle to an irrational dimension, when usual concepts of material balances and positional values gave way for a while to concrete calculation and a dynamic evaluation of the position based on the degree of the pieces' activity. In such circumstances, key was to constantly create threats, even one-move ones. Obviously, it didn't make sense to base the entire game strategy on this, but when a highly complex and non-standard situation arises in which your chances of survival are limited, the principle of "activity above all" is perfectly justifiable. So here black neglects the defense of the d6 pawn and begins pressing through one-move threats.

21.♕e2

Capturing another pawn with 21.♘xd6 would have unnecessarily increased the activity of the black pieces with 21...♖b6! 22.fxe5 ♗xe5 23.♘c4 ♗xg3+ 24.♔g1 ♖bf6 25.♗g2 ♖f2 26.♘e3 ♗xh3. One can conclude that having captured one pawn and placed the knight under constant rifle-point Korchnoi rejected further pawn grabbing, correctly preferring to ensure harmony among his pieces and strengthen his position.

21...♕b6(23) 22.♘a3 ♖be8

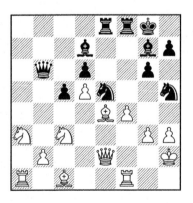

Now was the critical and most tense moment of the fight. Black had squeezed all he could out of his pieces, and there was no obvious way

to further strengthen. Petrosian, with his heightened sense of danger, would surely have played 23.♕g2 here, removing his queen from the guns of the rook on e8. This was the maneuver that Garry also feared the most. Once back in Moscow we found a chain of best moves in this critical line – 23...♕b4 24.♘c2 ♕b8 25.♘e3 ♘f7 26.♘c4 ♗xc3 27.bxc3 ♘f6 28.♗f3 ♗f5, where white retains an advantage but black has some activity in compensation.

Nevertheless, it would not be right to condemn Garry for the move 13...♘e5 and all the confusion that followed. His risky opening strategy fully matched his playing style. In those years he bravely steered for complications and knew how to mix up almost any situation. After the game, Korchnoi said: "Playing such complex positions with Kasparov is incredibly difficult – each time you have to find the only move."

The fourth hour of nervous calculation ended. Viktor was known as a fantastic calculator, but he couldn't withstand the pressure on this occasion. He relaxed after noticing a tempting way to improve his piece harmony while at the same time chasing the black queen from his camp. He was sure that only a madman would take on b2.

23.♗d2? ♕xb2!(7)

And yet! The "deadly" and obvious 24.♖fb1 is refuted by the no less deadly but quite unobvious 24...♘f3+!! The loss of this extra and, moreover, "anchor" pawn would force white to completely revise his strategy. But he didn't have time to rearrange his thought process, only to kick himself...

24.fxe5?(4)

This double mistake is understandable given Korchnoi's character. Shocked and angry he didn't even consider moves such as 24.♖a2 or 24.♘c2 and decided to immediately execute this nasty knight, as though a little wooden figure could have been guilty of his predicament. He chose the very worst moment for the execution and white's game quickly unraveled.

24...♗xe5   25.♘c4   ♘xg3 26.♖xf8+ ♖xf8 27.♕e1!

Korchnoi defends with desperation as his ship continues to sink. In a fierce time scramble, in a position where any move looked bad, he sets his opponent, already tasting victory, what might be his last test – to choose the best of two apparently equally promising moves – and this almost saves him.

27...♘xe4+   28.♔g2   ♕c2 29.♘xe5 ♖f2+?

This is just what white was counting on. Kasparov mixes up his lines. He had quickly calculated 29...♘xd2! 30.♘xd7 ♘f3+ 31.♕e2 ♘h4+ 32.♔g1 ♕xc3 33.♕e6+ ♔h8 34.♘xf8 ♕g3+ 35.♔f1 ♕g2+ 36.♔e1 ♘f3+ 37.♔d1 ♕d2#, but in reply to the king's other retreat 32.♔h2 he failed to find the decisive blow 32...♖f2+! It came to him in the post-mortem. He had only minutes left on the clock and decided to capture white's queen, considering the rest of the white army to be unfit for battle.

30.♕xf2! ♘xf2!

By pure intuition black rejects the temptation to give the intermezzo check 30...♗xh3+? and, as subsequent analysis proved, he was right. After 31.♔g1 ♘xf2 32.♖a2! ♕b3 33.♖a8+ ♔g7 34.♖a7+! white emerges unscathed, as 34...♔f6 is met by the quite unpleasant 35.♘f3! threatening 36.♗g5#.

The vastly experienced Petrosian told the kids when we analyzed this game at the next session of our school: "I also wouldn't have removed the bishop from the seventh rank, where it carried out the role of a tree log in the path of the white rook. In time trouble the king's safety is more valuable than material gains."

31.♖a2! ♕f5 32.♘xd7 ♘d3

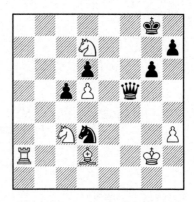

This is the position that Kasparov was aiming for, believing it won. However, the position on the diagram resembles a study. The white pieces, scattered in the far reaches of the board, don't look capable of withstanding the harmonious destructive operations of the two black pieces. However, it's white to move and this should save him: 33.♖a8+ ♔g7 34.♖a7! ♕f2+ 35.♔h1 ♕xd2 36.♘e5+! ♔f8 37.♖a8+ ♔e7 38.♖a7+ ♔d8 39.♖a8+. Now black cannot play 39...♔c7? due to 40.♘b5+! ♔b7 41.♖a7+ ♔b6 42.♘c4+, and therefore black should make do with a repetition of moves with 39...♔e7 40.♖a7+ and so on.

33.♗h6?

Age begins to tell, and in time trouble Korchnoi's play was not as faultless as it used to be. Yet the winner defended him: "The tension of the fight was so high that by the fifth hour of play the board was flickering before my eyes and it sometimes seemed that the pieces were rocking back and forth, even though I really enjoy this type of chess. My opponent was awfully tired..."

33...♕xd7 34.♖a8+ ♔f7 35.♖h8

He could have resisted better with 35.♘e4, all the more so as Garry wanted to meet it with 35... g5 and choose a complicated path to victory. He would have won much more easily with 35...♕e7! 36.♘g5+ ♔f6 37.♖f8+ ♔e5, but again we only found this line in Moscow.

35...♔f6!

The black king's march was totally unexpected by Korchnoi. In the confusion with his flag hanging he instinctively attempted to halt the king's raid. However, after:

36.♔f3 ♕xh3+ white lost on time.

Both spectators and other tournament players, who had formed a thick circle around their table, gave the winner an ovation. But the biggest reward came later. The effect caused by that grandiose and fierce battle was so stunning that international chess journalists awarded the Chess Oscar that year to Garry Kasparov for the first time.

Games 10

G. KASPAROV – E. VLADIMIROV
Training game. 23.01.1983
Queen's Gambit [D53]
Commentary by Dorian Rogozenco

1.d4 [00] **♘f6** [00] **2.c4 e6 3.♘f3** [02] **d5** [01] **4.♘c3 ♗e7** [02] **5.♗g5** [03] **h6** [03] **6.♗xf6** [04]

A big part of the theory of this move is based on games played by Kasparov and Karpov in their

World Championship matches. But that was to happen later. At the moment when the present game was played Kasparov was just starting to explore the finesses of the positions after 6.♗xf6.

6...♗xf6 7.e3 [07] **dxc4** [07]

This looks too early. In the fourth game of this mini-match Vladimirov played the main continuation 7...0-0.

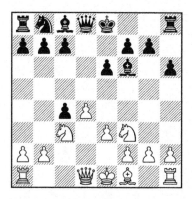

8.♘e4 [25]

It is amazing that instead of automatically taking back on c4 (which happened in all available games with this line) Kasparov spent 18 minutes here and makes a conceptual move, preventing black from the quick ...c7-c5.

8.♗xc4 c5 must have been the reason for Kasparov's choice. Indeed, it is not obvious how white can achieve any sensible advantage here, let's say after the most natural continuation 9.d5 exd5 10.♘xd5 0-0 (10...♗xb2 11.♖b1 ♗f6 12.♕c2 0-0 13.0-0 ♘c6 14.♖fd1 offers white an initiative for the pawn).

8...♘d7 [09]

Black shows his intention to play...c7-c5 quickly. 8...0-0 9.♗xc4 b6 10.0-0 ♗b7 11.♕c2 ♘d7 and then ♕e7, ♖ac8, ♖fd8 and c5 looks like a solid alternative for black.

9.♗xc4 c5 [19]

After 10 minutes of thinking Vladimirov decides to make this advance before castling, intending to give a check on a5 if white takes on c5.

Nevertheless, there was nothing wrong with castling before advancing the c-pawn: 9...0-0 10.0-0 c5, not fearing 11.dxc5 ♗xb2 12.♖b1 ♗a3 and black is fine.

10.d5 [33]

10.♘d6+ ♔e7 brings white nothing. 10.dxc5!? ♕a5+ 11.♕d2 ♕xd2+ 12.♘fxd2 ♗xb2 13.♖b1 ♗e5 (13...♗a3 14.♗b5 ♔e7 15.♖b3±) 14.♔e2 leads to an endgame where due to the undeveloped queenside black still hasn't equalized completely.

10...♘b6 [37]

10...♕a5+ now makes little sense due to 11.♘fd2; 10...exd5 here is bad because of 11.♘d6+ ♔e7 12.♕xd5+−, but 10...♗xb2!? 11.dxe6 (11.♖b1 ♘f6! is also unclear) 11...♘b6! 12.exf7+ ♔e7 leads to a complete mess, where black's chances don't seem to be worse.

11.♗b5+ [36] **♔f8** [47]

This is too much. Black is playing with fire and will be severely punished. After 11...♗d7 12.♗xd7+ ♕xd7 13.♘xf6+ gxf6 black is just slightly worse.

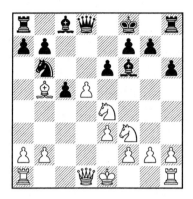

12.d6 [57]

Now black won't be able to connect rooks in the near future and therefore his position is difficult. White should try to open files on the queenside and use the better coordination of his pieces. As long as the pawn on d6 is alive and well protected, there is little hope for black to survive.

12...♗d7 [58]

12...♗xb2 13.♖b1 ♗f6 14.♖c1!?±; 12...g5 13.0-0 ♔g7 14.♖c1+−

13.a4 [68] **♗xb5** [62] **14.axb5 ♕d7** [63]

Good or bad, black had to continue 14...♗xb2 15.♖a2 ♗f6 16.0-0 c4, intending g6 and ♔g7. After 17.♕e2 white has excellent compensation, but at least a pawn up black has something to suffer for. In the game white continued to develop the initiative without even having to sacrifice anything.

15.♕e2 [76] **c4** [65] **16.♖a5!** [77]

Protects the pawn and prepares to double rooks on the a-file after castling.

16...♘d5 [87]

16...♘c8   17.♕d2±   (17.0-0? ♘xd6 18.♖d1 ♕c7).

17.0-0 [84] **b6** [88]

17...g6 18.♘xf6 ♘xf6 19.♕d2+−.

After 17...c3 white can choose between 18.b6 ♘xb6 19.bxc3 with a clear advantage, or 18.bxc3 ♘xc3 19.♘xc3 ♗xc3 20.♖a3 ♗b4 21.♖d3 ♕xb5 22.♖fd1, with excellent compensation for the pawn (22...♗xd6? 23.♔f1+−).

18.♖a4 [85] **♕xb5** [89]

18...g6 19.♖xc4 ♔g7 20.♖c6 ♖hc8 21.♖fc1+−

19.♖xc4 [90] **♕xb2** [91] **20.♖c2** [86] **♕b4** [92] **21.♕a6** [87]

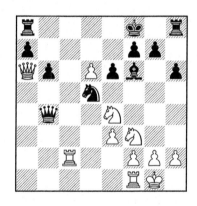

The pawn on d6 is still alive, the files on the queenside are open and white threatens ♖c8+. In order to hide the king and connect rooks black must weaken the long diagonal, which will allow Kasparov to win by a direct attack.

21...g5 [96]

21...♔g8   22.♕d3! (preventing ...♔h7) 22...♖d8 23.♖fc1 g6 24.♖a2 ♖d7 25.♖b1 catches the queen on b4. 21...g6 was somewhat better, because in the game the pawn on g5 allowed white to implement an additional winning plan later. Still, after 21...g6 white wins as well with 22.♘xf6 ♘xf6 23.♖c7 ♘d5 (23...♕xd6 24.♕b7+−) 24.♖d7 ♔g7 25.♘e5 ♖hf8 26.♕b7+−

22.♘xf6! [117]

Kasparov invested half an hour to calculate a forced win.

22.♖c8+? ♖xc8 23.♕xc8+ ♔g7 24.d7 doesn't work because the knight on e4 is hanging: 24...♕xe4−+

22...♘xf6 23.♕a1! [118]

The most convincing way to victory.

23...♔g7 [97] **24.d7** [128]

The same plan as in the game works immediately, too: 24.♘e5 ♕xd6 25.f4+− and black loses

quickly, but Kasparov prefers to keep the d-pawn alive.

24...♖hd8 [106] **25.♘e5** [129] **♕a5** [109]

25...♔g8 26.♘c6+−

26.♕b2 [133] **♕d5** [110] **27.f4** [135]

Thanks to the pawn on g5 white has this elegant way to finish the game. The opening of the f-file creates decisive threats against black's king. 27.♘g4 ♕f5 28.f3 ♖xd7 29.e4 ♕g6 30.♘e5 wins as well.

27...♔h7 [120]

Or 27...g4 28.♖d2 ♕e4 29.♘xg4 ♕f5 30.♖f3 h5 31.♘xf6 ♕xf6 32.♖g3+

28.fxg5 [140] **♘xd7 29.♘xf7**

Black resigned before getting mated after 29...♖f8 30.♖d2 ♕c6 31.♕b1+ ♔g7 32.gxh6+

1983	23.01				
Game No.	1	2	3	4	Score
Kasparov	1				1
Vladimirov	0				0

Game 11

G. KASPAROV – E. VLADIMIROV
Training game. 24.01.1983
Queen's Gambit [D36]
Commentary by Dorian Rogozenco

1.d4 [00] **d5** [01] **2.c4 e6 3.♘c3** [01] **♘f6 4.cxd5** [03]

The Exchange Variation of the Queen's Gambit Declined (in the former Soviet Union it's better

known as the Carlsbad Variation) was one of Kasparov's favorite ways to meet the Queen's Gambit.

4...exd5 5.♗g5 c6 [02] **6.♕c2** [05]

Preventing the bishop's sortie to f5. These days white usually plays 6.e3, meeting 6...♗f5 with 7.♕f3, which leads to a slightly better endgame for white.

6...♘a6 [06]

A principled reaction, trying to exploit the early development of the queen on c2. Black wants to provoke a2-a3, after which the knight will go via c7 to e6 later on.

7.e3 [10]

And the most principled reply by Kasparov, who doesn't wish to waste time on the move a2-a3.

7...♘b4

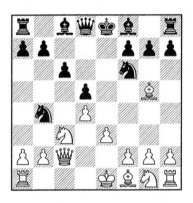

8.♕d1 [25]

This surprising retreat of the queen is in fact considerably stronger than it appears. It looks like white just lost time by playing ♕d1-c2-d1, but there are hidden tricks in the position. Kasparov spent 15 minutes thinking before playing 8.♕d1 and as we'll see he understood the position much better than his opponent.

Another good move for white to fight for an opening advantage is

8.♕b1 with the idea 8...g6 and only now 9.♕d1! ♗f5 10.♖c1, reaching the same position as in the game, but with the black pawn on g6 instead of g7. Then if 10...a5 white continues 11.a3 ♘a6 12.♕b3 and black is in deep trouble because there is no good way to protect the pawn on b7: everywhere white has a clear advantage. Therefore, instead of 9...♗f5 the right continuation is 9...a5 immediately, when after 10.a3 ♘a6 11.♗d3 white is just slightly better.

Sixteen years after the present game Kasparov played 8.♕d2, which is the usual choice of white players in practice. But after 8...♗f5 9.♖c1 a5 10.a3 ♘a6 in contrast to the game white does not have the move ♕d1-b3. The variation can continue 11.♘ge2 ♗e7 (11...h6 happened in G. Kasparov – V. Ivanchuk, Wijk aan Zee 1999, which ended in a draw) 12.♘g3 ♗g6 13.f4 (or 13.h4 h6) 13...♘g8 14.♗xe7 ♘xe7 with approximate equality

8...♗f5 [14]

Black's main idea (played with tempo!) will turn out to be an inaccuracy, because it weakens the pawn on b7. 8...a5 9.a3 ♘a6 10.♗d3± is preferable.

9.♖c1 a5

Played instantly by Vladimirov. Now Kasparov demonstrates the drawbacks of black's entire set-up.

10.a3 [27] ♘a6 [15]

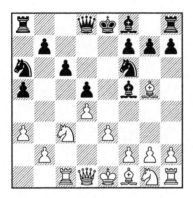

11.♕b3! [30]

Only here Vladimirov must have realized that black can't avoid making big concessions in order to keep material equality. He spent more than half an hour on his next move, but there is no acceptable way for black to protect the pawn on b7.

11...♘c7 [47]

Just like its alternatives this move doesn't prevent white from spoiling black's pawn structure. 11...♖b8 12.♗xf6 ♕xf6? (12...gxf6 13.♘f3±) 13.♗xa6+−; 11...♖a7 12.♗xf6 ♕xf6 13.♕b6+−; 11...b5 12.♗xf6 ♕xf6 13.♘xb5 cxb5 14.♗xb5+ ♗d7 15.♕xd5 ♖d8 16.♗xd7+ ♖xd7 17.♕b5+−. Even 11...♗c8 has a tactical drawback. Apart from 12.♘f3 or 12.♗d3 with better chances in a quiet middlegame, white has 12.♗xa6 ♖xa6 13.♗xf6 and black must either take 13...gxf6 again, or allow 13...♕xf6 14.♘xd5, hoping to prove some compensation for the lost central pawn.

12.♗xf6 [36]

White now achieves a clear positional advantage. Not 12.♕xb7?

♖b8 13.♕xc6+?? (13.♕a7=) 13...♗d7 14.♗xf6 gxf6−+

12...gxf6 [48] 13.♘ge2 [37]

Another plan to explore black's broken pawn structure is 13.♘f3± followed by ♘f3-h4. In both cases white takes control over the f5 square. Again 13.♕xb7? ♖b8 would favor black.

13...♖b8 [57] 14.♘g3 [42] ♗g6 [60] 15.♕d1 [45] ♘e6 [65] 16.h4 [53]

A standard move. White's strategical advantage is obvious and the next part of the game is an instructive example of how to play such positions.

16...h5 [72] 17.♗d3 [57] ♗d6 [73] 18.♘f5 [58] ♗c7 [75]

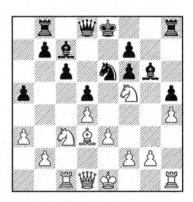

19.♕c2 [72]

Kasparov spent 14 minutes on this move, rejecting the more typical 19.♕f3. The explanation is that black's weaknesses on the kingside are close to each other and at the moment his kingside is well protected. White needs to create another weakness on the queenside (the classical principle of the two weaknesses). In the game Kasparov chose the standard plan of a minority attack and for that purpose the queen is better placed on the queenside. Another factor in favor of 19.♕c2 is that black can try to fight for control of the f5 square (by means of ♔f8, ♘g7 and ♕d7) and in that case it might be important to keep the d3 bishop protected. With other work at this moment the queen on c2 appears to be more useful for the upcoming battle than it would be on f3.

19...♔f8 [76] **20.♘a4** [76] **♔g8** [85]

With the white queen on c2 black must be careful to avoid the check on c5 in different variations.

21.b4 [83] **axb4** [98] **22.axb4 b5** [100]

Rather than wait for white to play b4-b5xc6 black decides to at least create a weakness for his opponent as well. This makes perfect sense, since in the future white will have to keep an eye on his b4 pawn. After 22...♘g7 23.0-0 black still cannot fight for the f5 square, because 23...♕d7 runs into 24.♘c5, while 23...♕c8 is not possible due to the fork on e7.

23.♘c5 [86] **♘xc5** [102] **24.♕xc5** [87] **♗xf5 25.♗xf5 ♖b6** [103] **26.0-0** [99] **♗d6** [104] **27.♕c3** [100] **♕e7 28.♖b1** [102] **♔g7** [105]

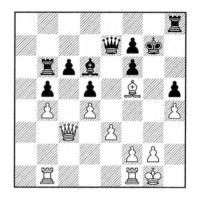

Both sides have achieved the maximum they could: white has created another weakness on black's queenside and has absolute control over the f5 square. Besides, the pawn on h5 needs permanent protection. Black on his part has blockaded the weakness on b4, reduced material and can hope to use the drawish tendency of the opposite-colored bishops.

So how to evaluate the diagram position? The fact that Kasparov managed to win in just another 11 moves by creating a mating attack on the kingside provides the answer that at least from the practical point of view black's situation is very difficult.

29.♖fe1 [104] **♖a6** [109] **30.e4**

This advance is the quickest way for white to switch his pieces to the kingside.

30...dxe4 [110] **31.♖xe4** [110] **♕d8** [112] **32.♖be1** [120]

Kasparov improves the position as much as possible before advancing the g-pawn. However, the immediate 32.g4 was good enough too, offering white a strong attack.

32...♗b8 [115]

32...♖a4 was better, after which 33.♕xc6 ♗xb4 34.♕xb5 ♕a5 35.♕xa5 ♖xa5 36.♖b1 leaves black with good chances to draw a position a pawn down either in a four-rooks endgame after 36...♖xf5, or in an endgame with rooks and bishops after 36...♗d6. If white doesn't like it, he can return the rook to b1 (33. ♖b1) and then continue g2-g4, as mentioned above.

33.♕f3 [129] **♖a4** [132]

33...♕d6 34.g4 ♕h2+ 35.♔f1 doesn't help black. For instance, 35... ♕xh4 loses on the spot after 36.gxh5 ♕xh5 37.♕g2+ ♔h6 38.♖4e3.

34.g4!+− [133]

Decisively opening the g-file for attack. As is often the case in positions with major pieces on the board, the opposite-colored bishops only increase the power of the attack. Black is defenseless.

34...♖xb4

34...♕d6 35.gxh5 ♕h2+ 36.♔f1+−

35.gxh5 ♖c4 [139] **36.♔f1** [137] **♔h6** [148] **37.♖g4** [144] **♖e8 38.♖xe8** [145] **♕xe8 39.♗e4** [148]

Black resigned

An opening fiasco for Vladimirov. He probably could have defended the position with the opposite-colored bishops better, but the outcome of the game was never in doubt.

1983	23.01	24.01			
Game No.	1	2	3	4	Score
Kasparov	1	1			2
Vladimirov	0	0			0

Game 12

G. KASPAROV – E. VLADIMIROV
Training game. 25.01.1983
Slav Defense [D17]
Commentary by Dorian Rogozenco

1.d4 [01] **d5** [00] **2.c4 c6 3.♘f3** [02] **♘f6 4.♘c3 dxc4** [02] **5.a4** [03] **♗f5** [03] **6.♘e5** [06]

Until 1983 Kasparov used to play exclusively the 6.e3 variation here. In the present game he is testing 6.♘e5 against the Slav for the first time.

6...e6 [04] **7.f3 ♗b4** [05]

7...c5 8.e4 cxd4 9.exf5 ♗b4 10.♗xc4 ♕d6? 11.♗b5+ saw a large advantage for white in G. Kasparov – A. Shirov, Dos Hermanas 1996.

8.♘xc4 [09]

8.e4 is the main continuation.

8...0-0 9.♗g5 [13]

In modern theory 9.♔f2 is considered to be white's only attempt to fight for an advantage in the 8.♘xc4 line.

9...b5!? [15]

9...h6 10.♗h4 c5 is nowadays the established way to neutralize 9.♗g5. Vladimirov's 9...b5 has never been played in a grandmaster game even up to the present, but it also seems to be a good move for black. The problem is that from a practical point of view 9...b5 is rather difficult to play, since it leads to positions where the price of each mistake is very high.

10.axb5 [29]

10.♘e5 h6 11.♗h4 c5 12.dxc5 ♕c7 is not a real option for white,

because he is practically forced to continue 13.♕d6 ♕xd6 14.cxd6 ♗xd6 15.f4 (15.♗g3 ♘h5∓), leaving black with many attractive possibilities in a good position.

10...cxb5 [16]

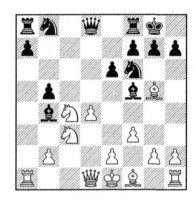

11.♘a3 [32]

Exchanging on b5 on the previous move (which provides the c6 square to the opponent's knight) and then retreating the knight to a3 looks quite a dangerous strategy. White hasn't castled yet and such play can easily backfire. But Kasparov trusts his outstanding calculating abilities and as long as he does not see a concrete refutation, he always plays principled moves. White's opening play is actually based on a very simple and healthy strategy: to occupy the center with pawns and limit the activity of the opponent's light-squared bishop. The retreat of the knight to a3 attacks the pawn on b5 and at the same time prepares to consolidate the position with e2-e4 and ♘a3-c2.

11.♘e5 allows black to wrest the initiative with 11...h6! (11...♕c7 12.♗d2!) 12.♗h4 (or 12.♗xf6 gxf6!) 12...♕c7 13.♖c1 ♘d5.

11...♘c6 [27]

An interesting alternative is 11...h6 12.♗h4 (12.♗xf6 ♕xf6 13.e4 is no good in view of 13...♗xa3 14.bxa3 ♘c6 15.exf5 ♘xd4 16.♗d3 ♖fd8 17.0-0 ♘xf5 with an advantage for black) 12...g5 (or 12...♘c6 13.e4 ♘xd4!? 14.exf5 exf5 and unclear) 13.♗g3 ♘d5 and unclear.

12.e4 [35]

Of course not 12.♘axb5 a6.

12...♗g6 [58]

Generally it was not typical of Vladimirov to think for long in these games, but this retreat of the bishop alone took him more than half an hour. Most certainly he was trying to make the bishop sac work: 12...♘xd4 13.exf5 exf5 14.♗xb5 ♕e7+ 15.♔f1 ♖fd8 is indeed interesting. The main problem is that in this line white also has other options, for instance, to leave the bishop hanging on f5 for the moment and start with 13.♗e3, or take the pawn with 13.♘xb5. In the arising variations it is impossible to calculate everything over the board. Black will be a piece down without entirely clear compensation, so after a long thought Vladimirov decided

to keep material equality (which is objectively the correct decision).

13.♘c2 [39]

Finally, white consolidates the center and can be optimistic about the future. Under these circumstances black should usually try to create some tactical counterplay, otherwise he will have to defend a passive and strategically inferior position. And this is exactly the problem in such positions for black: to keep the balance between strategic play and try to feel the right moment for starting complications.

13...♕b6 [59] 14.♘xb4 [47]

If white planned to place the bishop on e3 on the next move, then it made sense to do it at once in order to have it protected by the knight and not allow e6-e5.

14...♘xb4 15.♗e3 [58]

The path to an advantage is quite narrow here: 15.♗xb5 ♖fd8 (15...♕xd4 16.♕xd4 ♘c2+ 17.♔f2 ♘xd4 18.♗a6 ♖ab8 19.♖a2±) 16.♖a4! (16.♗e3 e5, or 16.♕e2 a6 17.♗c4 ♕xd4 is less clear) 16...♖xd4 17.♕e2±

15...e5 [65] 16.♔f2 [60]

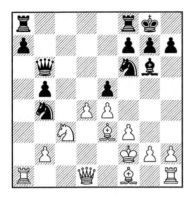

It seems that black must exchange on d4, but Vladimirov finds a strong tactical way to keep the board on fire.

16...♘c2! [66]

16...exd4   17.♕xd4   ♕xd4 18.♗xd4 ♘c2 19.♖d1 ♘xd4 20.♖xd4 a6 21.♗e2 leads to a better endgame for white.

17.♕xc2 [62] **exd4 18.♕d3** [63] **♖fd8** [81]

Possibly black missed that after 18...dxe3+ 19.♕xe3 ♕b8 20.♗xb5 he has 20...♗xe4!= This means that instead of taking the pawn on b5 white should play 20.♗d3 or 20.♗e2, but then black continues 20...b4 followed by 21...♖e8, which is very close to equality.

But 18...♖ad8! 19.♗e2 b4 20.♘a4 is even stronger (in case of 20.♘b5 dxe3+ 21.♕xe3 ♕b8 black has good play everywhere; for instance, white is already worse after 22.♘xa7 ♖de8), followed by 20...dxe3+ 21.♕xe3 ♕b8. This is the point of 18...♖ad8: the queen does not block the rook on a8, while the king's rook will go to e8, helping to create different tactical

ideas. Black is by no means worse: 22.♖ad1 (22.g3 ♖fe8 with double-edged play) 22...♖xd1 23.♗xd1 ♖c8 24.g3 h5 25.♖e1 h4=

19.♗e2 [64]

Now white's prospects are preferable.

19...a6 [88]

White also has an advantage after 19...b4 20.♘a4 (20.♘b5!?) 20...dxe3+ 21.♕xe3 ♕b8 22.g3, although black retains chances to save the game here as well.

20.♗xd4 [79] **♖xd4** [89] **21.♕e3 ♕d8** [95]

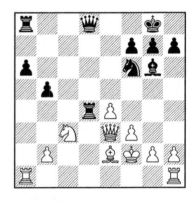

22.e5 [95]

The immediate 22.♘xb5? would be a mistake in view of 22...♘g4+ (even stronger than 22...♘xe4+ 23.♔g1) 23.fxg4 ♖xe4, but 22.♖hd1 ♖xd1 23.♖xd1 ♕c7 24.♕d4 is an attractive alternative, leaving the bishop out of play on g6.

22...♘h5? [97]

This apparently active move was probably based on the wrong assessment of the position. Black is not able to provide any serious activity and as a consequence the knight will remain totally misplaced on h5.

22...♞e8 was correct, keeping chances to hold the position, even if white's superiority after 23.g3 (23.♞xb5 ♜d2∓) 23...♞c7 24.♜hd1 ♜xd1 25.♜xd1 ♛e7 26.♜d6 ♜e8 27.f4 is beyond question.

23.♞xb5 [100] ♜b4 [102]

The variation 23...♜d2 24.♞d6 ♜xb2 25.g3 shows the difference between the knights: white has a mighty knight on d6, while the black knight on the edge of the board is out of play.

24.♜ad1 [101] ♛h4+ [110]

24...♛e7 25.♞c3 ♞f4 26.g3 ♞xe2 27.♞d5+−

25.g3 ♛h3

A blunder in a lost position.

26.♛d2 [102]

A double attack which ends the game immediately.

Black resigned

1983	23.01	24.01	25.01		
Game No.	1	2	3	4	Score
Kasparov	1	1	1		3
Vladimirov	0	0	0		0

Game 13

G. KASPAROV – E. VLADIMIROV
Training game. 26.01.1983
Queen's Gambit [D55]
Commentary by Dorian Rogozenco

1.d4 [00] ♞f6 [00] 2.c4 e6 3.♞f3 [07] d5 [01] 4.♞c3 ♝e7 [02] 5.♝g5 h6 [03] 6.♝xf6 [08] ♝xf6 7.e3 0-0 [04] 8.♛d2 [09]

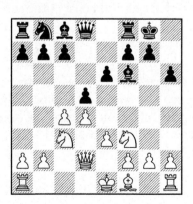

Korchnoi's move from 1965, which started to gain popularity when Petrosian played it twice in the World Championship versus Spassky in 1969. This system was a part of Kasparov's main opening repertoire for white in the years 1981-1983, and he tested it in training games both against Vladimirov and Timoshchenko. White's main idea behind 8.♛d2 is to use the d1 square for the rook and discourage his opponent's quick c7-c5. Moreover, in some variations white can castle long and start an attack by advancing his kingside pawns.

8...a6 [09]

Previously Kasparov had been confronted only with 8...♘c6 and 8...c6 in his tournament practice: 8...♘c6 9.cxd5 (9.♖c1 was better, after which theory recommends 9...a6 for black) 9...exd5 10.♗e2 ♗f5 11.0-0 ♘e7 12.b4 c6 13.♖fc1 a6 14.a4 ♕d6 15.♕b2 ♖fe8 16.♕b3 ♘g6 17.♖a2 ♗e7 18.b5, draw agreed in G. Kasparov – A. Karpov, Moscow 1981; 8...c6 9.h4 ♘d7 10.g4 ("At a training session for the Soviet team before the student world championship, with this dashing attack on the king I won numerous blitz games against Vladimirov" – Kasparov in his book *Garry Kasparov on Modern Chess, Part 2: Kasparov Vs Karpov 1975-1985*, 2008) 10...♖e8 11.0-0-0 b5 12.cxb5 cxb5 13.♗xb5 ♖b8 14.g5+− and white was already winning in G. Kasparov – A. Duer, student world championship, Graz 1981.

9.♖d1 [41]

This strong move took Kasparov 32 minutes. 9.♖c1 ♘c6 leads to the line mentioned above (see 8...♘c6 9.♖c1). Then the main variation continues 10.♗e2 dxc4 11.♗xc4 e5 12.d5 ♘a7! I suspect that after black's rare 8...a6 Kasparov wanted to achieve more than transposing to a known variation and he decided to act differently. Placing the rook on d1 is in the spirit of the 8.♕d2 system, preventing black's quick pawn advances in the center.

9.0-0-0 would offer black good play by allowing him to implement the main idea of his previous move: 9...dxc4 10.♗xc4 b5 11.♗d3 ♗b7 followed by ♘d7, c5 and ♖c8 etc. with good attacking prospects against the white king.

9...♘c6 [19]

Another important possibility for black is 9...dxc4 10.♗xc4 b5 11.♗d3 ♗b7 12.♗e4 ♕c8.

10.♕c2 [43]

In case of 10.a3 black can continue with the standard 10...dxc4 11.♗xc4 e5 12.d5 ♘e7 (12...♘a7!?) 13.♘e4 ♘f5. After Kasparov's move black is suddenly faced with the fact that he cannot carry out his main plan to take on c4 and play e6-e5. Now it was Vladimirov's turn to take a deep think.

10...b6 [58]

And black also makes a good choice: the development of the bishop on the long diagonal is the best way for black to continue. However, everything has its price: such a plan was less familiar to Vladimirov, who spent 39 minutes on his last move – time that he would miss at the end of the game.

Sticking to the initial idea with 10...dxc4 11.♗xc4 ♕e7 12.0-0 e5 is worse, because the e7 square isn't optimal for the queen here. White has a pleasant choice between 13.♘d5 ♕d6 14.♘d2 and 13.d5 ♘a7 14.♘d2, in both cases with better prospects.

11.a3 [50] **♗b7** [60] **12.cxd5** [66]

Judging by the time spent by the players on the first twelve moves it becomes clear how hard it is to make strategic decisions in such a flexible pawn structure, when both sides have several possible plans. By taking now on d5 Kasparov finally settles the structure in the center. The reason for his decision is that with the black bishop developed on b7 such an exchange makes most sense for white.

Now the game enters another phase: a strategic battle with the pieces in the middlegame.

12...exd5 13.♗d3 [69] **♖e8** [71] **14.0-0** [70] **♕d6** [74] **15.♖fe1** [76] **♖ad8** [75] **16.b4** [77] **g6** [83]

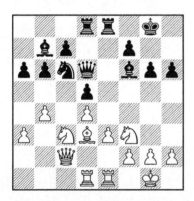

Such middlegames with a fixed pawn structure and same minor pieces on the board can arise from different opening variations. It is very difficult here for either side to show activity, but usually it is white who has more possibilities in this sense. Black's only real option to open the position – the advance of the c-pawn to c5 – can be easily

prevented by his opponent. On his part white can combine two ideas: pressure on the queenside with the advance e3-e4 (the latter only after provoking the move ...c7-c6). With the next moves both sides will continue to improve the position of their pieces, trying to find the most optimal squares for them.

17.♖c1 [85] **♖e7** [90] **18.♕b3** [93] **♗g7** [99]

One of black's methods of fighting against the advance e3-e4 is to keep the pawn on d4 under attack. That's why the apparently passive dark-squared bishop has an important prophylactic role on the long diagonal.

19.♖ed1 [98] **♘a7** [105] **20.♘e2** [103] **♘c8** [107] **21.a4** [105]

This creates the positional threat b4-b5 and forces black's reply.

21...c6 [112]

21...♕d7 22.b5 axb5 23.axb5 ♘d6 24.♘f4±

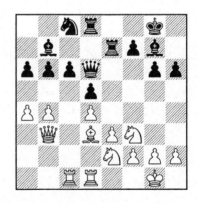

22.h4! [128]

Another important rook's pawn advance. In such situations it is always unpleasant for black to allow his opponent the option of further advancing the h-pawn and thus weaken the light squares in black's camp.

22...h5 [127]

Fifteen minutes of thinking is too much for this typical response. The approaching mutual time trouble will soon influence the logical outcome of the game.

23.♕c3 [132] **♕b8** [132] **24.♘f4** [134]

That's why Kasparov needed to blockade the kingside pawn structure: his knights have now got the f4 and g5 squares. Black's solid position is starting to become critical: with active knights on the kingside supported by the long-range queen and bishop white can create dangerous tactical threats.

24...♖de8 [133] **25.♕c2** [135] **♕d6** [135] **26.♘g5** [140] **♖d8** [130]

26...♕xb4   27.♗xg6   fxg6 28.♕xg6+−

27.b5 [143]

With this advance white opens the c-file and intends to take full control of it after transferring the bishop to the c8-h3 diagonal.

27...cxb5 28.axb5 a5 [140]

28...axb5 29.♗xb5±

29.♕b3 [145]

In time trouble Kasparov places the queen on the standard square b3, where she exerts pressure along the a2-g8 diagonal and forces black to reckon all the time with the advance e3-e4. But 29.♕e2± preparing g2-

g4 was very strong, with a powerful attack on the kingside.

29...♖ed7 [142] **30.g3** [146] **♗f6** [145]

It is obvious that white has numerous tactical ideas and the culmination is hastened by the fact that both sides have less than five minutes left for ten moves.

31.♗f1 [147] **♖c7** [146] **32.♗h3 ♖xc1** [147] **33.♖xc1 ♘e7 34.♖c3** [149] **♖a8?**

34...♗xg5 35.hxg5 ♖a8 was the right way, with good chances to defend successfully.

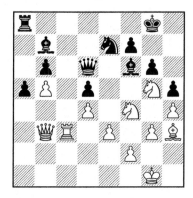

35.♕c2

With less than one minute on the clock it is no wonder that Kasparov missed 35.♘xf7!! ♔xf7 36.♕c2 and white wins due to the fact that black is unable to prevent the invasion of the rook to c7, after which the g6 pawn falls and black gets mated or loses a lot of material. One possible variation is 36...a4 37.♖c7 a3 38.♕xg6+ ♔f8 39.♕h6+ ♔e8 40.♘e6 a2 41.♕f8#.

The final part of the game was played in severe time-trouble and the evaluation of the position changes several times.

35...a4? [148]

35...♗xg5 36.hxg5 a4=

36.♖c7?

36.♘xf7 ♔xf7 37.♖c7+−

36...a3?

Here it was black who would have taken a full point after 36...♗xg5 37.hxg5 a3.

37.♘xf7+− ♕xc7 [149] **38.♕xc7 a2 39.♗e6?**

39.♘g5 a1=♕+ 40.♔g2 is winning for white: 40...♕b1 (40...♗c8 41.♗xc8 ♖xc8 42.♕xb6+−) 41.♕xb7 ♖a1 (41...♖f8 42.♘xd5+−) 42.♕b8+ ♔g7 43.♘fe6+ ♔h6 44.♕f8+ ♗g7 45.♕xg7#

39...a1=♕+ 40.♔g2

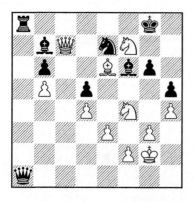

40...♗c8?

When making the last move in this wild position Vladimirov lost on time, but now white is winning again after 41.♘h6+! A few nice variations are: 41...♔h8 (41...♔g7 42.♘f5+! gxf5 43.♘xh5+ ♔g6 44.♘xf6 ♔xf6 45.♕e5+ ♔g6 46.h5+ ♔h7 47.h6 ♔xh6 48.♕f6+ ♔h7 49.♕xe7+ with mate soon) 42.♕d8+ ♔g7 (42...♔h7 43.♘g8!) 43.♘f5+! ♔h7 44.♕f8! ♗xe6 45.♕h6+ ♔g8 46.♘xe7+ ♔f7 47.♕h7+ ♔e8 48.♘g8! and white either wins material or mates the black king.

In the diagram position the only move to save the game was 40...♕b1!! Then 41.♘g5+ ♔g7 42.♗d7! (the inclusion of the moves ♗e6 and ♔g7 proves fatal for white in the variation 42.♕xb7 ♖a1−+, because there is no check with the queen on the 8th rank. Compare it with 39.♘g5 from above) 42...♖a1 43.♘fe6+ ♔h6 44.♘f7+ ♔h7 45.♘fg5+ with a draw by repetition.

Black lost on time.

1983	23.01	24.01	25.01	26.01	
Game No.	1	2	3	4	Score
Kasparov	1	1	1	1	4
Vladimirov	0	0	0	0	0

Game 14

G. TIMOSHCHENKO – G. KASPAROV
Training game. 03.02.1983
Queen's Gambit [D34]
Commentary by Dorian Rogozenco

1.d4 d5 2.c4 e6 3.♘c3 c5

Using this training mini-match Kasparov prepared the Tarrasch Defense as a big surprise for the upcoming candidates match versus Beliavsky, which was about to start in less than a month. The present game is Kasparov's first practical test with the Tarrasch as black.

4.cxd5 exd5 5.♘f3 ♘c6 6.g3 ♘f6 7.♗g2 ♗e7 8.0-0 0-0 9.♗g5

The main line. In the next game Timoshchenko would play 9.♗e3.

9...cxd4 10.♘xd4 h6 11.♗e3 ♖e8 12.♕a4

At the beginning of the eighties this move was at the height of its popularity and there is no wonder that 12.♕a4 was tested in the training match. Kasparov and his coaching team had great foresight: when met with the Tarrasch for the first time in the candidates match, Beliavsky would play similarly up to move fourteen (spending a lot of time in the opening on the way).

12...♗d7 13.♖ad1 ♘b4 14.♕b3 a5 [06]

The only move, otherwise black loses the d5 pawn.

15.a4 [09]

Only here Beliavsky would deviate in the candidates match

and play 15.♖d2 instead. That game continued 15...a4 16.♕d1 a3 17.♕b1 ♗f8 18.bxa3 ♖xa3 19.♕b2 ♕a8 20.♘b3 ♗c6 21.♗d4 ♘e4 22.♘xe4 dxe4 23.♖a1 ♗d5 and Kasparov won convincingly, A. Beliavsky – G. Kasparov, Moscow (m/2) 1983. In fact in that game Beliavsky lost on time in a lost position, so the Tarrasch proved to be a truly wise decision by Kasparov and his team.

15.♘xd5? doesn't work in view of 15...♘bxd5 16.♗xd5 ♘xd5 17.♕xd5 ♗h3 and after 18.♕xd8 ♖axd8 19.♖fe1 ♗b4 white loses the exchange.

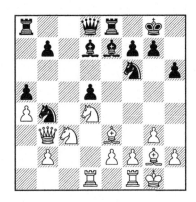

15...♗c5 [28]

All this was already known to Kasparov (the games mentioned below had been published in issues of *Chess Informant* before this match), nevertheless he spent more than 20 minutes on the last move. Possibly Kasparov was just recalling or checking the known variations, but maybe he was feeling that here black could try to find more attractive alternatives than giving up the pawn on d5 and achieve a draw from a slightly inferior position. Indeed, the move 15...♖c8 soon came to eclipse 15...♗c5 and became black's main continuation in the diagram position. After 15...♖c8 taking on d5 is still no good for white: 16.♘xd5 ♘bxd5 17.♗xd5 ♘xd5 18.♕xd5 ♗xa4 and it is the first player who must fight for a draw.

16.♘c2 is best answered by 16...b5! 17.♘xb4 bxa4 18.♘xa4 ♗xb4 19.♘c3 ♗xc3 20.bxc3 a4 with good counterplay for black, which was played by Ehlvest later in 1983.

Probably the best try for white to keep at least some life in the position after 15...♖c8 is 16.♘db5 ♗e6 17.♗d4 ♗c5 18.♗xc5 (18.♖d2 b6=) 18...♖xc5 19.♖d2 with complex play but equality.

16.♘xd5 [14]
Now the massive exchanges will lead to a position where white's extra pawn doesn't really offer him winning chances. The alternative 16.♘c2 keeps the position more complicated, although here too black should not have particular problems: 16...♗xe3 17.♘xe3 ♕b6 18.♘c2 ♗g4 (18...♖ad8 was played in V. Chekhov – V. Eingorn, Tallinn 1980) 19.♘d4 ♖ad8 20.h3 ♗h5

21.♖d2 ♘e4 22.♘xe4 dxe4= A. Mikhalchishin – V. Eingorn, Soviet Union 1981.
16...♘fxd5 [39] 17.♗xd5 ♘xd5 [40] 18.♕xd5

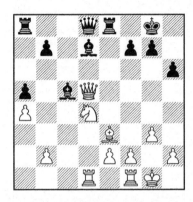

Black's bishop pair and opponent's exposed pawn on a4 secure him enough compensation for a draw. He just needs to play accurately in order to neutralize white's slight pressure on the d-file.

18...b6 [41]
Formally only this move was a novelty. In the game K. Lerner – V. Eingorn, Soviet Union 1982 black played 18...♕c8 19.♘f3 ♖xe3 20.fxe3 ♗xe3+ 21.♔h1 ♗xa4 22.♘e5 ♗xd1 and lost after 23.♖xf7! ♔h8 24.♖f8+ ♕xf8 25.♘g6+. However, black's play can be improved in several ways, for instance instead of taking the pawn on a4 the continuation 21...♗c6! 22.♕e5 ♗b6 would have offered black excellent compensation for the exchange.

19.♘c6 [45]
19.♘b3 ♗xa4 20.♕xd8 ♖axd8 21.♖xd8 ♖xd8 22.♗xc5 (or

22.♘xc5 bxc5 23.♗xc5 ♗d1) 22...
♗xb3 23.♗xb6 ♖d2 24.♗xa5 ♖xb2
25.e4 ♗c2 followed by ♖b1 is an
immediate draw.

19...♗xc6 20.♕xc6 ♕c8 [42]
21.♕xc8 [50] **♖axc8**

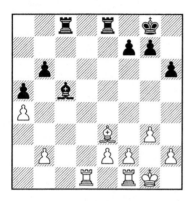

22.♖d7 [56]

In case of 22.♗xc5 ♖xc5 23.♖d2
(or 23.e3 ♖e4 24.b3 ♖c3 25.♖b1
♖b4) 23...♖e4 24.b3 g5 black's
activity compensates for the pawn
and a draw is inevitable.

22...♗xe3 [49] **23.fxe3 ♖xe3**
[50] **24.♖fxf7** [58] **♖xe2** [51]
25.♖xg7+ [60]

This apparent action is illusory:
the game quickly ends with a
theoretical draw.

25...♔f8 [52] **26.♖df7+** [62]
♔e8 27.♖c7 [63] **♖xc7** [53]
28.♖xc7 ♖xb2 [54] **29.♖h7** [64] **b5**
[57] **30.axb5** [69] **a4 31.♖a7 ♖xb5**
[58] **32.♖xa4 ♔f7**
Draw agreed

Game 15

G. TIMOSHCHENKO – G. KASPAROV
Training game. 04.02.1983
Queen's Gambit [D34]
Commentary by Dorian Rogozenco

**1.d4 d5 2.c4 e6 3.♘c3 c5 4.cxd5
exd5 5.♘f3 ♘c6 6.g3 ♘f6 7.♗g2
♗e7 8.0-0 0-0** [02] **9.♗e3** [01]

This move invented by Salo
Flohr back in 1931 has its logic:
just like with 9.♗g5 white forces
his opponent to take a decision in
the center. Nevertheless, 9.♗e3 was
never on the same level as the main
lines 9.♗g5 and 9.dxc5.

9...c4 [06]

9...♘g4 is met with 10.♗f4±; 9...
cxd4 10.♘xd4±

10.♘e5 h6 [08]

Officially, Kasparov introduced
this move only four years later,
when it quickly gained popularity
and became the main alternative to
10...♗e6, which was played almost
automatically until then. With 10...h6
black prefers to find a better job for his
light-squared bishop than place it on
e6 in order to protect the pawn on d5.

11.b3 [20]

In two games from Kasparov's
later practice white played

differently: 11.h3 ♗b4 12.♕a4 ♗xc3 13.bxc3 ♗f5 14.g4 ♗h7 15.♗f4 (15. ♘xc6 ♕d7=) 15...♖e8 16.♖ad1 a6 17.♗g3 b5 18.♕a3 ♕b6 and black was already preferable in V. Hort – G. Kasparov, Cologne 1988.

11.♕a4 a6 12.♘xc6 bxc6 13.b3 ♖b8 14.bxc4 ♖b4 15.♕d1 ♖xc4 was B. Larsen – G. Kasparov, Brussels 1987. Both these games were won by Kasparov.

The advance 11.f4 looks somewhat strange without the black bishop on e6 and it can be simply answered with 11...♗f5 or 11...♗b4. Therefore, after 20 minutes of thinking Timoshchenko went for the most standard plan in this system.

11...cxb3 [12] 12.♘xc6 [30]

In case of the immediate 12.axb3 black can consider 12...♘b4 13.♕d2 ♗f5 and unclear; 12.♕xb3 is another important option for white, which leads to a complicated middlegame after 12...♘a5. I don't think that black's prospects are worse here.

12...bxc6 13.axb3

13.♕xb3 ♗f5 14.♗f4 ♕a5=

13...a5 [13]

White's plan here is ♕c2, ♘a4, ♖fc1 and ♘c5. Black can place his light-squared bishop either on a6 or f5, the other bishop on b4 and create some pressure on the b- and e- files. He has sufficient possibilities for active play and Kasparov must have been happy with the opening outcome. The chances are about equal in the diagram position.

14.♗c1 [32]

An ambitious move. White plans to exchange the bishops via a3, which is positionally sound (it underlines the weakness of the c5 square even more), but Timoshchenko will fail to do so in the game. Therefore, 14.♕c2 appears to be more logical, continuing with the mentioned plan.

14...♗b4 [22] 15.♘a4 [36] ♖e8 [25] 16.♗d2 [40]

In case of 16.♗a3 the reply 16...♗g4 is quite unpleasant, using the fact that the e1 square is not available for the rook.

16...♗a6 [39]

16...♗g4 17.♖e1 ♗f8 18.♕c2=

17.♖e1 [41] ♗f8! [41]

White is slowly being strategically outplayed.

18.♕c2 [62] ♘e4 [55] 19.♘c3 [65]

19.♗f4 is no good in view of 19...♗b4 20.♖ec1 ♘xf2! 21.♔xf2 ♖xe2+ 22.♕xe2 ♗xe2 23.♔xe2 ♕f6, with a decisive attack after 24.♗e5 ♕f5 25.♖xc6 ♖e8. Also 19.♗xe4 dxe4∓ or 19.♗e3 ♗b4 20.♖ec1 ♗b5∓ leave black with the upper hand.

19...♘xd2 [65] 20.♕xd2 ♗b4

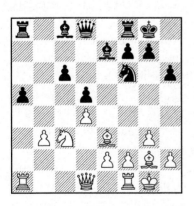

It was worth considering 20...♖b8 21.♖eb1 (21.♕c2 ♕b6! 22.♖eb1 ♕xd4 23.♖xa5 ♗c8∓) 21...♗c8∓

21.e3 [69]

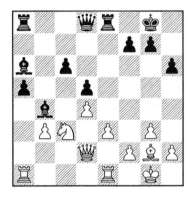

21...c5 [92]

White has a very solid position and after a long think Kasparov decides to start concrete play. He opens up the position in the center, trying to exploit the knight pin. Analysis shows that activity on the kingside brings black no advantage: 21...h5 22.h4 g5 23.e4! gxh4 (23... dxe4 24.♗xe4 gxh4? 25.♕h6+−) 24.exd5 ♕f6 25.dxc6 hxg3 26.fxg3 with a messy position, where any result is possible. Also 22...♖e6 (instead of 22...g5) 23.♕c2 (23. ♖ec1 g5 is weaker for white) 23... g5 24.hxg5 ♕xg5 25.e4 h4 is not convincing due to 26.exd5 cxd5 27.♖xe6 fxe6 28.♘xd5! exd5 29.♕c6 with sufficient counterplay for white.

22.♖ec1 [77] **♖c8** [96] **23.♕d1**

Finally unpinning the knight and threatening to take on d5. Useful waiting moves like 23.h3 or 23.h4 were also logical.

23...cxd4 24.♕xd4 [81] **♕c7** [97] **25.♘a2** [88]

Timoshchenko is taking unnecessary risks by placing the knight on the edge of the board. After 25.♘e2 black has nothing better than 25...♗c5 26.♕d2 ♗xe2 (26...♕b6 27.♘d4 is obviously not dangerous for white) 27.♕xe2 d4, but then 28.e4 ♕b6 29.♕d3 and a peaceful outcome is not far off.

25...♗c5 26.♕xd5 [92] **♕b6** [121] **27.♖c3** [103] **♖ed8** [127] **28.♕f5** [106] **♖d2** [130]

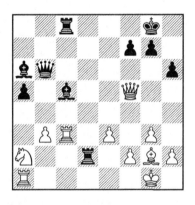

White's main problem in this position is his knight on a2, which is difficult to bring into play. This gives black excellent compensation for the sacrificed pawn, because even after a hypothetical exchange of queens the knight could remain a headache for white. On the other hand the mutual weaknesses of the back ranks and the pin on the c-file make the position very tactical: everything depends on concrete variations. At this moment Timoshchenko had 44 minutes left and Kasparov 33, so there is no sign of time-trouble.

29.b4? [127]

With this move, played after a long think, Timoshchenko hopes to solve the problem of the knight in the most radical way. The idea is nice, because now 29...axb4 30.♘xb4! ♕xb4 (or 30...♗xb4 31.♖xc8+ ♗xc8 32.♕xc8+) 31.♖xa6 ♖d1+ 32.♗f1 solves all the problems indeed and even leaves white with a healthy extra pawn. But Kasparov will show that 29.b4 has a tactical drawback.

Therefore in the diagram position 29.♖ac1 is better (29.♗d5 is also good enough for equality, with the idea after 29...♖c7 to play 30.b4!) and the only important point is that after 29...♖xa2 (29...♖cd8 30.♖xc5 ♖d1+ 31.♗f1; or 29...g6 30.♕e5 ♖xa2 31.h4=) white doesn't have to take on c5 immediately, because black will lose the c5 bishop anyway. A possible variation is 30.♗d5 ♔h8 (the only move; 30...♖c7? 31.♖xc5+−) 31.♗e4 g6 32.♕e5+ f6 33.♕d5 and it is black who must find the right way to keep the balance: 33...♖xf2! 34.♔xf2 ♗xe3+ 35.♖xe3 ♖c1 36.♕f7 ♖f1+ 37.♔g2 ♕xe3 38.♕f8+ ♔h7 39.♕f7+ ♔h8=.

29...♕d8! [132]

This queen retreat must have come as a shock for Timoshchenko. Black protects his rook with tempo and unpins the c5 bishop.

30.♗f1 [140]

30.h4 loses due to 30...axb4 31.♖xc5 ♖xc5 32.♕xc5 ♕f6.

30.♗f3 g6! (30...axb4 31.♖xc5 ♖xc5 32.♕xc5 ♕f6 33.♖d1! ♕xf3 34.♖xd2 ♗b7 35.♔f1=; 30...♗xb4 31.♘xb4 axb4 32.♖xc8 ♗xc8=) 31.♕e4 ♗f8! 32.♖xc8 ♗xc8 and the threat of ...♗g7 secures black a large advantage.

30...♗xb4 [143]

A nice trick: white has no time to take the bishop on a6, because the rook on c3 is hanging.

30...♗xf1? 31.♖xf1 leaves the c5 bishop pinned again, but the computer shows that 30...g6 was the strongest way to continue: 31.♕f3 ♗xf1 32.♔xf1 (32.♖xf1 axb4+−) 32...♗f8 (again, this idea is best; 32...axb4? 33.♘xb4 ♗xb4? 34.♖xc8 ♕xc8 35.♖a8+−) 33.♖ac1 (33.bxa5 ♗g7 34.♖xc8 ♕xc8−+) 33...♖b8 34.♖c7 ♖d7 35.♖xd7 ♕xd7∓ 36.bxa5? ♕d2−+.

31.♘xb4 [147]

31.♗xa6 ♗xc3−+

31...axb4 32.♖b3

The right decision. It is more difficult for white to defend after 32.♖xc8 ♗xc8 33.♕b1 (or 33.♕f3 b3) 33...♕f6 34.♕e1 ♖c2.

32...g6 [146]

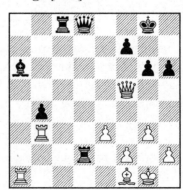

Timoshchenko had consumed almost all his time on his last defensive moves and he now blunders under severe time pressure.

33.♕e4?? [149]

After the correct 33.♕f3 ♗xf1 34.♖xf1 white should be able to save the game.

33...♕f6

A double attack on a1 and f2.

White lost on time.

Game 16

G. TIMOSHCHENKO – G. KASPAROV

Training game. 05.02.1983
Sicilian Defense [B44]
Commentary by Dorian Rogozenco
[Thematic rapid (15'), first game]

1.e4 c5 2.♘f3 ♘c6 3.d4 cxd4 4.♘xd4 e6 5.♘b5 d6 6.c4 ♘f6 7.♘1c3 a6 8.♘a3 ♗e7 9.♗e2 0-0 10.0-0 b6 11.♗e3 ♗b7

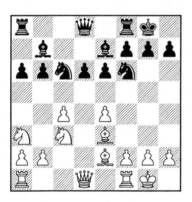

This is the starting position of the four thematic rapid games, played on the same day. It is curious that in his entire career Kasparov played this position only once: in the third game of his first World Championship match versus Karpov, see below.

12.♕b3

The main continuation of this Sicilian line. Its idea is to provoke the move ♘f6-d7 before the other knight can be transferred there from c6.

12...♘d7

12...♘a5. This unfortunate novelty from the first World Championship match versus Karpov didn't find many followers since it offers white a better endgame: 13.♕xb6 ♘xe4 14.♘xe4 ♗xe4 15.♕xd8 ♗xd8 16.♖ad1 d5 17.f3 ♗f5 18.cxd5 exd5 19.♖xd5 ♗e6 20.♖d6 ♗xa2 21.♖xa6 ♖b8 22.♗c5 ♖e8 23.♗b5 ♖e6 24.b4 ♘b7 25.♗f2 ♗e7 26.♘c2 ♗d5 27.♖d1 ♗b3 28.♖d7 ♖d8 29.♖xe6 ♖xd7 30.♖e1 ♖c7 31.♗b6 and black resigned, A. Karpov – G. Kasparov, Moscow 1984.

13.♖fd1 ♖e8

It seems that Kasparov's main goal in the rapid match was to improve his general feeling for these complex hedgehog-type positions, rather than prepare a specific variation for his opening repertoire. 13...♘c5 is the main theoretical line.

14.♖d2

A standard plan, preparing to retreat the queen to d1.

It is more common though to bring the queen to f2. Here is one example from Karpov's practice before 1983: 14.♖ac1 ♗f8 15.♗f1 ♖c8 16.♕c2 ♘ce5 17.h3 ♕c7 18.f3 ♘f6 19.♕f2 ♘ed7 20.♘c2 d5 21.cxd5 exd5 22.exd5 ♗d6 23.♘d4 ♗g3 24.♕d2 ♕e5 25.♘de2 ♗h2+ 26.♔h1 b5 27.♗d4 ♕d6 28.f4+− A. Karpov − O. Romanishin, Moscow 1981.

14...♖c8 15.♕d1 ♕c7 16.♖c1 ♘ce5

In these positions the c6 square is not optimal for the knight and black is usually happy to relocate it. Kasparov brings it to g6.

17.f3 ♘g6 18.♔h1 ♕b8 19.♗f1 ♗c6

19...h5!?

20.♘c2 ♗a8

20...b5 21.cxb5 axb5 22.♘b4±

21.♘d4 ♗f6

Now that the d6 pawn is not under attack black improves the position of his dark-squared bishop. This slightly provocative plan with ♗e7-f6-e5 was deployed in several games by Grandmaster Romanishin. A more common standard route for the dark-squared bishop in this type of position is to go via d8 to c7, which was played in rapid games three and four of this mini-match.

22.♘c2 ♗e5 23.♗g1 h5 24.♘e3 ♗f4 25.♘e2 ♗e5 26.b3 ♘f6

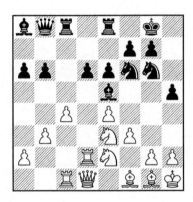

Both sides have made typical moves and the fight hasn't really started yet. With an active bishop on e5 and good control over the dark squares black seems to have decent prospects in the upcoming battle. The next moves are not recorded on the scoresheet, only the result. **Black went on to win**

Game 17

G. TIMOSHCHENKO – G. KASPAROV
Training game. 05.02.1983
Sicilian Defense [B44]
Commentary by Dorian Rogozenco
[Thematic rapid (15'), second game]

1.e4 c5 2.♘f3 ♘c6 3.d4 cxd4 4.♘xd4 e6 5.♘b5 d6 6.c4 ♘f6 7.♘1c3 a6 8.♘a3 ♗e7 9.♗e2 0-0 10.0-0 b6 11.♗e3 ♗b7

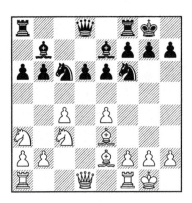

12.♖c1

In games 2-4 of this mini rapid match Timoshchenko switched to this continuation, which those years was equally popular. Recent decades have proved that black's play is easier here compared with 12.♕b3.

12...♘e5 13.f3 ♖e8

The d5 square is already controlled by sufficient black pieces, but the problem with the immediate advance 13...d5 is that white has 14.cxd5 exd5 15.f4 with an advantage for white. For example: 15...♘c6 16.♘xd5 (16.e5? d4! 17.exf6 ♗xf6)

16...♘xd5 (16...♘xe4 17.♗xb6+–) 17.♕xd5 ♕xd5 18.exd5 ♘b4 19.d6 ♗xd6 20.♘c4±

14.♕d2?

This natural move turns out to be a serious mistake.

14...d5!

With the queen on d2 black is able to carry out this break and achieve a comfortable position right away.

15.cxd5 exd5 16.exd5

Here after 16.f4 black has 16...♘eg4 with a large advantage.

16...b5 17.♘c2 b4 18.♘e4 ♘xd5 19.♗d4 ♘c6 20.♗f2 ♘f6 21.♕xd8 ♖axd8 22.♗b6?

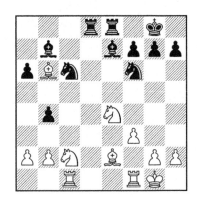

With the accurate move 22.♘g3 white would have been very close to equalizing completely.

22...♘xe4! 23.♗xd8?

The second mistake loses at once. Better was 23.fxe4 ♖d2 24.♗f3 ♘e5∓

23...♗c5+   24.♔h1   ♘f2+
25.♖xf2 ♗xf2–+

and **black went on to win**, again no more moves were recorded.

Game 18

G. TIMOSHCHENKO – G. KASPAROV
Training game. 05.02.1983
Sicilian Defense [B44]
Commentary by Dorian Rogozenco
[Thematic rapid (15'), third game]

1.e4 c5 2.♘f3 ♘c6 3.d4 cxd4 4.♘xd4 e6 5.♘b5 d6 6.c4 ♘f6 7.♘1c3 a6 8.♘a3 ♗e7 9.♗e2 0-0 10.0-0 b6 11.♗e3 ♗b7

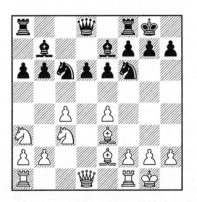

12.♖c1 ♘e5 13.f3 ♖e8 14.♗d4 ♕c7

14...♘c6 15.♗f2 d5 16.cxd5 exd5 17.exd5 (17.♘xd5 ♘xd5 18.♕xd5 ♕xd5 19.exd5 ♘b4=) 17...♘b4 18.♕b3 is possible for black here and now instead of 18...♗xd5 19.♘xd5 ♘bxd5 20.♖c2 ♘b4 21.♖d1 with an advantage for white in A. Beliavsky – V. Liberzon, Baden 1980, black

achieves good compensation for the pawn with 18...b5 19.♖fd1 ♗d6.

15.♕d2 ♖ac8 16.♖fd1 ♘ed7 17.♗f1 ♕b8

Both sides are making standard moves. The position is about equal.

18.♔h1   ♗d8   19.♘c2   ♗c7 20.♗g1

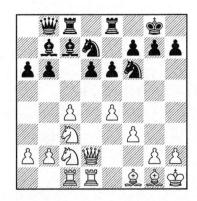

20...d5

Again, Kasparov succeeds in implementing this standard break. He sacrifices the d-pawn in order to free all his pieces. Unfortunately, it is not enough for black to create an advantage: white will return material and simplify the position with complete equality.

21.cxd5 exd5 22.♘xd5

22.exd5 ♗f4 23.♘e3 (23.♗e3? ♗xh2∓) 23...b5 with compensation.

22...♗xd5

This somewhat surprising decision to exchange the bishop offers white hopes for an advantage. There was nothing wrong with 22...♘xd5 23.exd5 ♗f4 24.♘e3 ♖xc1 25.♕xc1 (or 25.♖xc1 ♘f6 26.d6 ♗xd6 27.♖d1 ♗f4 28.♕d4=) 25...

♘f6 26.d6 ♗xd6 27.♘f5 ♗f4 28.♕c3 ♗c8 29.♗d3 b5=

23.exd5 ♗f4 24.♘e3

24.♗e3? allows 24...♖xc2! 25.♕xc2 ♗xe3.

24...♖xc1 25.♕xc1 ♕e5 26.♖e1

Here white could try to play for more than a draw with 26.♘c4 ♕g5 (26...♗xc1 27.♘xe5+−; 26...♕f5 27.♗e3±) 27.♕c2 b5 (27...♘xd5 28.g3 ♗b8 29.f4 ♕h5 30.g4+−) 28.g3, which is very messy.

26...♘xd5   27.♕d1   ♗xe3 28.♗xe3 ♘xe3 29.♕xd7 b5

Draw agreed in an equal position.

Game 19

G. TIMOSHCHENKO – G. KASPAROV
Training game. 05.02.1983
Sicilian Defense [B44]
Commentary by Dorian Rogozenco
[Thematic rapid (15'), fourth game]

1.e4 c5 2.♘f3 ♘c6 3.d4 cxd4 4.♘xd4 e6 5.♘b5 d6 6.c4 ♘f6 7.♘1c3 a6 8.♘a3 ♗e7 9.♗e2 0-0 10.0-0 b6 11.♗e3 ♗b7

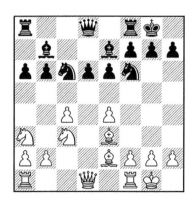

12.♖c1 ♘e5 13.f3 ♖e8 14.♗d4 ♕c7 15.♕d2 ♖ac8 16.♖fd1 ♘ed7 17.♗f1 ♕b8 18.♔h1 ♗d8 19.♘c2 ♘e5

In the last game of this mini rapid match Kasparov doesn't want to simplify the position and prefers to keep all his pieces on the board. He brings the knight to g6, hoping to create an attack on the kingside later on.

19...♗c7 was played in the previous game.

20.b3

20.♘e3? Cuts off the bishop's way back, which allows black to exchange it with 20...♘c6∓

20...♗c7 21.♗g1 ♖cd8 22.♘e3 h5

With the advance of the rook's pawn black is fighting for more space on the kingside and would like to secure some squares for his knights.

23.♕e1 ♘g6 24.♕d2

24.♗f2?! h4 25.♗xh4 ♘xh4 26.♕xh4 d5 27.cxd5 ♗f4 28.♖e1 exd5∓

24...♘e5 25.b4

Repeating moves and agreeing a draw is certainly not the idea of a training game, so in the spirit of the position Timoshchenko rightly decides to go for some activity on the queenside.

25...h4

With the idea of ...h4-h3.

26.h3 ♘h5 27.♘e2 ♘g6 28.♗f2 ♕c8

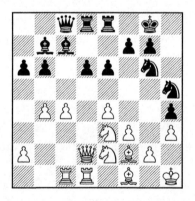

Unfortunately, the game record ends here. Black's last move shows his intention to bring the queen to e7 and then transfer it closer to his opponent's king, to f6 or g5. White is very solid for now, but his plan is not very clear and in a rapid game it might be easier to play with black, who also has ideas to open files with f7-f5, or d6-d5.

It must be said that the last move is an inaccuracy though, because the queen's way to the kingside via d7 and e7 is too long and in the diagram position white can play 29.♘g4! with the idea 30.♕g5, which is unpleasant for black. Therefore, instead of 28...♕c8 more precise was 28...♖d7!, which shortens the route of the black queen to f6 or g5. Black intends either ...♕d8-f6/g5, and perhaps ...♗d8-g5.

In any case **black went on to win** this game as well, as shown on the scoresheet, Kasparov thus winning the mini rapid match with a score of 3.5-0.5.

Game 20

Garry always found it easy to play against Alexander Beliavsky, one of the hardest-working chess players I knew, but whose approach is always overly direct and who relies heavily on home prep for each game.

This encounter began with Beliavsky already losing 3:4 and just three games were left in the match. We expected Garry's opponent to attempt to win this game in order to save the match, as he had the white pieces. Black decided to dampen his opponent's aggressive intent, applying a rare opening setup that wasn't part of his repertoire and which Beliavsky had naturally not prepared for the match. Garry also saw an advantage for himself in that white had to capture a pawn in this opening. That would force his opponent to put a stop to the aggressive scenario he had mapped out at home and instead solve a difficult psychological challenge. On the one hand, being a decent pawn up increased white's chances of winning. But on the other hand he had to accept losing the initiative and switching to defense in order to retain his minimal material advantage.

The need to sharply alter his playing mood proved to be torture for Beliavsky, which was evident from his very first moves.

A. BELIAVSKY – G. KASPAROV
Moscow. Candidates Quarter-Final Match, game 8. 15.03.1983
King's Indian Defense. [E81]

1.d4 ♘f6 2.c4 g6 3.♘c3 ♝g7 4.e4 d6 5.f3 0-0 6.♝e3 a6 7.♝d3 c5 8.dxc5 dxc5 9.♝xc5 ♘c6 10.♘ge2?!

White doesn't sense any trap and makes a typical move for such positions, which in this specific line turns out to be misplaced. He should have retreated his bishop with 10.♝e3, intending to meet 10...♘d7 with 11.f4 and develop the unlucky knight on f3.

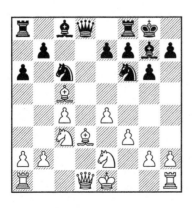

10...♘d7! 11.♝f2?!(41!)

Such a long think in the opening, and one which was far from complicated, pointed to the player being unhappy with the position on the board and that his mind was not at ease. Beliavsky really didn't want to switch to defense, all the more so against such a master of attack. He was still thinking about how to play actively and wanted to avoid his bishop coming under attack after 11...♘de5 12.♘c1 ♘b4 13.♘d5 ♘bxd3+ 14.♘xd3 ♘xc4 while preparing the counter sac 15.b3! ♝xa1 16.♕xa1, so he decided to move his pieces temporarily to some awkward squares.

11...♘de5(05)   12.♘c1 ♝h6!(24)

The downside of white's artificial opening strategy is shown up immediately – the black bishop has become the master of the c1-h6 diagonal.

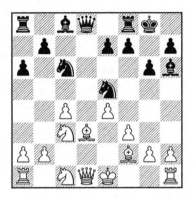

13.♘d5?(26)

The obtuseness of Beliavsky's thinking makes itself felt. He didn't want to put up with switching to defending, though that was dictated by the position. After the better 13.♗e2 ♕xd1+ 14.♘xd1 ♘b4 15.0-0 ♘c2 16.♖b1 ♗e6 17.b3 black had the option of repeating moves with 17...♘a3 18.♖a1 ♘c2, and that is what stopped Alexander.

The psychological discomfort that he had felt since the start of the game led to his ignoring the real potential of his position in favor of his "pre-programmed" aim to play for a win at all costs. Beliavsky hence throws his knight into attack. On its own. To certain death.

13...e6 14.♗b6 ♕g5 15.0-0

Alas, the knight's retreat loses immediately: 15.♘e3? ♘d7! White is forced to mix things up.

15...exd5!(14)

The primitive 15...♘xd3 16.♘xd3 (16.♗e3 ♕xe3+!) 16...exd5 17.cxd5 ♘b8 would also have eventually affirmed black's superiority. However, Kasparov finds a much more effective and elegant solution.

16.f4 ♕h4! 17.fxe5 d4!

A wonderful tactic! Instead of illusionary hopes with 17...dxe4 18.g3 or 17...♘xe5 18.cxd5 white sees his bishop locked out of the game, faces nasty barbed wire on d4 and has to put up with an enemy military base in the very middle of his territory.

18.♘e2 ♗e3+ 19.♔h1 ♘xe5 20.♗c7

The game was essentially over, as by now white only had thirty minutes left on the clock and he had no counterplay against black's growing attack.

20...♕e7   21.♗xe5   ♕xe5 22.♕e1 ♗d7(08) 23.♕g3 ♖ae8 24.♘f4 ♗c6(25) 25.♘d5 ♕xg3 26.hxg3 ♖e5! 27.g4 h5 28.♘f6+ ♔g7 29.gxh5 ♖h8 30.g3

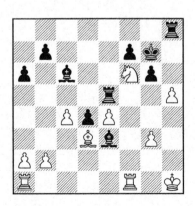

30...♖exh5+(11)

With his opponent in desperate time trouble black decides to hasten victory, sharply changing the nature of play. There was a more effective way to increase his advantage, relying less on psychology: 30...♗g5! 31.♘d5 f5! 32.exf5? ♖xd5!

31.♘xh5 ♖xh5+ 32.♔g2 f5 33.♖ae1

White had just one minute left on his clock and spectators were focused on whether Beliavsky would manage to make his

remaining seven moves before his flag fell.

33...fxe4 34.♗b1 ♖c5 35.b3 b5 36.♖xe3 dxe3 37.♖e1 bxc4 38.bxc4 ♖xc4 39.♖xe3 ♖b4! 40.♖b3 e3

Time trouble was now over, but so was the battle. White had no chance to save this bishop ending. The rest was obvious and requires no commentary.

41.♔f1 ♗b5+ 42.♔e1 a5! 43.♗e4 ♖xb3 44.axb3 ♔f6 45.♔d1 g5 46.♔c2 ♔e5

White resigned.

Game 21

G. TIMOSHCHENKO – G. KASPAROV
Training game. 07.07.1983
Queen's Gambit [D34]
Commentary by Dorian Rogozenco

1.d4 d5 2.c4 e6 3.♘f3 ♘f6 [01] **4.g3 c5** [04] **5.cxd5** [01] **exd5 6.♗g2 ♘c6 7.0-0 ♗e7** [05] **8.♘c3** [03] **0-0 9.♗g5 cxd4** [06] **10.♘xd4 h6 11.♗e3 ♖e8** [07] **12.♖c1** [04] **♗f8** [10] **13.♕c2** [05]

Eleven years after the present game Kasparov faced the Tarrasch with the white pieces. The game G. Kasparov – M. Illescas Cordoba, Linares 1994, continued 13.♘xc6 bxc6 14.♘a4 ♗d7 15.♗c5, which is the main line of the Tarrasch Defense.

13...♗e6 [11]

Sometimes black provokes the move h2-h3 with 13...♗g4 14.h3 and only then goes for 14...♗e6, but

playing it here is rather doubtful, because the pawn on h3 is useful for white. After 15.♖fd1 ♕d7 16.♘xe6 (16.♔h2 is also possible) 16...fxe6 white has the interesting option 17.♘e4 with better prospects.

14.♖fd1 [12] **♕d7** [21] **15.♘xe6** [13]

An important point: after completing the development of his pieces Timoshchenko decides to change the pawn structure, which defines a new strategic stage of the game. Another option to change the structure was 15.♘xc6 bxc6 16.♘a4 with a slight plus for white.

15...fxe6

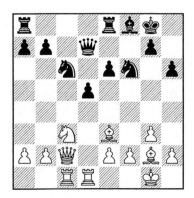

In this position, in order to make use of his better positional factors (the bishop pair and the more compact pawn structure) white must play e2-e4 at some point, otherwise it is difficult to make any progress. This will very likely force his opponent to reply d5-d4 (because any other reaction is strategically inconvenient for black) and after that white will try to use the weakened light squares around his opponent's pawn on d4 to further improve the position of his pieces. Black's task is to prepare for all this and compensate for his positional deficiencies with dynamic play.

16.♗d2 [18]

At first sight this looks passive and strange, but it's not bad at all: white follows the main plan of preparing the e2-e4 break. Another way to free the path for the e-pawn is 16.h3 ♕f7 17.f4 ♖ad8 18.♗f2 and here black must continue 18...e5 with sufficient counterplay.

16...♕f7 [27] **17.♗e1 ♖ad8** [31] **18.♕b3** [23]

18.e4 d4 19.♘e2 ♘g4 20.♘f4 ♘ge5 and unclear

18...♘a5! [44]

Starting with this moment Kasparov displays an amazing fight for the initiative, bringing his pieces and pawns forward and conquering more and more space.

19.♕b5 [26]

Returning the queen to c2 is more prudent. Then black would have had little better than to come back with the knight to c6, because 19.♕c2 ♘c4 (19...♘c6=) 20.e4 d4? 21.♘b5 loses the pawn on d4.

19...♘c4 20.e4 [30] **a6** [47] **21.♕b3 b5 22.♕c2** [70]

Black is well prepared for 22.exd5 exd5 and unclear, but 22.a4 looks more to the point for white, trying to justify the position of the queen on b3.

22...d4 [52] **23.♘b1** [71]

White's position is becoming very dangerous if he is forced to make such moves. After 23.♘e2 e5 it is not clear what to do next: the white pieces obviously lack coordination. For instance, after 24.b3 black already has tactical solutions: 24...♗a3 25.♖b1 (25.bxc4 ♗xc1 26.♘xc1 bxc4∓) 25...♘b2! 26.♖xb2 d3 27.♖xd3 ♖xd3∓

23...♕h5 [85]

Played after 33 minutes of thinking. Black activates the queen and already here Kasparov must have taken into consideration that black will very likely have to sac the knight on g4 later on.

There was a strong alternative: 23...♖c8! 24.♕e2 (24.♖xd4 e5 25.♖d3 ♘e3 26.♕d2 ♘xg2 27.♖xc8 ♖xc8 28.♔xg2 ♘xe4 29.♕e2 ♘c5 30.♖d1 ♕xa2 31.♕xe5 possibly offers better chances to defend) 24...♗c5 25.♔h1 ♗b6∓

24.h3 [79] **♘e5** [87]

By threatening 25...♘f3+ black prepares the further advance of the d-pawn.

25.♕b3 [83]

25.f4 ♘f3+∓; 25.g4? ♘fxg4 26.hxg4 ♕xg4! (26...♘xg4 27.♖d3) 27.♘d2 ♗d6 leads to a decisive attack for black.

25...d3 [89] **26.♘d2** [90]

26.♗c3 ♗c5 27.♗xe5 ♕xe5 28.♖xd3 ♖xd3 29.♕xd3 ♘h5 followed by ...♖f8 offers black powerful compensation for the pawn.

The best continuation for white is 26.♗a5!, which leaves black with several attractive options. He can quietly remove the rook to d7, b8 or a8, or sac the exchange positionally with 26...♖d4 27.♗c3 and then play 27...♖xe4 or 27...♗c5, in both cases with compensation and double-edged play.

26...♖d4 [93]

Following the same strategy of bringing his pieces forward. The rook on d4 is very disturbing for white, who now must also reckon with the possibility of ...♖b4.

27.f4 [105]

After 27.a3 black can prepare the move ...♗c5 by playing 27...♘fd7.

27...♘c4 [111]

Using the fact that white cannot win the pawn by taking on c4, because the rook on d1 needs protection. The alternative 27...♖b4 28.♕c3 ♘c4 allows white to centralize the queen with 29.♘xc4 bxc4 30.♕e5! which unexpectedly attacks the rook on b4 with the bishop from e1. Then 30...♗c5+ 31.♔h1 ♕xe5 32.fxe5 ♖xb2 33.exf6 ♖c2 offers black compensation only sufficient for equality. For instance: 34.♖xc2 (34.e5 ♗e3 35.♖b1 d2=) 34...dxc2 35.♖c1 ♖b8 36.♖xc2 ♖b1 37.♗f1 ♖xe1 38.♔g2=

28.♗f2 [108] **♗c5**

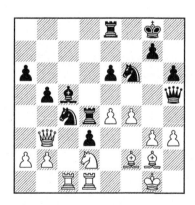

It is amazing that this wild position is objectively equal.

29.g4 [120]

After 29.♗xd4 ♗xd4+ 30.♔h1 black can gain a draw with 30...

♘g4 (30...♗e3 31.♘xc4 bxc4 32.♖xc4 ♘g4 33.♖xd3 ♘f2+ 34.♔h2 ♘g4+ is similar) 31.♘xc4 ♘f2+ 32.♔h2 ♘g4+. Playing for a win with 30...♘e3 31.♕xd3 e5 is an interesting alternative, even if white is objectively no worse after 32.fxe5 ♕xe5 33.♘f3 ♕xg3 34.♖d2.

29...♘xg4 [117]

Forced, as retreating the queen allows white to take on c4: 29...♕g6? 30.♘xc4 bxc4 31.♖xc4 ♖xc4 32.♕xc4 ♗xf2+ 33.♔xf2+−

30.hxg4 ♕xg4 31.♕c3 [126]

31.♘f3 ♖xe4 32.♗xc5 ♖e2 33.♘h4! was correct Then after the best moves 33...d2 34.♖b1 ♕xh4 35.♕f3 ♖e1+ 36.♗f1 ♖xd1 37.♖xd1 ♖d8 38.♗f2 ♕f6 the pawn on d2 and the open position of the white king compensate for the missing piece. The position is objectively equal.

31...e5

A good alternative is 31...♖ed8. With his last move Kasparov creates an impressive concentration of black pieces in the center.

32.b3? [137]

The computer shows the strongest defensive move as 32.♖f1! after which it is difficult for black to find a clear continuation for his attack. Perhaps the best continuation is the prophylactic 32...♔h8. Then a possible variation is 33.♘f3 d2 34.♖cd1 ♖xe4 35.♗xc5 ♖e2 36.♖f2 ♖xf2 37.♔xf2! e4 38.♖xd2! exf3 39.♗xf3 ♕h4+ 40.♔g2 ♘xd2

41.♕xd2 ♕f6 with a draw the most likely outcome.

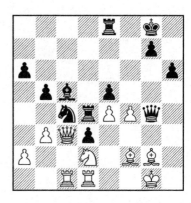

32...exf4 [126]

Both sides missed the idea 32...♖d6! and white gets mated quickly: 33.f5 (or 33.♗xc5 ♖g6) 33...♘e3 34.♗xe3 ♗xe3+ 35.♔h2 ♕f4+ 36.♔h3 ♗f2.

33.bxc4 [141] **♖dxe4**

Again, 33...♖d6 wins on the spot.

34.♖f1? [143]

White could escape here with 34.♕xd3 ♗xf2+ (34...♖e2? 35.♕d5+ ♔h8 36.♕xc5+−) 35.♔f1!! with equality in all variations: 35...♖e3 (35...♖e2 36.♕f3 ♕g6 37.♕xe2 ♖xe2 38.♗d5+ ♖e6 39.♔xf2 ♕g3+ 40.♔f1 ♕h3+ 41.♔g1 ♕g3+=) 36.♕d5+ ♔h8 37.♔xf2 ♖8e5 38.♕a8+ ♔h7 (38...♖e8 39.♕d5=) 39.♗e4+ g6 (39...♖5xe4 40.♕xe4+ ♖xe4 41.♘xe4 is also a draw) 40.♕b7+ ♔h8 41.♕b8+ ♔h7 42.♕xe5 ♕e2+ 43.♔g1 ♖g3+ 44.♔h1 ♖h3+ 45.♔g1=

34...♖e3! [127]

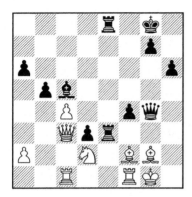

The rook moves very nicely to the dark squares and white is helpless against its further transfer to g3.

35.cxb5 [148]

White must open the a2-g8 diagonal, because the only way to defend against mate on g2 is to bring the queen to the long diagonal.

35...♖g3 [129] **36.♕c4+ ♔h7** [133] **37.♕d5 ♖e5!** [134]

That's why on the previous move Kasparov went with the king on h7 and not h8. With the king on the 8th rank white would have now had a check on a8, followed by ♖xc5.

37...f3? makes no sense due to 38.♕xd3+ ♔h8 39.♕xf3.

38.♕f3

White gets mated after 38.♕c6 ♖g5 39.♕e4+ ♖g6.

38...♖xf3   39.♘xf3   ♗xf2+ 40.♖xf2 ♖xb5

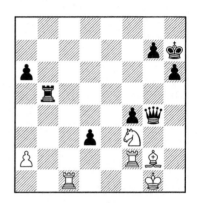

Here the game was adjourned, but didn't resume. Black is winning: the queen and four pawns are much stronger here than a rook and two minor pieces (the machine shows -4.63 at a depth of 49). So I guess it won't be too wrong to consider the game as a victory for Kasparov.

White resigned.

Game 22

G. KASPAROV– G. TIMOSHCHENKO
Training game. 08.07.1983
Queen's Gambit [D55]
Commentary by Dorian Rogozenco

1.d4 [01] **♘f6 2.c4 e6 3.♘c3** [05] **d5** [01] **4.♗g5 ♗e7 5.♘f3** [06] **h6** [02] **6.♗xf6** [07] **♗xf6 7.e3 0-0** [03] **8.♕d2** [08]

Kasparov also played this system in the training match against Vladimirov in January 1983 (see the annotations to the fourth game of that match).

8...b6 [09]

One of the most popular continuations. Vladimirov played the rare move 8...a6.

9.♖c1 [22]

Just like in the mentioned game against Vladimirov Kasparov's idea is to wait for his opponent's bishop to come to b7, before he exchanges on d5. After the immediate 9.cxd5 exd5 10.♖c1 black can consider keeping the bishop on the c8-h3 diagonal with 10...♗e6!?

The sharpest attempt to create problems for black after 8...b6 is the move 9.0-0-0, which leads to double-edged positions.

9...♗b7 [12] **10.cxd5 exd5**

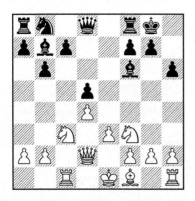

11.b4

An (over)ambitious continuation. This advance is similar to the variation 6.♗h4 (instead of 6.♗xf6) 6...0-0 7.e3 b6 8.♗e2 ♗b7 9.♗xf6

♗xf6 10.cxd5 exd5 11.b4 and compared with it white is even a tempo up in the diagram position: he has played ♕d2 and ♖c1 instead of ♗e2. However, the point is that the bishop on e2 is more useful for white than the two other moves combined, because with the pawn on b4 the rook is often better off on b1 than on c1 and the queen is better placed on b3 than on d2.

Experiencing many of the Queen's Gambit's opening subtleties in a training match was useful for Kasparov in his later World Championship encounters versus Karpov.

11.♗e2 c5 12.0-0 is about equal.

11...♗e7 [18] **12.b5** [28]

This is already an inaccuracy, and it allows black to grab the initiative. 12.♖b1= was better.

12...♗a3!

Fixing the pawn on a2. The immediate 12...a6 13.a4= was less accurate.

13.♖c2 [34] **a6!** [30] **14.♗e2 c6**

14...axb5?! allows white to exchange his opponent's important dark-squared bishop after 15.♘xb5, but 14...c5 was another good option for black.

15.bxa6 [36]

The strategically preferable 15.bxc6 has concrete drawbacks: it helps black to develop a quick initiative after 15...♘xc6 (threatening 16...♘b4) 16.♕d1 b5 17.0-0 ♖c8.

15...♘xa6 16.♕d1 b5 [50]

Impressive play by Timoshchenko. The somewhat surprising advance of the b-pawn is a good strategical decision, because black increases the pressure on the a-file and retains many options to further improve the position of his pieces. Apart from all that, it will be more difficult for white now to prepare one of his important ideas in such structures – the e3-e4 advance – because black can always drive the knight away from c3 by means of b5-b4 and thus increase control in the center.

An alternative way to treat this position with black is 16...♘c7 17.0-0 c5.

17.0-0 ♗d6 18.♕b1 [43]

18.e4? loses a pawn: 18...♘b4 (18...b4 19.e5) 19.♖b2 dxe4 20.♘xe4 ♖xa2∓

18...b4 [58]

It was not necessary to hurry with this break and offer white the a4 square for his knight. White's task to equalize would have been considerably more difficult after 18...♗c8 (threatening 19...♗f5) 19.♖b2 (19.e4? b4 20.e5 bxc3 21.exd6 ♗f5–+) 19...♕a5 20.♕c2 ♗d7 and black will later advance...b5-b4 under much better circumstances.

19.♘a4

Now the position is equal.

20...♕a5 20.♕b3 c5 [60]

20...♘c7 21.♘c5 ♗xc5 22.dxc5 ♗a6=

21.♘xc5 [50] **♘xc5** [63] **22.dxc5 ♗xc5**

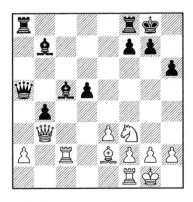

23.a3 [53]

Both sides underestimate the power of black's passed a-pawn after the reply ...b4xa3. 23.♖fc1 or 23.♖d1!? hoping for an edge was preferable.

23...♖fb8 [93]

Black could have forced white to fight for a draw with 23...bxa3 24.♕xb7 a2 25.♖cc1 (or 25.♖a1 ♖ab8 26.♕xb8 ♖xb8 27.♖cxa2 ♖b1+ 28.♖xb1 ♕xa2 29.♗d3∓) 25...♗a3! 26.♖a1 (26.♖cd1 ♖fb8 27.♕d7 ♗b2∓) 26...♖fb8 27.♕xb8+ (27.♕c6 ♗b2 28.♗d3 ♖xa1 29.♖xa1 ♖c8 30.♕b5 ♕c3–+) 27...♖xb8 28.♖xa2 ♕c3∓

24.♖fc1? [57]

24.axb4=

24...♕xa3 [99]

Missing 24...bxa3! 25.♖xc5 ♕xc5 26.♖xc5 a2 27.♖c1 a1=♕ 28.♖xa1 ♖xa1+ 29.♗d1 (29.♗f1 ♖xf1+ 30.♔xf1 ♗a6+–+) 29...♗c8! 30.♕c2 ♗f5 31.♕e2 ♖b2 32.♘d2 ♗d3–+

25.♕xa3 [59] **bxa3 26.♖xc5 a2 27.♖a1 ♗a6 28.♗xa6** [60] **♖b1+ 29.♖c1 ♖xc1+ 30.♖xc1**

♖xa6 31.♖a1 ♖b6 32.♘d2 ♖b2 33.♘f1

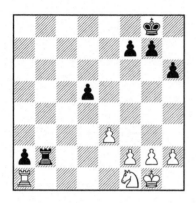

After a forcing variation initiated by black (24...♛xa3) the players have reached an interesting endgame, which Timoshchenko most likely rightly assessed as a draw. Now it was time to stop and think carefully in order to understand exactly what to do next. Instead of that, Timoshchenko continued to play quickly.

33...♚f8? [101]

This straightforward move allows white to implement his only winning plan: to bring the king to f3 and the knight to g3 as quickly as possible. After that white will threaten to put the knight on e2, which together with ideas like ♘c3 or ♘c1 will win the pawn on a2.

Black can reach a draw in several ways, but in order to see clearly the problems from the game I will show how to reach a draw by playing 33...h5. In fact any other black move with a pawn to the fifth rank leads to a draw as well,

even 33...g5 34.g4 f5. But we'll stick to the advance of the rook's pawn: 33...h5 34.g3 (otherwise it is not clear how to make progress with white. 34.h3 is a bad mistake in view of 34...h4 and white is suddenly in deep trouble. 34.h4 is better. Then 34...♚f8 35.g3 ♚e7 36.♚g2 ♚d6 37.♘h2 ♚c5 38.♘f3. White has blockaded the d-pawn, but he is passive and black saves himself: 38...♚b4 39.♘d4 ♚a3 40.♖d1 ♖b1 41.♖d2 ♖c1 42.♘b5+ ♚b3 43.♘d4+ ♚a3=) 34...♚f8 (following a similar plan from the game, although here 34...g5 35.h3 g4= is a very simple plan to draw) 35.h3 ♚e7 36.♚g2 ♚d6 37.g4 hxg4 38.hxg4 ♚c5 39.♘g3 d4 (39...♚b4 is sufficient as well, because white does not bring the knight to c1 in time: 40.♚f3 ♚a3 41.♘e2 ♖b1 42.♖xa2+ ♚xa2 43.♘c3+ ♚b2 44.♘xb1 ♚xb1 leads to a draw in a pawn endgame) 40.exd4+ ♚xd4 41.♘f5+ ♚c3 42.♘xg7 ♖c2. Now we have a position from the game but without the h-pawns (and the little yet important factor that the white king is on g2 instead of f3). This difference changes the evaluation: white has no pawn to win on h6 and therefore the position is a draw.

34.g4! [61]

Kasparov doesn't let his chance slip away. He plays perfectly from here until the end of the game, without giving black any hope of saving himself.

34...♔e7

After 34...g6 35.♔g2 f5 36.gxf5 gxf5 white must be careful not to play 37.♘g3? due to 37...f4! 38.exf4 d4 allowing black to create counterplay and escape. Instead, 37.♔f3 leads to a winning rook endgame: 37...♖b1 38.♖xa2 ♖xf1 39.♔f4+−

35.♔g2 ♔d6 36.♘g3 [65]

Obviously, white cannot leave the knight unprotected: 36.♔f3? ♖b1=

36...♔c5 [111] 37.♔f3 [71] d4 [115]

In case of 37...♔c4 (or 37... g6) white transfers the knight to c1: 38.♘e2 ♔b4 39.♘c1 winning easily in many ways. Even the pawn endgame is hopeless for black (after exchanging rooks by sacrificing the knight on a2).

38.exd4+ ♔xd4 39.♘f5+ ♔c3 [72] 40.♘xg7 ♖c2 [120] 41.♘f5 ♔b2 42.♖xa2+ ♔xa2 43.♘xh6

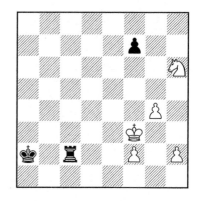

White is easily winning here, because the black king is too far from the kingside.

43...♖c7 [124]

43...f6 44.h4 ♔b3 45.♘g8 ♖c6 46.h5+−

44.g5 [74] ♔b3 45.h4 ♔c4 46.♔e4 ♖e7+ 47.♔f5 ♔d5 48.f4 [75]

Black resigned

Although Kasparov won this game, the opening outcome clearly favored black and must have left an unpleasant feeling. Possibly that is one of the reasons why Kasparov never played the 8.♕d2 system in his career again.

Game 23

G. TIMOSHCHENKO – G. KASPAROV
Training game. 10.07.1983
Queen's Gambit [D36]
Commentary by Dorian Rogozenco

1.d4 d5 2.c4 e6 3.♘c3 ♘f6 [01] 4.cxd5 [01] exd5 5.♗g5 ♗e7 [02] 6.e3 [02] 0-0 7.♗d3 ♘bd7 8.♕c2 [03] **♖e8 [06] 9.♘ge2 [05] c6 [12] 10.0-0 [07] ♘f8 [13]**

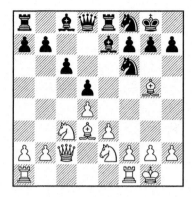

When I saw the opening of this game I had to check the scoresheet again: the position on the diagram used to be one of Kasparov's favorite opening variations with the white pieces. It is remarkable that in this game Kasparov was on the black side: he never played this variation with black in his practice. My explanation is that Kasparov was preparing to face the Queen's Gambit with both colors for the upcoming candidates/ World Championship matches and therefore also wanted to accumulate experience from the other side of the board.

11.♖ab1

As white, Kasparov used to play 11.f3 here.

11...a6 [27]

A very rare move, played after 14 minutes of thinking. Usually black prefers 11...a5. However, in that case white has an interesting option to return to the plan in the center by playing 12.f3. The point is that after white's f2-f3 black's counterplay is often based on the c6-c5 break. With the pawn on a5 the advance of the c-pawn becomes less attractive for black due to the weakness of the b5 square.

Here is one recent example, where a Swiss grandmaster changed white's initial plan to play on the queenside: 11...a5 12.f3!? g6 13.♗h4 ♘e6 14.♖bd1 ♘g7 15.e4 ♗e6 16.h3 ♘fh5 17.♗xe7 ♕xe7 18.♕d2 ♘f6 19.♖de1 ♖ed8 20.g4 b5 21.e5 ♘d7 22.♘g3 ♕h4 23.♔g2 with a clear advantage for white in S. Bogner – A. Mindlin, Batumi 2018.

12.b4 [10] ♗g4 13.a4 [12]

"13.♘a4 ♘h5! 14.♗xe7 ♕xe7 15.♘c5 ♖ad8 16.a4 ♖d6! and unclear" is a variation mentioned on Kasparov's scoresheet.

In case of 13.f3 ♗h5 14.♘f4 ♗g6 15.♘xg6 hxg6 the chances are about equal for both sides.

13...♖c8

Black prepares to meet b4-b5 with the advance of the c-pawn.

14.♗f5 [16]

A toothless move. The voluntary exchange of bishops is a sign that in the present game Timoshchenko wasn't even trying to fight for an opening advantage. 14.b5 axb5 15.axb5 c5 is equal as well. The best attempt is 14.f3 ♗h5 15.♘g3 (15. ♗f5 ♗g6=) 15...♗g6 16.♘f5 ♗xf5 17.♗xf5 ♖c7 (17...♘e6? 18.♗xf6 ♗xf6 19.♗xh7+) 18.♗h4 ♘h5 19.♗f2. Here white at least has the bishop pair and can try to exploit it in the future.

14...♗xf5 [36] 15.♕xf5 g6 [38]

After 15...♘e4 16.♘xe4 dxe4
17.♗xe7 ♕xe7 18.♖fc1 white's
position is slightly more pleasant.

16.♕d3 [17] **♘g4** [40] **17.♗xe7**
[19]

17.♗f4 ♘e6 18.♗g3 ♗d6=

17...♕xe7 [42] **18.h3** [20] **♘f6**
19.b5 axb5 20.axb5 c5 [43] **21.dxc5**
[22] **♖xc5** [44]

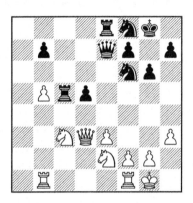

In this equal position black can
claim a slight initiative thanks to his
control of the c-file.

22.♘a4 [31]

In case of 22.♘d4 ♖ec8 23.♘ce2
♖c4 white still cannot simplify the
position completely. For instance,
24.♖fc1 ♘e4 25.♖xc4 dxc4 26.♕c2
♘d7 27.♘c3 ♘xc3 28.♕xc3 ♕e4
29.♖c1 ♘e5 and black continues to
keep some pressure.

22...♖c7 [46] **23.♖fc1** [32] **♘e6**
[50] **24.♖xc7** [35] **♕xc7 25.♖c1**
[37] **♕a5** [56] **26.♘ac3** [40] **♖c8**
[57] **27.♕d1** [48]

27.♘d1? ♖xc1 28.♘xc1 ♕e1+
29.♔h2 ♘e4∓ 30.♕xd5? ♘d2–+.
A good plan is 27.f3 ♖c5
28.♔f2=

27...♖c5 [60] **28.♕b3** [50] **♘e4**

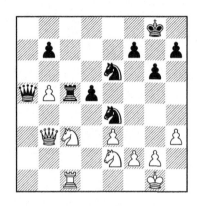

29.♘xe4 [62]

A concession, not just improving
black's pawn structure, but also
opening access to e1 and/or d2 for
the black queen. Now the position
will require more accuracy from
white in order to keep the balance.

Instead of exchanging on e4
white could have calmly played
29.♕b2. Then after 29...♘xc3
30.♖xc3 the pawn on b5 is indirectly
protected, because 30...♖xb5?
31.♖c8+ ♘f8 32.♕e5 ♕a3 33.♘f4
gives white a decisive initiative.
30...♕xb5 31.♖b3 ♕a5 32.♖xb7
with an equal position is better.
Black can't continue 32...♕e1+?
33.♔h2± ♕xf2 due to 34.♖b8+ ♘f8
35.♕e5+–

29...♖xc1+ [64] **30.♘xc1 dxe4**
31.♕c2 [73]

31.♔f1 ♕d2∓

31...b6 [77] **32.♕c6** [83]

It is not easy to decide which
pawn to give up, b5 or f2. In both
cases black has the initiative, which
is not enough for a victory, though:

32.♘a2 ♕xb5 33.♕xe4 ♘c5 (33...
♕b2 34.♘b4, or 33...♕e2 34.♕b1!)
34.♘c3!? ♘xe4 35.♘xb5 and
black's passed b-pawn gives him only
a symbolic advantage.

32...♕e1+ [87] **33.♔h2 ♕xf2
34.♕xb6** [99] **h5** [97]

34...♘g5? loses the knight
due to the check on d8, but 34...
h6 preparing ♘e6-g5-f3 could be
quite unpleasant for white. He must
find the defence 35.♘b3! (35.♕d6
♘g5!) 35...♘g5 36.♘d4 ♕xe3 (36...
♘f3+ 37.♘xf3 exf3 38.♕b8+ ♔h7
39.♕g3) 37.♕f6=

35.♕d6 [110] **♔h7** [98] **36.♘b3**
[120]

36.♕e7 ♔g7 37.b6 ♕xe3
38.♕d6= is more accurate.

36...♕xe3

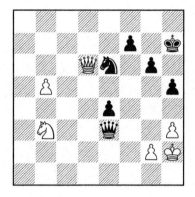

The notation of the game ends
here with no result. Timoshchenko
had consumed 2 hours up to this
point, Kasparov – one hour and 38
minutes. Possibly white lost on time
(the time control in this game may
have been 2 hours for 40 moves).
Anyway, a pawn up and with the
exposed position of the opponent's
king black has an advantage,
although after the precise 37.♕g3!
with the idea 37...♕b6 38.♕e5 white
can put up tough resistance.

Game 24

Bobby Fischer descended from chess Olympus in 1975 of his own free
will when refusing to play a match against Karpov. The latter could merely
try to justify his so easily earned champion's title by posting tournament
victories. Victories are what he indeed chalked up, spectacular and
convincing ones, and the world agreed that the new chess king was a real
one, and not a champion on paper. Little was said about the true nature
of such convincing wins – unfortunately. Those tournament victories by
Karpov were to a large extent driven by the champion's ability to strike
down opponents with the power of his team's huge preparation for his
match against Fischer. As a result, grandmasters who had only recently
fought with him on an equal footing for first place in tournaments suddenly
transformed into timid apprentices.

Now Kasparov unexpectedly found himself in a similar situation, and not by his own volition His semi-final against Korchnoi had been indefinitely postponed by malicious intrigues with the aim of keeping Karpov on his throne. Its chances of taking place looked extremely slim, but the energy and strength that Garry had built up preparing for that match couldn't bear the uncertain wait and needed an outlet. Well, a strong tournament in Niksic came up, although nobody had planned on Kasparov taking part in it.

Not that long before, games against the vastly experienced Hungarian grandmaster had proved to be a serious trial for Garry. Well, see what happened this time, when a heavily armed tank charged at Portisch.

G. KASPAROV – L. PORTISCH

Niksic. International grandmasters tournament. 27.08.1983
Queen's Indian Defense. [E13]

1.d4 ♘f6 2.c4 e6 3.♘f3 b6 4.♘c3 ♗b7 5.a3 d5 6.cxd5 ♘xd5 7.e3 ♘xc3 8.bxc3 ♗e7 9.♗b5+ c6 10.♗d3 c5 11.0-0 ♘c6 12.♗b2 ♖c8 13.♕e2 0-0 14.♖ad1 ♕c7 15.c4 cxd4 16.exd4 ♘a5

The opening is over and the game has reached a typical middlegame position where the hanging pawns on c4 and d4 add heightened dynamism to the position and lead to a looming culmination of the battle. How quickly the game ends depends on the playing style of the player with the white pieces as well as on the vigilance of black, who has not yet achieved full equality.

Portisch's last moves were perfectly natural, but one of them, 14...♕c7, proved to be premature, and that significantly hastened a crisis. Garry sensed in time that he now had to take decisive measures. Sensing the place and time for the main battle was a key component of Kasparov's ability, raising him above the level of other supergrandmasters.

17.d5! exd5

Portisch "believes" his opponent and selects a continuation where events are then forced right to the very end. However, to decide on making a break in the center white had to assess the consequences of the pawn sac after 17...♘xc4. I wonder who among the readers would have calculated the variation that Kasparov demonstrated immediately after the game: 18.♕e4! g6 19.♗xc4 ♕xc4 20.♕e5 f6 21.♕xe6+ ♖f7 22.♖c1 ♕a6 23.d6 ♖xc1 24.♖xc1 ♗d8 25.♘g5! fxg5 26.♖c7!! ♗xc7 27.♕e8+ ♖f8 28.♕e5, with a win.

18.cxd5 ♗xd5 19.♗xh7+ ♔xh7 20.♖xd5 ♔g8

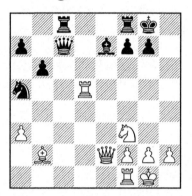

Although there's a big hole in the black fortress on h7, the decisive maneuvers of the white pieces are less obvious than the threat of the black queen invading on c2. In reality, though, black's position is critical, and it needs just one move to demonstrate that. Its base is Emanuel Lasker's famous combination. Garry thought here for 26 minutes before deciding on deploying this motif. At first, his intuition wanted him to move his knight to e5, but in that case the white bishop would have found itself locked out of the battle.

21.♗xg7!! ♔xg7 22.♘e5! ♖fd8

Black is crushed quickly after both 22...f5 23.♖d7 ♕c5 24.♘d3 ♕xa3 25.♖xe7+ ♖f7 26.♕e5+ and 22...♖h8 23.♕g4+ ♔f8 24.♕f5 f6 25.♖e1 ♘c6 26.♘d7+ ♔f7 27.♖xe7+ ♔xe7 28.♕xf6+.

23.♕g4+ ♔f8 24.♕f5! f6 25.♘d7+! ♖xd7 26.♖xd7 ♕c5 27.♕h7 ♖c7

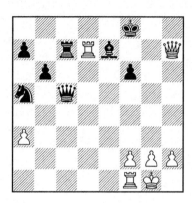

28.♕h8+!

An important move! Immediately playing 28.♖d3 misses the win due to an amazing resource: 28...♕xf2+!! 29.♔xf2 (but not 29.♖xf2?? ♖c1+! 30.♖f1 ♗c5+! 31.♔h1 ♖xf1!#) 29...♗c5+ 30.♔g3 ♖xh7 31.♖xf6+ ♔e7, and black is perfectly safe.

28...♔f7 29.♖d3 ♘c4 30.♖fd1! ♘e5?

Black is tired of defending and loses immediately. The only way to defend is to block the d-file with 30...♗d6 31.♖d5! ♕c6. But then white's passed pawn marches with a decisive effect: 32.h4!

31.♕h7+! ♔e6

King walks like this are usually highly dangerous, but Portisch has no choice here. 31...♔f8 loses to 32.♖d8+.

32.♕g8+ ♔f5 33.g4+! ♔f4 34.♖d4+ ♔f3 35.♕b3+!

Black resigned. Torture after 35...♕c3 36.♕d5+ ♔e2 37.♕e4+ is unbearable and pointless.

Game 25

Before the start of the match both opponents tried as objectively as possible to figure out their advantages and disadvantages compared to each other, and to build a match strategy on their basis. A short team meeting between Garry and his coaches held after the victorious sixth game led to the conclusion that Korchnoi could no longer claim any advantage in playing complicated strategic middlegames or endgames. All he had left was the confidence that his experience granted him some advantage in understanding the opening systems deployed in the match. So we had to deprive him of this confidence as well by shocking him in the opening, just as Korchnoi had himself done in the first game. We decided that it was time to introduce an unusual opening trick that we nick-named "cross-fire".

The idea of this effective but risky ploy was to stick to a single opening in potentially all of the match games, but on the condition that this be a key weapon in the opponent's opening arsenal with one of the colors. In this case, once the opponent had played the opening with his "favorite" color, he would have to face his own weapon the very next day, demonstrating the best method of defense. And in the game after that he would have to show how to break down the bastions built using his own design, and so on. The psychological effect from deploying this trick was powerful, but only if we knew all the nuances of the opening, otherwise sorry confusion would result.

Gennady Timoshchenko was our chief expert in the Catalan. Evgeny Vladimirov also had a fine grasp of its nuances. He spent many hours going through disparate material on the opening with Garry when preparing for the match. The dress-rehearsal for this cunning ploy was seen in games four and five, and Korchnoi naturally assumed that this happened ad-hoc at a difficult point in the match for Garry. He certainly didn't expect us to plan to deploy the Catalan in most of the remaining games.

The effect exceeded all expectations. "Cross-fire" stunned Korchnoi while allowing Kasparov to gain confidence and quickly take control of the match.

G. KASPAROV – V. KORCHNOI
London. Candidates Semi-Final Match, game 7. 06.12.1983
Catalan Opening. [E04]

1.d4 ♞f6 2.c4 e6 3.g3 d5 4.♝g2 dxc4 5.♞f3 ♝d7?!

Korchnoi's losing move was to show up to this game! He should have taken a time-out. The twenty hours separating the start of game seven from the end of such a disappointing second session of the previous game was quite insufficient for him to regain his strength and adapt to the thought that the match was effectively starting over again, but now a match of just six games.

He misread white's repetition of the opening system that he had deployed without success in game five, and simply decided that his opponent was also tired and had no objection to a quick draw. However, the setup that white selected was hardly appropriate for such a goal.

6.♕c2 c5 7.0-0 ♗c6 8.♕xc4 ♘bd7 9.♗g5 ♖c8

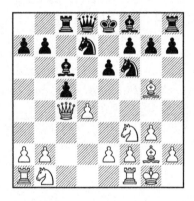

10.♗xf6!

The start of an effective series of exchanges that was totally unexpected by black. Now any capture has positional drawbacks. Almost half an hour of thought convinced Korchnoi not to object to the simplifications. Kasparov considered capturing by the pawn to be the best reply.

**10...♘xf6	11.dxc5	♗xf3 12.♗xf3	♗xc5	13.♕b5+	♕d7 14.♘c3!**

White is simply attempting to gain an advantage through having a larger number of pieces in play.

14...♕xb5?! 15.♘xb5 ♔e7

Black's plan is also simple – to carry out exchanges and wait for peace talks.

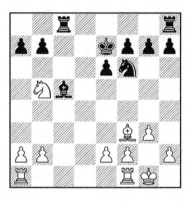

16.b4!

To gain equality black is short of a move that would enable him to chase the knight away and stabilize the situation on the queenside. Aware of the fragility of his advantage, Kasparov finds an original trick with the idea of opening files to his advantage.

16...♗xb4 17.♘xa7 ♖c7?

A superficial decision, but black did not want to think that evening (or could not) and hence he failed to sense danger. After 17...♖a8! 18.♖fb1! ♖xa7 19.♖xb4 ♖b8 20.a4 ♘e8 (or even 20...♘d5 21.♗xd5 exd5) 21.a5 ♘d6 the reciprocal pawn weaknesses on a5 and b7 promised an approaching draw.

18.♖fc1!

Now the idea behind 16.b4! is fully justified. White takes control of the c-file and his advantage turns ominous.

18...♖d7 19.♖ab1 ♗d2 20.♖c2 ♖hd8 21.♗xb7

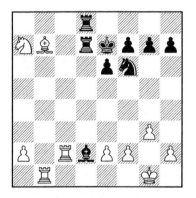

Garry has managed to win a pawn without surrendering a gram of his positional superiority in return. Now it's time for him to demonstrate how to convert this minimal material advantage into a full point.

21...♔f8 22.♞c6 ♖c7! 23.♖bb2 ♖d6 24.a4 ♗e1 25.♖b1

Black's threats are not serious, and this could have been highlighted by the elegant 25.a5 ♞g4 26.a6! ♗xf2+ 27.♔g2. Kasparov instead carries out his plan prepared earlier.

25...♞d5 26.♗a8 ♖c8 27.♗b7 ♖c7 28.♖c4! ♞e7 29.♞e5!

The battle is over and black could have resigned here. However, Korchnoi fights to the bitter end and allows Garry to demonstrate his improved technique.

29...♗a5 30.♖b5 ♞g6 31.♞c6! ♖d1+ 32.♔g2 ♗e1 33.a5 ♞e7 34.a6 ♞xc6 35.♖xc6 ♖xc6 36.♗xc6 ♖a1 37.♖b8+ ♔e7 38.♖b7+ ♔d6 39.♗b5 ♗c3 40.♖xf7 ♗f6 41.♖d7+ ♔c5 42.♗d3 h6 43.♖b7 ♖a3 44.a7 ♔d5 45.f3 ♔d6 46.♖b6+

Black resigned. After 46...♔c5 47.♖a6 the pawn queens.

Game 26

The Candidates Final proved to be Kasparov's best match on his path to meeting Karpov. Wise Vasily Vasilevich knew even before the games began that he had almost no chance against his young, relentless opponent who was improving with every match. So he forgot about sporting calculations and played unusually freshly and inventively. Losing 4:7, Smyslov made a final attempt here to avoid being bageled. To do this he first had to penetrate what appeared to be an impregnable opening wall.

V. SMYSLOV – G. KASPAROV

Vilnius. Candidates Final Match, game 12. 07.04.1984
Queen's Gambit. [D34]

1.d4 d5 2.♘f3 c5 3.c4 e6 4.cxd5 exd5 5.g3 ♘f6 6.♗g2 ♗e7 7.0-0 0-0 8.♘c3 ♘c6 9.♗g5 cxd4 10.♘xd4 h6 11.♗e3 ♖e8 12.a3 ♗e6

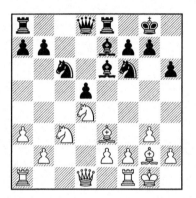

The ex-world champion countered his young opponent's encyclopedic opening knowledge with a deep understanding of the subtleties of those openings that he regularly played. Smyslov began the battle in four of his games as white from this position, which reduced the number of moves left to time control and helped the 63-year-old grandmaster preserve his energy and withstand the fighting tension commendably.

13.♘xe6

Smyslov's key idea had previously involved a setup beginning with the quiet move 13.♔h1. After that, white played f2-f4, hid his bishop away on g1 and pushed his e-pawn forward. In the second game of the match

Kasparov had some difficulties in withstanding the attack, and grandmaster Makarychev, at the time an important member of Karpov's team, hastily called the ex-champion's idea "novelty of the year".

Vladimirov and I, the "guardians" of the Tarrasch Defense, were forced to work hard before suggesting to our charge that he reply with the effective counter 13...♗g4! Smyslov twice attempted to improve on white's play, but to no avail. So now he decided to deploy plan B, and a cunning one at that.

13...fxe6 14.♕a4 ♔h8(37) 15.♖ad1 ♖ac8(14) 16.♔h1 a6(04) 17.f4 ♘a5!(16)

Black starts counterplay at the right time. He would have met the obvious-looking 18.♗g1 with 18...♘c4! 19.♕b3 ♗c5! 20.e4 ♗xg1 21.♖xg1 ♘e3, and white would have problems to solve. Smyslov finds a different way to attack d5.

18.f5! b5(13)

I wasn't delighted at Kasparov's reply here, as it allowed white to strengthen his attacking potential on the kingside. Obviously, 18...♘c4 was weak due to 19.♗c1!, after which black's walls in the center collapse. However, the logical continuation of his maneuvers was 18...♖c4, chasing white's queen to a less active position. Kasparov was afraid of falling under attack after 19.♕c2 e5 20.♕d2 d4 21.♗xh6 dxc3? 22.♕g5! However, he had failed to spot the strong move 21...♘g4! forcing white to head for complications with 22.f6, which was more to black's advantage.

19.♕h4! ♘g8

Black now needs to hurriedly build a defense on that section of the board which was quiet just a couple of moves earlier. But what else could he have done here? The knight charge 19...♘c4? would have been suicidal: 20.♗xh6 ♘h7 21.♕h5 gxh6 22.fxe6 ♘e3 23.♖f7. The move 19...♖c4 is now useless due to 20.♕h3!

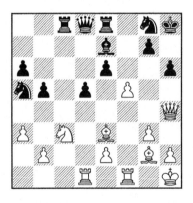

20.♕h3(05!) ♘c4 21.♗c1 ♗g5 22.fxe6 ♗xc1 23.♖xc1

Here 23.♖xd5 had no effect, as there was no threat to g7, thereby allowing black to calmly dismantle white's queenside with 23...♕b6 24.♖xc1 ♘xb2. Smyslov instead found an excellent way to maintain the pressure.

23...♘e3 24.♘xd5! ♘xf1! 25.♖xf1 ♖f8!

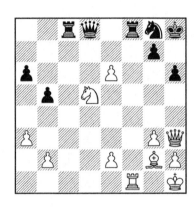

The critical point of this great game. Although white is the exchange down, his powerful knight in the center of the board ensures him equality. Kasparov believed that after 26.♗e4 white retained sufficient compensation for the exchange, but in making that move gave up chances of winning. The logical move 26.♖d1 led to an unclear position.

Smyslov knew that he couldn't save the match as a whole, and obviously immediately rejected an exchange. Hoping to score a win at last he goes all out. However, this sporting spirit leads to disaster.

26.♘f4? ♘e7 27.♕g4?

As is well known, mistakes don't happen alone. Smyslov decided to bring his queen into play and prevent the black queen from invading on d4! Evidently, he should have played 27.♗f3 and accepted that his chances of winning had passed him by.

27...g5!(13)   28.♕h3   ♖f6!

29.♘d3   ♖xf1+   30.♗xf1   ♔g7!
31.♕g4 ♕d5 32.e4 ♕d4! 33.h4 ♖f8
34.♗e2   ♕e3   35.♔g2   ♘g6   36.h5
♘e7 37.b4 ♔h7! 38.♔h2 ♖d8 39.e5
♖xd3 40.♗xd3 ♕xd3.
White resigned.

Game 27

The mood was desolate in the Kasparov camp before the start of game seven. The previous evening, Garry had failed to save his position as white after several painful hours in the post-adjournment session – a game which had at first looked so promising. Instead of being equal, the match score was now a depressing 0:2.

We began to torture ourselves in the morning over which opening to select. The challenger paced from room to room angry at his fate... and at his coaches. We seconds were all convinced that Karpov would "switch hands" that day and play 1.d4. All our doubts and vacillations circled around the question of whether to play the Tarrasch Defense.

We had prepared this opening specially for Kasparov's candidate matches. We attached a high value to the deployment of unexpected openings in those short matches, as there was insufficient time for the opponents to find the right antidotes. The well-known strategic risk inherent in this opening setup was more than compensated for by the lad's energetic and confident play, leading to astonishing results.

While preparing for the final, we faced tons of other chess problems, and any alternative to such a favorable opening was put together only reluctantly and kept getting postponed indefinitely. However, the start of the match, which had progressed quite unfortunately, led to unpleasant psychological consequences. Karpov grew in the eyes of his opponent with every passing day, and by game seven had reached the size of a cyclops. Moreover, the strategic risk of this opening, which Garry had previously failed to recognize, had grown to a similar size. The isolated d5 pawn, which only recently had led him to war, had suddenly turned into a problem child.

Now that the time had come to decide whether to continue with the Tarrasch, silence descended on our apartment HQ. Nobody wanted to become the target of "unconstructive" criticism by the annoyed challenger. As chief second, it fell to me to begin: "Garry, there is no point in rejecting the Tarrasch," I said, "as it has never let you down. It will give you confidence that you are clearly lacking. Zhenya (Vladimirov) and I have again checked the main lines and we guarantee that this opening is sound." "Who cares about your guarantees?" grumbled the lad, and, accepting the notebook that I proffered, withdrew, making it clear that joint prep for this game was now over.

A. KARPOV – G. KASPAROV

Moscow. World Chess Championship. Game 7. 05.10.1984
Queen's Gambit. [D34]

1.d4 d5 2.c4 e6 3.♘f3 c5(07)

Now that Garry had no intention of rejecting the planned opening, this time spent thinking, or, rather, hesitating, suggested that his soul was not at peace. Watching the events unfold from the ninth row of the stalls, I tried to appear confident and lively, yet inside me a feeling of alarm began to emerge.

4.cxd5 exd5 5.g3 ♘f6 6.♗g2 ♗e7 7.0-0 0-0 8.♘c3 ♘c6 9.♗g5 cxd4 10.♘xd4 h6 11.♗e3 ♖e8 12.♕b3 ♘a5 13.♕c2 ♗g4

We had guessed precisely the path that Karpov would follow after the first well-known opening moves. The powerful analytical team of grandmasters built around the world champion had easily found the most aggressive opening setup, under which black's pieces would lack harmony for some time.

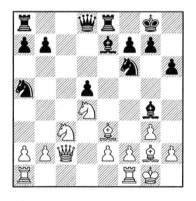

14.♘f5!

Karpov made this sharp and relatively new move like all his previous ones, without thought, demonstrating that he was very familiar with the position on the board. I wasn't sure exactly how Kasparov had prepared for the game psychologically, but I noticed at this point that Garry was downhearted at his opponent's confident moves. We had spent a fair bit of time analyzing this very position, and it would have been naive to think that the champion's seconds hadn't done the same.

14...♖c8(20)

Meanwhile, we thought that here there was no alternative move, as we assessed the complications after 14... ♗b4 15.♗d4! ♗xc3 16.♗xc3 ♖e2 17.♕d1! d4 18.♘xd4 ♖xf2! 19.♕a4! ♖xg2+ 20.♔xg2 as being better for white. Garry was convinced of this for some time, until another Tarrasch adherent, grandmaster Illescas, demonstrated in 1990 that white's advantage was illusory: 20...♕d5+! 21.♔g1 ♘c4 22.♕b5! a6! 23.♕xd5 ♘xd5. This happened at Linares when he was playing black against... Kasparov.

15.♘xe7+(21)

Garry had spent those twenty minutes refreshing his memory and checking the methods of defense against the line that was considered the most dangerous: 15.♗d4 ♗c5 (oh, how his lack of confidence was annoying!). Karpov had evidently found at the board something he didn't like in the main continuation and decided to opt for a secondary line, postponing the principled battle for another time. The voluntary exchange of his active knight was certainly no achievement for white, yet it produced an astounding effect. Garry didn't think for a moment that this move was unplanned. His photographic memory opened up in his head the page analyzing the wide-reaching consequences of 14...♖c8, on which a discussion of 15.♘xe7+ occupied a single sentence ending in the equals sign. Garry looked up and at me at this point, expressively. It was obvious that the lad was angered by the small amount of analysis created on this second-rate line and was now cursing himself for listening to his coaches about which opening to select. Our woes were deepened by the fact that his opponent visibly perked up and even seemed to be having fun while observing this theater of a single and somewhat inept actor. The doubts that had seized Karpov disappeared without trace.

Garry assessed quickly that black had a strong position yet refused to trust his own evaluation – "It wasn't for nothing that Karpov played that move" – and continued to check our short analysis time and time again, trying to find holes in it. He was angry at both himself and his seconds to the extent that only the most short-sighted of spectators could have missed it. The lad eventually captured the knight, though his alarm at Karpov's choice had not died down.

15...♖xe7(31!)

He could also have played 15...♕xe7, which could have led to sharp play after 16.♗xa7 b5! 17.♗d4 b4. However, such a turn of events would have required a calm state of mind, which Kasparov no longer possessed. Therefore, he selected a less committal but no less comprehensive plan.

16.♖ad1(31) ♕e8!(21)

A great example of how to defend actively. Black could have achieved equality by begging: 16...♖d7 17.h3 ♗e6, but the counterplay he plans against the pawn on e2 is more active and promises equal chances quickly.

17.h3(07)

The apparently solid continuation of the battle 17.♗d4 promises little after 17...♘e4! Karpov instead takes a risky strategic decision to capture a pawn, taking into account above all his opponent's troubled and unconfident state of mind. The immediate capture would have been dangerous: 17.♗xd5? ♗h3! 18.♗g2 ♗xg2 19.♔xg2 ♖xe3! 20.fxe3 ♘c4! So first he had to weaken his king's bunker, granting black new targets of attack.

17...♗h5! 18.♗xd5 ♗g6 19.♕c1 ♘xd5 20.♖xd5 ♘c4 21.♗d4(06)

White has to be vigilant. 21.♗f4 is met by the strong 21...♘b6! followed by 22...♘a4 or 22...♖xe2.

21...♖ec7!(31)

A great solution to a complicated problem. The tempting 21...b5 is countered by the reciprocal charge 22.b4!, creating an outpost on c5 that kills black's counterplay along the c-file. White also has a neat refutation to black's attempt to strengthen his attack with an exchange sac: 21...♖xe2? 22.♘xe2 ♕xe2 23.♖e1 ♕f3. The modest move 24.♖c5! destroys all of black's illusions, as 24...♖xc5 is met by the stunning 25.♖e8+ ♔h7 26.♖h8+!! ♔xh8 27.♕xh6! ♔g8 28.♕xg7#.

Grandmaster Averbakh considered it quite sufficient to continue 21...♖d7 as well, which is evidence that the players had equal chances at this point in time.

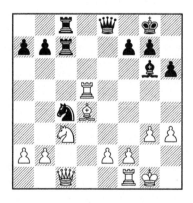

22.b3?!(21)

The culmination of a fierce battle. Despite his extra pawn, white does not have a comfortable position, as black's pieces are very active. White can still force a draw with 22.♘b5 ♖d7 23.♖xd7 ♕xd7 24.♘xa7 ♕xh3 25.♘xc8 ♗e4 26.f3 ♕xg3+ and so on. Another option was 22.♕f4, which after 22...f6! 23.b3! ♘b6 24.♗xb6 ♖xc3 25.♗xa7 ♕xe2 26.♖d2 ♕e6 leads to a highly complicated position that is hard to evaluate over the board.

Karpov wanted to ensure that his rook stuck in the center had good prospects. However, nothing is free of charge here. Moving the pawn deprives the white knight of protection, and Kasparov skillfully exploits this barely noticeable flaw in white's idea.

22...♘b6 23.♖e5 ♕d7 24.♕e3 f6! 25.♖c5 ♖xc5 26.♗xc5 ♕xh3

At last, Kasparov manages to restore material equality while retaining the activity of his remaining pieces. His chances of fighting for an advantage here cannot be considered worse, as the white king's bunker has a big hole in it, which black's queen is already contemplating thoughtfully. She needs just one piece to come to help her, but it's quite unclear how black can achieve this, as white controls the center of the board and thereby prevents his opponent from engaging in aggressive regrouping.

In the middle of the fourth hour of play a new phase of the maneuvering struggle begins, where success depends on correctly selecting new targets, concentration and maintaining a cool head. It's here that the challenger loses this latter attribute.

27.♖d1(08) h5?(07)

Oh, no! After Garry had wonderfully navigated a highly complex episode of the game and won back the sacrificed pawn, he calmed down and relaxed. This impulsive pawn thrust shows that he didn't yet have a clear action plan in the new situation. In fact, black had a rich set of choices for the first time. He could have gone for the quiet 27...♗f7 28.♗d6 ♕e6, the prophylactic 27...♔h7, or the sharp and logical 27...♗e8 28.♗xb6 ♗c6! 29.♘d5 ♖e8! 30.♕d3 ♖e5! 31.e4 (31.♘xf6+ ♔f7) 31...axb6, giving him excellent counterplay.

28.♖d4!(10)

Karpov's elegant reply nails the pawn to the h5 square, where it will not only require defense but will prevent its own rook from reaching the h-file and coming to support the queen.

28...♘d7?(05)

The general of the black pieces couldn't gather his thoughts and makes another pointless move, now switching to passive defense. He again missed an attempt to gain counterplay, with 28...♗e8! 29.♖h4 ♕f5 30.♗xb6 axb6 31.♘d5 ♔h7! 32.♘e7 ♕b1+ 33.♔h2 ♖c5!

29.♗d6 ♗f7 30.♘d5(03) ♗xd5 31.♖xd5

In the last five moves Karpov had more than grabbed the initiative, taking advantage of black's lack

of plan. Yet white didn't have a serious advantage here. Black had no weaknesses and it shouldn't be hard for him to regain equality.

Kasparov, however, realizing that the initiative had swung to his opponent, again became nervous. He only had ten minutes left to reach move forty, yet he fretfully fidgeted on the chair, and his eyes kept switching between the board and the clock face. He found it impossible to concentrate – he had spent too much energy and nerves on his internal battle in the game's first hours. His state of mind was no secret to his opponent here, who sat with the utmost concentration. Karpov wasn't going to let this chance slip away.

31...a6 32.♗f4 ♘f8 33.♕d3 ♕g4 34.f3 ♕g6 35.♔f2

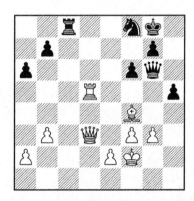

Black had now managed to make nearly half the remaining moves required to reach time control after getting into time trouble without worsening his position. Kasparov's two remaining minutes should have been enough to reach the adjournment and achieve an easy draw. All the more so, as the chain of saving moves 35...♛xd3 36.♜xd3 ♜c2 37.a4 g5 appeared in his mind in an instant.

Well, Garry can still not explain what outside force led him to make the second move in the line straight away. We saw him shake in horror when, after moving the rook to c2 but before letting go of it, he noticed that the white queen was still on the board. He desperately looked around for a more appropriate square for his piece, but, not finding one, he angrily pressed his clock.

35...♜c2??

The rest didn't require commentary.

36.♛e3! ♜c8 37.♛e7 b5?
38.♜d8 ♜xd8 39.♛xd8 ♛f7 40.♝d6
g5 41.♛a8 ♚g7 42.♛xa6

Black resigned.

The winner had demonstrated a tough character, immense self-belief, an ability to concentrate deeply at critical moments and total domination in a battle of nerves. Karpov's win in this game was no fluke.

Game 28

What's so great about this game, you may ask? Well, don't jump to conclusions. It is arguably the most important one that Kasparov every played. His third and last win in the marathon first match that lasted nearly half a year, but with a unique effect in the history of sport.

The game after this one was postponed for a week on various premises, and once it became clear that Karpov was unable to continue the match FIDE president Campomanes called it off!

G. KASPAROV – A. KARPOV
Moscow. World Chess Championship. Game 48. 08.02.1985
Petroff Defense. [C42]

1.e4 e5 2.♘f3 ♘f6 3.♘xe5 d6
4.♘f3 ♘xe4 5.d4 d5 6.♝d3 ♘c6
7.0-0 ♝e7 8.c4 ♘f6

Our new deployment of the "cross-fire" was highly effective at this critical point in the match. Karpov, who had now waited more than two months for his precious final victory, was forced in game 41 as white to apply against Garry what he considered his best way to fight for an advantage in this line. Yet he failed to win that game. And now, like a form of punishment, he had to either wait with the black pieces for Kasparov to improve on his, Karpov's, play in that unfortunate game, or else turn off the beaten track first and head knowingly into an inferior path. Karpov took the second option and soon regretted it.

9.♘c3 0-0

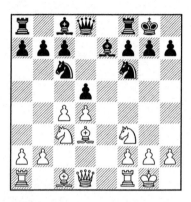

10.h3!

A useful prophylactic move that restricts the bishop's movements and condemns black to passive defense.

10...dxc4(28) 11.♗xc4 ♘a5 12.♗d3 ♗e6 13.♖e1(17) ♘c6(10)

Having chased white's bishop from the a2-g8 diagonal, the knight returns to the center. However, black still doesn't have decent counterplay, so he has a long wait for events to unfold, which only white can initiate. Realizing this, Kasparov acts in a markedly unhurried fashion.

14.a3(08) a6(10) 15.♗f4(17) ♕d7(15) 16.♘e5!(10)

Judging by Karpov's unusually long think over his next move, he underestimated this invasion that forces him to adapt to a new situation on the board and devise a new framework.

16...♘xe5(25)   17.dxe5(05) ♘d5 18.♘xd5 ♗xd5 19.♕c2 g6(13) 20.♖ad1

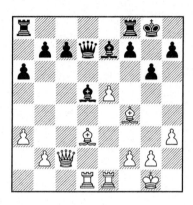

20...c6?(0)

Only 20...♕c6 would have allowed black to maintain the defense. Karpov pushed his pawn immediately. Evidently, tiredness had again afflicted him, in just the third hour of play, and to the extent that he couldn't even calculate a couple of moves ahead.

21.♗h6 ♖fd8 22.e6! fxe6

22...♕e8 is met by the unpleasant 23.♕c3 f6 24.f4! with a strong attack.

23.♗xg6 ♗f8 24.♗xf8 ♖xf8 25.♗e4 ♖f7 26.♖e3(18)

White's solid advantage is down to the weakness of the black pawns and the black king's lack of a safe bunker.

26...♖g7 27.♖dd3!

Anybody can move their rooks to an open file, but up until now Karpov had faced no equal at clearing ranks for rooks to work along them in order to raise their mobility and work-rate. Well, now Kasparov had attained this level of skill in the match. Here, his rooks worked to fantastic effect.

27...♖f8(15)   28.♖g3!   ♔h8 29.♕c3! ♖f7 30.♖de3!(07)

White's rooks are working miracles, combining threats to the king and to the e6 pawn. Having used up almost all his remaining time, Karpov decides to give up the pawn to get his king out of danger. He can be criticized for this, as the rook endgame promised few chances of survival. However, while in game two he managed to fight off Kasparov's attack with just five minutes left on the clock he was unable to repeat this feat after five months of exhausting battle.

30...♘g8(10)   31.♕e5   ♕c7 32.♖xg7+(08)   ♖xg7   33.♗xd5 ♕xe5 34.♗xe6+ ♕xe6 35.♖xe6

White is winning this endgame due to his huge pawn majority on the kingside and active rook.

35...♖d7   36.b4   ♔f7   37.♖e3 ♖d1+ 38.♔h2 ♖c1 39.g4 b5 40.f4 c5 41.bxc5 ♖xc5 42.♖d3!

It's useful to divert the king from the right hand side of the board to make it easier to queen a white pawn.

42...♔e7 43.♔g3 a5 44.♔f3 b4 45.axb4 axb4 46.♔e4 ♖b5 47.♖b3 ♖b8 48.♔d5 ♔f6 49.♔c5 ♖e8 50.♖xb4 ♖e3 51.h4 ♖h3 52.h5(23) ♖h4

Our analysis at the adjournment had stopped once we got to this position, considering it won and not needing further analysis. While Garry thought over his next move, grandmasters in the press-center, moving the pieces about, quickly found a simple path to victory: 53.g5+ ♔f5 54.h6 ♖h1 55.♔d6 ♖e1 56.♖b8! ♔xf4 57.g6! hxg6 58.h7 ♖h1 59.h8=♕ ♖xh8 60.♖xh8 g5 61.♔d5 g4 62.♔d4 ♔f3 63.♔d3! g3 64.♖f8+. However, Garry was afraid of miscalculating tempos – he had also been playing for five months without a break – and after forty minutes of thought chose a differing, slightly longer path, that he knew to be reliable from his days at the Botvinnik school.

As we know, the competition was cancelled on the premise that both players were tired. The chairman of the match's organizing committee, expressing the view of "highly-placed" spectators, told Garry that proof of his tiredness was... his messy conversion of a material advantage that evening!

53.f5(15) ♖h1 **54.♔d5** ♖d1+
55.♖d4 ♖e1 **56.♔d6** ♖e8

The game would have gone on for a few more moves had black played 56...♖g1 here, but in this case the winning plan is still easy to find: 57.♔d7 ♔f7 58.♔d8 ♖g2 59.h6 ♔f8 60.♔c7! ♔f7 61.♖d7+ ♔g8 62.♖g7+ ♔h8! 63.♖e7! ♔g8 64.♔d7! ♖xg4 65.♔e6 ♔f8 66.♖a7 ♖e4+ 67.♔f6 ♖e8 68.♖xh7 and so on.

57.♔d7 ♖g8 **58.h6(15)** ♔f7
59.♖c4 ♔f6 **60.♖e4** ♔f7 **61.♔d6**
♔f6 **62.♖e6+** ♔f7 **63.♖e7+** ♔f6
64.♖g7 ♖d8+ **65.♔c5**

The fight is over, all that's left is agony.

65...♖d5+

65...♖h8 meets a swift end: 66.♔d4 ♖d8+ 67.♔e4 ♖e8+ 68.♔f3 ♖h8 69.♔f4 ♖e8 70.g5#.

66.♔c4! ♖d4+

66...♖a5 is best met with 67.♔b3! ♖b5+ 68.♔c3 ♖c5+ 69.♔d3 ♖d5+ 70.♔e3 ♖e5+ 71.♔f3

67.♔c3!

This move proved to be the last in a match that had looked like it would go on forever. 67...♖f4 would be met by the now familiar maneuver 68.♔d3 ♖d4+ 69.♔e3 ♖e4+ 70.♔f3 ♖f4+ 71.♔g3! and curtains.

Black resigned.

Game 29

The two matches between the two great Ks held at the end of 1985 and 1986 stood out from their other matches due to the spectacular and powerful play of both sides. At least half the games of both those matches belong to the collection of all-time great games. They set benchmarks for grandmaster play and are wonderful text-book examples.

Kasparov considers game 16 of the 1985 match to have been his greatest work. He was facing a professional of the highest class who forced him to mobilize all of his strength and ability, while the sporting significance of their dual was particularly important. The special destiny of this game was highlighted by the interesting and instructive circumstances preceding it.

After Garry's win in game 11 of the match, we decided it was the perfect time to deploy one of his key opening novelties. The effect of playing this Kasparov specialty was stunning and basically changed the course of the match. Karpov had shown up to game twelve buzzing and ready for an uncompromising battle. He had no intention of ending the first half of the match with an equal score, realizing that the closing stages of the match would be tough for him. Garry's opening surprise immediately knocked the stuffing out of his opponent's aggressive mood.

Karpov quickly steered the game to a draw, postponing a principled battle until later.

In game 14 the champion then checked whether Garry was ready to repeat his novelty, and, discovering that he was, quickly switched to a reserve line. Karpov wasn't, though, inclined to waste his white games, and it was obvious to us that the enemy camp was engaged in intensive and, evidently, what they considered to be successful analysis to refute Kasparov's idea. Hence the main battle would come when the challenger once again played the black pieces, i.e. in game 16.

At last, the long-awaited evening was upon us. Judging by the confident gait with which Karpov appeared on stage, he was ready to crush his opponent: the refutation to the "Kasparov Gambit" had been found.

I have a good idea of which grandmasters were mobilized to refute the gambit, and I know who was in charge of the project. About ten days before that game, the head of the Karpov team let slip in a moment of anger that grandmaster Geller, the best opening expert on the Karpov team, had been ordered to focus on countering the Sicilian (game 12 was held on 3 October and game 16 on 15 October). This information implied that Geller, a classical chess player, needed to find and prove to Karpov the correct line in which white returned the pawn but remained slightly better until the end of the game. At the same time, we came to the conclusion that in such a short time Karpov's seconds would find it hard to correctly assess another, truly gambit idea, in which black developed an initiative without worrying about winning the material back. This was the idea that we polished in advance of the key fight.

The possible situations arising after the opening moves were so complicated that navigating them without home preparation was impossible. Having spent dozens of hours analyzing them, we were only able to establish what the main technical ploys would be, and we figured out that the combinations of pieces worked particularly effectively in them. During the game, Garry skillfully and effectively made use of the fruits of our analysis, creating a fine work of art. He managed to mask so wonderfully well the sudden turning point leading from an unclear position to disaster for Karpov, that the latter only realized where he was heading when it was too late to do anything about it.

We watched with awe and pity as the world champion failed to find a useful move after just 24 moves even though he was a good pawn up with a solid pawn structure. His pieces were deprived of coordination and were frozen to the spot. The game was like a flight to the stars for Garry but a nightmare for his opponent.

A. KARPOV – G. KASPAROV

Moscow. World Chess Championship. Game 16. 15.10.1985
Sicilian Defense. [B44]

1.e4 c5 2.♘f3 e6 3.d4 cxd4 4.♘xd4 ♘c6 5.♘b5 d6 6.c4 ♘f6 7.♘1c3 a6 8.♘a3

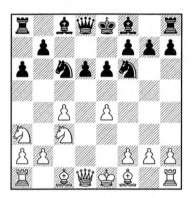

This position had first arisen between the players in game 3 of the abandoned 1984 match. After the well-known moves 8...♗e7 9.♗e2 0-0 10.0-0 b6 11.♗e3 ♗b7 12.♕b3 Garry went for a questionable exchange sac with 12...♘a5, which he had invented at home and jealously guarded from his coaches. Karpov's reply 13.♕xb6 had shocked him like a bucket of ice-cold water and the game quickly turned pear shaped. That opening disaster had severely wounded our charge's pride, and he started to think up ideas that would give black principally new opportunities. Finally, in summer 1985 on a flight to Baku, a passenger suddenly turned to his neighbor and joyfully told her: "Mum, I've come up with a brilliant idea!"

This time, work on adding meat to the new opening super-bomb was more painstaking, and his seconds' attempts to disprove some of the author's lines were no longer treated as an attempt to slander him.

The justification of this daring central pawn sacrifice was in the time white spent on transferring the knight from g1 to the other edge of the board. However, there was huge risk in the sacrifice: success depended on concrete calculation, and any mistake in the lines we analyzed could have quickly led to disaster.

8...d5!? 9.cxd5 exd5 10.exd5 ♘b4 11.♗e2

The first time that he came across the novelty, in game 12, Karpov played 11.♗c4, but after 11...♗g4! he chose not to hold on to the pawn in positions such as that after 12.f3 ♗f5 13.0-0 ♗c5+ 14.♔h1 0-0 15.♗g5 b5. Instead he went for the solid continuation 12.♗e2 ♗xe2 13.♕xe2+ ♕e7 14.♗e3, which left him no opening advantage.

11...♗c5(0)

When we first began our analysis, we intended to continue with the modest bishop development 11...♗e7, which led after 12.0-0 ♘bxd5 13.♘xd5 ♘xd5 14.♗f3 ♗e6 15.♘c2 (and then ♘d4) to stale positions in which white had a tiny but stable advantage. We only managed to

improve on black's moves here (12...
♞fxd5! 13.♞xd5 ♛xd5) leading to
a firm "=" in our assessment about a
year later. But by then Karpov has
stopped playing 1.e4 against Garry.

Kasparov would have hardly
played 8...d5 in this match had he
not found another idea that turned
play into a pure gambit. Now there's
no point complaining that among
our veritably strong analytical
brigade, so enchanted by the beauty
of the lines we had uncovered, there
was no skeptic who stood up and
exclaimed: "Guys, I don't like this
beauty! Let's try and find a hole in
our analysis."

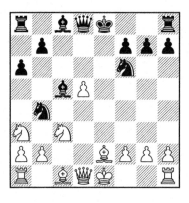

12.0-0?(05!)
We had no doubt that the
Karpov team wouldn't view the
gambit path as the main line. Garry,
though, developed his bishop to c5
confidently and without thought,
which left Karpov downhearted.
He now realized that this was a
particularly important line, that his
team's extensive analysis was in the
wrong line, and that he would now

have to carry out the lion's share of
the work as his clock ticked, while
his opponent would continue to
pull new surprises from his memory.
In such unexpected and tricky
situations Karpov would always
make solid moves, strengthening his
position. Having seen in game 12 the
dangers that his king could face if it
remained in the center, he decided
to transfer him to his bunker before
starting to think about serious plans.

In this match, the champion's
opening prep was clearly inferior to
ours, and, sensing this, he sometimes
overestimated the quality of
Kasparov's novelties. Actually, the
Kasparov Gambit was unsound. As
soon as Garry placed his bishop on
c5, I immediately saw a refutation,
just like five years earlier in Minsk:
12.♝e3 ♝xe3 13.♛a4+!! We had
missed this cunning check and
its continuation 14.♛xb4! Later,
Kasparov tried to prove that after
13...♝d7 14.♛xb4 ♛b6 15.♛xb6
♝xb6 black had compensation, but
only sufficient for a draw. Towards
the end of the match, Ukrainian
master A. Kostyuchenko published
a brief analysis in a local newspaper
beginning with the moves 12.♝e3
♝xe3 13.♛a4+! By then, though,
Garry had switched to another, more
reliable but just as exciting system in
the Sicilian Defense.

12...0-0 13.♝f3(13)
Karpov, seeking to justify his
mistake, now says that he could
have counted on an advantage had

he here played 13.♗g5 ♗f5 14.♘c4 ♖e8 15.a3 ♘c2 16.♖c1 ♘d4 17.♗d3. However, that line contains errors, and the first improvement for black – 15...♘bxd5 16.♘xd5 ♕xd5 17.♗xf6 ♕xd1 18.♖fxd1 gxf6 – ensures him equal chances. The then champion had failed to notice the seriousness of his opponent's counterplay, and his decision to protect his gains with a natural move seemed perfectly logical and consistent with his playing style in such situations.

13...♗f5 14.♗g5 ♖e8!(17)

Black has achieved a lot: he has chased the white knights out of play while his own pieces are nicely placed. However, no serious danger to white can be foreseen here even in the distant future. To correctly assess such a complex position you need to sense its dynamics, which is impossible without insights into its secrets. Karpov only realized that he needed to find equality rather than an advantage when it was too late.

15.♕d2(10)

Again, that strategy of solid moves that don't ruin anything. Yet now we should actually place a "?!" sign against this move and advise white to return the pawn with 15.♘c4!? ♗d3 16.a3! ♗xc4! 17.axb4 ♗xb4!, leaving him with active pieces and equal chances in a complicated situation. However, even the grandmasters sitting in the press-center and calmly analyzing

the position, moving the pieces around, didn't seriously consider such continuations. You don't give back an extra pawn so easily...

15...b5!

Each black move deprived his opponent of another option somewhere or other and gradually wrapped the white pieces in a tight web. A quiet attack was progressing, unnoticed...

16.♖ad1?!(15)

Who would criticize this move, bringing the rook into play? Yet just a few moves later it will be clear that it's as useless here as it was on a1. The point at which it's hard to give white any decent advice is fast approaching. Kasparov believed that white had to exchange queens here: 16.♕f4 ♗g6 17.♗xf6 ♕xf6 18.♕xf6 gxf6. However, this would have been unlikely to save white from problems, for example: 19.♖ad1 ♘d3 20.d6 ♖ad8 21.d7 ♖e5 22.♖d2 ♘xb2 23.♘axb5 ♘c4 and so on.

16...♘d3!(09)

Now white has lost control over f4.

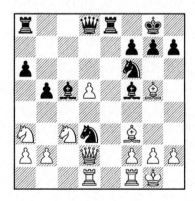

It's only now that Kasparov's grand idea is becoming clear. This fierce black knight has paralyzed the white army. Concrete threats have now appeared, foretelling the approaching storm.

17.♘ab1?(08)

It's now evident that white is worried about black's growing activity. But he continues to underestimate the degree of danger and hence doesn't wish to give up the pawn. Karpov hopes to chase away this terrible knight by retreating his bishop to e2 and after that to restore the coordination of white's pieces, which has been catastrophically disturbed.

The only way to salvation was to give up the pawn with 17.d6, in reply to which Kasparov planned an exchange sac: 17...♕xd6 18.♗xa8 ♖xa8, in return retaining prospects of launching a fierce attack.

17...h6(04)   18.♗h4   b4!(05) 19.♘a4(11)   ♗d6(06)   20.♗g3(05) ♖c8(26) 21.b3(05)

The black pieces have taken up great positions. However, the board gives the impression that the balance of potential attack and defense has been retained, and one more attacking unit is needed by black, capable of tilting the balance. So where is it, this attacking unit? The black queen, kept on its starting square, is ready to jump into the hottest point of battle, but not in the role of a scout! Meanwhile, a white knight threatens to destroy the

attacking units by transferring to b2. Black has to hurry...

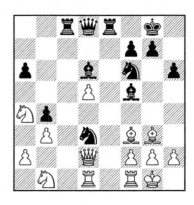

21...g5!!(14)

A brilliant, stunning solution. The modest pawn jumps into the fray, launching the key battle. White cannot try 22.♗e2 ♘e4! or 22.♘b2 ♘xb2 23.♕xb2 g4 24.♗e2 ♖c2 with a win.

22.♗xd6?!(16)

Bringing the g7 pawn into the attack was analyzed by Garry before the game, but before playing it he had to assess the consequences of the counter-strike 22.h4. He believed that here too he had a strong initiative. After figuring out that the consequences of 22...g4 23.♗e2 ♘e4 24.♕xh6! ♗f8 25.♕h5 ♘xg3 26.fxg3 ♗g6 27.♕xg4 ♖e4 28.♕f3 ♘e5 29.♕f2 ♗h6! 30.♘d2! ♗e3 31.♘xe4 were unclear, he intended to choose between 22...♘e4 23.♗xe4 ♗xe4 24.hxg5 ♗xg3 25.fxg3 ♕xd5 26.gxh6 ♖c6! with a new attacking wave, and 22...♘f4 23.hxg5 hxg5.

Karpov chooses a simple way to defend f4, and it looks like a good move. However, it creates new weaknesses in his own camp.

22...♕xd6   23.g3   ♘d7(11) 24.♗g2(04)

White just can't smoke out the knight from d3. After 24.♘b2 ♕f6! 25.♘xd3 ♗xd3 26.♕xd3 ♘e5!, his queen suddenly dies in the middle of the board.

24...♕f6!(04)

Now that b2 is fully under control, black's wide-scale attack develops without resistance. The battle is effectively over. What we now see, like during a Soviet-era military parade, is a "show of strength and power".

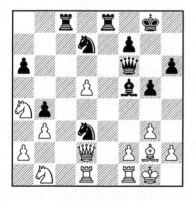

25.a3 a5 26.axb4 axb4 27.♕a2 ♗g6!(04)

Black acts consistently and firmly – white cannot play 28.♘d2 ♖e2 29.♗f3 due to 29...♕xf3! 30.♘xf3 ♖xa2. In desperation, Karpov finally decides to return the pawn, but black is already close to his targeted trophy.

28.d6(12) g4!(11)

Despite lots of pieces remaining on the board white can barely make a move!

29.♕d2   (08)   ♔g7   30.f3(04) ♕xd6   31.fxg4   ♕d4+   32.♔h1 ♘f6(04) 33.♖f4(05) ♘e4!(0)

An elegant finale to finish – and decorate – the game.

34.♕xd3(03)

Karpov barely had time left to think, but it wouldn't have made any difference by now...

34...♘f2+   35.♖xf2   ♗xd3 36.♖fd2   ♕e3!   37.♖xd3   ♖c1!! 38.♘b2   ♕f2!   39.♘d2   ♖xd1+ 40.♘xd1 ♖e1+

White resigned. Mate on f1 is inevitable.

Game 30

So the fate of the chess crown came to depend on the final, 24th game. In order to become world champion, Garry needed just a draw. But he dived into battle. One thought was firmly and unexpectedly embedded in his mind that his seconds had constantly instilled in him during walks for the past week: the world would recognize him as the undisputed champion were he to win in a true, manly fight, and demonstrate the play of a "king" in the decisive game. He had dictated the course of the second half of the match, and we had hoped that his 23rd game with white would decide the outcome. However, the fisher's hand shook again at the critical moment and the carp once again freed itself from the hook. So we reached game 24 and just had to make sure that the future king didn't burn out and retained his calm and confidence until it began.

With his first move Karpov showed that we had once again correctly anticipated the battle scene. In his search to create an early crisis the tired champion headed straight where we were waiting for him...

A. KARPOV – G. KASPAROV
Moscow. World Chess Championship. Game 24. 09.11.1985
Sicilian Defense. [B85]

1.e4 c5 2.♘f3 d6 3.d4 cxd4 4.♘xd4 ♘f6 5.♘c3 a6 6.♗e2 e6 7.0-0 ♗e7 8.f4 0-0 9.♔h1 ♕c7 10.a4 ♘c6 11.♗e3 ♖e8 12.♗f3 ♖b8 13.♕d2 ♗d7 14.♘b3 b6

15.g4!?

We had no doubt that Karpov would head for this line in his attempt to win. We had already used up all our brutal novelties and it was impossible to squeeze a brand new opening setup in the head of the tired challenger at the finishing line after such a long match. All we could do was sharpen one of the setups applied earlier. We had already

reached this position in game 18, but that time Karpov played the insipid 15.♗f2 ♗c8 16.♗g3 ♘d7 17.♖ae1 and quickly lost the initiative. In his final attempt to win he needed a "fat" target on a narrow portion of the board so that the outcome would be effectively determined in the first hours of battle. He might not have enough energy left for a longer fight.

15...♗c8 16.g5 ♘d7

About ten days before this game, a sports newspaper printed a fresh game between A. Sokolov and Z. Ribli played in France. After 17.♗g2 ♘a5 18.♕f2 ♗f8 19.♖ad1 ♘c4 20.♗c1 white developed a strong attack and won. We immediately placed this game under a powerful analytical microscope and found two holes. The first was that black could have improved his piece setup with 18...♘c4!, which meant he easily solved his opening problems. However, the second, more cunning trick was that white could significantly improve on his play one move earlier thanks to an imperceptible change of move order. We expected Karpov to find it.

A week of intense analysis enabled us to learn pretty well the nuances of the opening positions that arose and even some middlegames. Our work certainly didn't turn the challenger's play dry – the game is striking for its tension and complexity. But in both the opening and middlegame Garry felt much more confident than his opponent. We achieved that by constantly checking the variations of the opening that we had tried so hard to polish. The sporting significance of the upcoming game fully justified spending so much time on it.

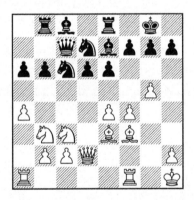

17.♕f2! ♗f8!(18)

White is the first to reveal his aces, but Garry remains vigilant and, avoiding the path with a trap 17...♘a5 18.♖ad1! ♘c4 19.♗c1, he sets up his pieces in a more promising fashion.

18.♗g2 ♗b7!

After this move Karpov clearly realized that his plan of a wide-scale fight was no surprise to his opponent. Garry rejected the defensive setup applied by Ribli without hesitation and placed his bishop on the long diagonal, demonstrating that he wasn't afraid of the f4-pawn advancing further.

19.♖ad1 g6!(04)

The striking cold-bloodedness with which black carried out his maneuvers faced with the menacing white armada firmly shook Karpov's confidence, which was so important for him to take critical decisions. For the first time in the game he took a long think, thereby signaling that his home prep had now ended.

20.♗c1(44)

Objectively this was a very strong move. The rook on d1 wants to take the journey d1-d3-h3. Other plans for white 20.♕h4 ♗g7 21.♖f3 ♘b4 22.♖h3 ♘f8 or 20.♘e2 ♗g7 21.c3 ♘a5 22.♗xb6 ♘xb6 23.♘xa5 ♗a8 promised less.

20...♖bc8?!(19)

Garry has a weakness for this maneuver and for some reason tries to carry it out early. Black has no problems here. Sitting in the hall, I considered 20...♘c5! 21.♘xc5 bxc5 22.♖d3 ♘d4 23.♖h3 ♕e7! 24.♕h4 h5! to be the best continuation. 20...♘b4 also seemed perfectly playable, as the obvious 21.♖d4 is met by the counterstrike 21...d5 22.e5 ♗c5 and then 23.♘xc5 bxc5 24.♖dd1 ♘c6! followed by transferring the knight to f5. Later analysis proved that I was right.

21.♖d3(04) ♘b4(16) 22.♖h3 ♗g7

Kasparov spent just two minutes thinking on his last move. This suggests he remained in the state of slight euphoria typical of him when he correctly guessed the opening and, even more so, when the game was going to the plan prepared at home.

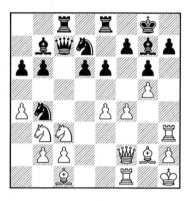

The critical point of the battle is now. White has managed to concentrate significant forces on the kingside, and now he needs to select the most appropriate moment to launch an attack.

23.♗e3(03)?

It was inexcusable to think just three minutes over such a fateful decision, that would impact the rest of the champion's life. Karpov played in his style – continuing to strengthen his pieces unhurriedly – and in doing so missed his sole chance to begin a dangerous attack.

His plan here is to exchange dark-colored bishops with 24.♗d4, and those three minutes were only sufficient for him to calculate the consequences of the pawn sac with 23...♗xc3? 24.bxc3 ♕xc3 25.♗d4

♕xc2 26.♖xh7! and plan further regrouping of his pieces.

Instead, he should have gone for the pawn break 23.f5! Kasparov had underestimated this possibility at the board, while Karpov, it seems, hadn't considered it at all. A couple of weeks later, he began to say with increasing audibility and frequency that Kasparov didn't deserve to win the match, as white could have won the final game.

Well, did the direct and definitely most energetic move 23.f5! force a win? Detailed analysis would have taken up several pages, so here I provide only the main line: 23...exf5 24.exf5 ♗xg2+! (24...♘e5? 25.♕h4 ♕c4 26.♖f4!) 25.♔xg2 ♕b7+ 26.♔g1 ♖c4! 27.fxg6 ♖g4+! 28.♖g3 ♖xg3+ 29.hxg3! (29.♕xg3? hxg6 30.♕f4 ♘e5! 31.♕xb4 ♘f3+) 29...♘e5 30.gxh7+! ♔h8! 31.♕f5 (31. ♘d4 ♘ed3! 32.cxd3 ♘xd3) 31... ♘xc2! 32.♕xc2 ♘f3+ 33.♖xf3 ♕xf3 34.♕f2 ♕d3. Was it really possible to give a definitive assessment of this position? All the more so, in white's favor? In order to head for such complications in a duel against a top player you need to believe in your ability and have strong nerves. At that moment in time, Karpov lacked both attributes, and neither did he think about launching such direct play.

23...♖e7!!(28)

Garry is proud of the regrouping of his major pieces that he executed that evening, and which hadn't even occurred to the grandmasters working in the press-center. The rook defends f7, meaning that the active continuations 24.f5 exf5 25.exf5 ♗xg2+ 26.♕xg2 (26.♔xg2 ♗xc3! 27.bxc3 ♕xc3 28.♕h4 h5!) 26...gxf5 and 24.♗d4 e5! 25.fxe5 dxe5 no longer have any effect. Nor are any new targets for attack evident. After a long think white makes a neutral move. He is playing a waiting game for now...

24.♔g1(29) ♖ce8(14)

The essence of Garry's great idea. Black's invention – doubling rooks on the smallest possible section of a closed file(!) – appears to be totally absurd. However, in fact he is preparing a cunningly camouflaged counterattack.

25.♖d1

White bids farewell to his plan of aggression on the kingside and plans to create play in the center, although black has no weaknesses there. This is basically an admission that his plan has gone wrong, but he has to pay for his mistakes. The failure of his attacking strategy also signals a loss of time enabling black to begin a counterattack.

25...f5!(08) 26.gxf6(04) ♘xf6!

A brave decision. Black sacrifices a pawn to further activate his forces. This came as an unpleasant event for Karpov: he now realized that his opponent had found his game at the worst moment for the defending champion. The final hour of a tense battle was now approaching – the time when figuring out Kasparov's

tricks became particularly difficult and perilous.

27.♖g3?!(07)

This rook retreat was a sign of approaching tiredness interfering with white's ability to calculate variations. Karpov has stopped trusting his own calculations and isn't brave enough to take the pawn. After that he still insisted that he had more than one opportunity to win the game. Let's see if that's true. If 27.♗xb6 black has a choice between 27...♘g4 28.♗xc7 ♘xf2 29.♗xd6! ♘xd1 30.♗xe7 ♖xe7 31.♘xd1 ♘xc2 32.e5 ♗xg2 33.♔xg2 g5! 34.♖c3 ♘b4 35.♖c8+ ♔f7 36.fxg5 ♗xe5 and 27...♕b8!, which is what Garry had planned. In that case, the complications 28.a5! e5! 29.f5 gxf5 30.exf5 ♗xg2 (or 30...♔h8!) 31.♕xg2 d5! 32.♗c5 ♖d7 33.♖h4 d4 were not easy to assess.

27...♖f7!(04)

A new surprise. It transpires that black doesn't intend to defend the pawn on d6, but is regrouping his forces to attack the pawn on f4.

Karpov has no choice other than to capture the pawn, albeit tardily, so that he at least knows in the approaching time trouble what his plan is.

28.♗xb6 ♕b8 29.♗e3(09) ♘h5 30.♖g4

White has no choice. 30.♖f3 is met by the strong 30...♗xc3 31.bxc3 ♘a2!

30...♘f6(04)

This ploy is fully justified in the final game. Black's prospects are no worse in the forthcoming battle, but he has no advantage so far and the players are engaged in a typical battle of nerves, to see who will flinch first. White cannot obviously repeat moves, and in rejecting a draw he is forced to place his rook on a clumsy square and grant his opponent new opportunities.

31.♖h4 g5!(04)

Black's counterattack is gaining strength. Moreover, he is progressing it with such inventiveness and skill that he gives the impression that it is he and not white who has to win.

32.fxg5 ♘g4!

Garry again makes a most unpleasant move. Now the standoff is over, and black starts to dictate the shape of the game.

33.♕d2(12) ♘xe3 34.♕xe3 ♘xc2 35.♕b6

White mustn't leave the g1-a7 diagonal.

35...♗a8!(03)

It's very hard to react decently to such an unexpected move in deep time trouble (Karpov had just two minutes remaining). Now his queenside – which had up to now seemed the most peaceful part of the board – is on fire.

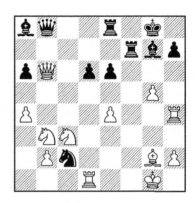

36.♖xd6?

With his flag falling Karpov makes a natural, yet losing move. However, the only defense that would have retained equal chances on the board could be found either in the quiet of a study room in home analysis, or else with super-sharp intuition over the board. The only way to prevent black from gaining a strong initiative and hence to save the game was 36.♕xb8 ♖xb8 37.♗h3!! A complex game would have ensued from both 37...♖xb3 38.♗xe6 ♗d4+! 39.♔h1 ♖xb2 40.♖f1 ♗xc3 41.♖xf7 ♘d4 42.♖a7+ ♘xe6 43.♖xa8+ ♘f8 44.♖xa6 ♗e5 and 37...♖e7 38.♖xd6 ♖xb3 39.♖d8+ ♔f7 40.♖xa8 ♖xb2.

36...♖b7!!

Who would have thought that the bishop made way for the rook?

37.♕xa6 ♖xb3

A strong move, but black could have wrapped up the game earlier with 37...♘b4! 38.♕a5 ♕xd6 39.e5 ♕d3! 40.♗xb7 ♕e3+ and so on.

38.♖xe6 ♖xb2 39.♕c4 ♔h8 40.e5?

White's last move to time control, with just seconds left, ends the game straight away. Karpov could have put up resistance with 40.g6 h6 41.♖xe8+ ♕xe8 42.♘d1 ♘a3 43.♕f7 ♕xf7 44.gxf7 ♖b1 45.♗f3 ♘c4 46.♖f4, but then black would have won upon the resumption.[4]

40...♕a7+ 41.♔h1 ♗xg2+ 42.♔xg2 ♘d4+!

Karpov loses his rook. **White resigned**.

What a fierce battle! The twelfth world champion extended his hand and admitted defeat, therefore becoming the first person to congratulate his opponent for winning the match. The deafening roar that broke out in the Concert Hall that very second definitively convinced Garry that these events weren't a wonderful dream, but were really happening. He raised his hands in victory like a football goal-scorer. The thirteenth world champion's joy was boundless and spontaneous. It was evident to everybody that the new chess king was just 22 years old.

Game 31

This was a full-scale battle that you could name Borodino or Waterloo, such was the tension and relentless striving to win that it contained. Although this dramatic match saw many tense games, this game stood out due to its truly tragic finale, which nevertheless you could not call accidental or unfair.

Attempting to take away the initiative from the hands of his inventive opponent, Karpov just for a second turned off the voice of his always practical common sense. Once he realized that something was wrong on the board it was too late... Now focused, Karpov sought a saving move but failed to find one – there simply wasn't one by then. The minute hand on his clock was already touching the red flag and slowly sliding towards the fateful edge. The general of the black army wasn't looking at the clock. At that moment time

---

[4] Kasparov demonstrates updated analysis in his book *Garry Kasparov on Garry Kasparov: Part II* where white can draw by perpetual check in the line given by Nikitin after playing 43.♖xh6+ (publisher's note)

ceased to exist for him – he was losing a game in which he had invested such great effort!

The Chief Arbiter brought him back down to Earth: "You've lost on time, Mr. Karpov." He had failed to make ten whole moves to time control! I don't recall Karpov having lost on time before, let alone missing so many moves...

G. KASPAROV – A. KARPOV

London. World Championship Return Match. Game 8. 15.08.1986
Queen's Gambit. [D35]

1.d4 d5 2.c4 e6 3.♘c3 ♗e7 4.cxd5(05) exd5 5.♗f4 ♘f6(10) 6.e3 0-0 7.♗d3(07) c5!

White has prevented black from developing the c8 bishop to an active square, but in doing so he has weakened control over d4. Karpov immediately exploits this almost imperceptible defect in his opponent's opening strategy and begins active play in the center.

8.♘f3(13) ♘c6 9.0-0 ♗g4(11) 10.dxc5 ♗xc5 11.h3!(16)

Realizing that he cannot retain control over d4, Garry decides to make do with the two bishops. In that case, the opening of the center after the inevitable d5-d4 will pose black new problems.

11...♗xf3(08)

He had no choice. The retreat 11...♗e6 is too passive, while 11...♗h5 leads to the loss of his central pawn after 12.g4! ♗g6 13.♗xg6 hxg6 14.g5! d4 15.gxf6 dxc3 16.fxg7.

12.♕xf3 d4 13.♘e4!

The attempt to win the queenside pawn with 13.exd4? ♘xd4! 14.♕xb7 would contradict the

logic of the unfolding events, and, as a consequence, would lead to exchanges unfavorable for white: 14...♘e6! 15.♖ad1 ♘xf4 16.♗xh7+ ♔xh7 17.♖xd8 ♖axd8.

13...♗e7!(23)

The natural 13...♘xe4 14.♗xe4 dxe3 would lead to complications after 15.♕h5 exf2+ 16.♔h1 f5 17.♗xf5 g6 18.♗xg6 hxg6 19.♕xg6+ ♔h8 20.♖ad1! that Garry evaluated to his advantage, for example: 20...♗d4 21.♕h5+ ♔g7 22.♕g4+ ♔h8 23.♗e3! ♗xe3 24.♖xd8 ♖axd8 25.♕h4+! ♔g7 26.♕g3+ and so on. Karpov selects the most rational and safest means of defense.

14.♖ad1!(22)

White has gradually strengthened his position in the center and the kingside, as the inevitable exchange of the e3 pawn will allow his f1 rook to enter the game directly.

14...♕a5!(30)

14...♕b6 looked more natural. However, in that case white would grab the initiative with 15.♗d6! ♘d5! (but not 15...♗xd6? 16.♘xf6+ gxf6 17.♕g4+ ♔h8 18.♕f5) 16.♕f5 ♗xd6 17.♘xd6 ♘f6 18.♘c4 ♕c7 19.e4. By developing his queen to the fifth rank, Karpov stamps out that idea. But why did he spend so long thinking about it?

15.♘g3!(17)

A logical and, evidently, the best decision. White avoids exchanges after 15.♗g5 ♘xe4! 16.♕xe4 g6! 17.♗xe7 ♖fe8 18.b4! ♕c7! and strengthens his attacking potential on the kingside.

15...dxe3 16.fxe3! ♕xa2!

So that's the operation that Karpov had planned prior to making his 14th move. Daring, precise calculation and belief in his ability were all contained in this far from reckless move. Black avoids weakening his king's pawn protection and strengthens his defense, relocating his queen via an unusual but "tasty" route. Note that the primitive 16...g6 would not have prevented white's knight from invading: 17.♗h6 ♖fe8 18.♘f5!

17.♘f5! ♕e6!(05)

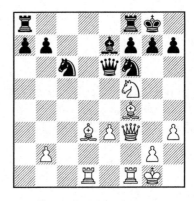

The concentration of the white pieces on the kingside looks dangerous, but black's fortress appears to have no weaknesses and he has enough defenders. For some time attack and defense prove to be each other's equals.

18.♗h6!(17)

He could have won back the pawn with 18.♘xe7+ ♘xe7 (18...♕xe7 19.♗d6!) 19.♕xb7 and after 19...♘g6 20.♗xg6 hxg6 21.♖d6 ♕c8 22.♕f3 ♕c4 23.♗e5 he could have mounted an attack at little risk. However, Kasparov didn't want to reduce the fighting tension. He is looking to kick up a storm.

18...♘e8 19.♕h5!(06) g6!(05)

The ex-champion defends superbly. He's willing to give up a rook for the dangerous bishop and then build a fortress with an outpost on e5.

20.♕g4(05) ♘e5!(07) 21.♕g3 (11)

Winning the exchange with 21.♘xe7+ ♕xe7 22.♗xf8 ♔xf8 23.♕f4 was perhaps objectively stronger, but then black would have had a clear defensive plan and a solid position. White continues to try and maintain the tension and unclear situation, given that Karpov had started to spend a long time thinking over his moves.

21...♗f6!(17) 22.♗b5(10)

An unexpected choice sharply raising the already high battle tension. White does everything possible to retain the escaping initiative, considering it his main trump card in the unfolding fight. Black, on the contrary, having eaten an extra pawn, tries to defuse the situation.

22...♘g7!(05) 23.♗xg7 ♗xg7 24.♖d6 ♕b3! 25.♘xg7 ♕xb5

So far black has defended successfully, retaining the extra pawn and strong defense around his king. However, his series of excellent defensive moves had engendered in Karpov a belief that fortune was on his side. From then on, despite his serious time shortage, he begins to ignore continuations that would have forced a draw.

26.♘f5 ♖ad8

It was simplest of all to force a draw with 26...f6! 27.♘h6+ ♔g7 28.♘f5+ ♔g8.

27.♖f6!(08)

Now the players are testing each other's character. White doesn't want to be the initiator of peace either: 27.♖xd8 ♖xd8 28.♕g5! ♖d7 29.♘h6+ ♔g7 30.♘f5+ and so on.

27...♖d2?!

It seems that Karpov got carried away with this game of nerves and

lost his objectivity. A perfectly safe continuation would have been 27...♔h8! 28.♘d4 ♕c5 29.♘e6! fxe6 with full equality. Black attempts to frighten his opponent, but in essence he only wastes time.

28.♕g5 ♕xb2?

In time trouble it's hard to sense the situation has changed and sharply reshape your playing strategy. A draw, while tougher to find, was still available: 28...♔h8! 29.♕h6 ♖g8 30.♘e7 ♕xb2 31.♕g5 ♖g7!!, for example: 32.♖e6! ♘d7! 33.♘xg6+! fxg6! 34.♖e8+ ♖g8 35.♖xg8+ ♔xg8 36.♕d8+ and so on.

I think that at this point Karpov had still not noticed that white could create serious threats. Had he done so, he would surely have found a reliable defense.

29.♔h1!

For a player in time trouble, such quiet and mysterious moves that don't mess anything up are particularly unpleasant. In a very sharp position, white finds time for prophylaxis, freeing up his queen from the need to carry out defensive functions. At the same time, he hasn't lost any of his attacking tempo, as it unexpectedly becomes clear that black's counterplay on the 2nd rank is illusory, hence his last two active moves have just wasted time.

It was probably now that Karpov realized he was in big trouble.

29...♔h8?!

The danger facing black is evident in the line 29...a5 30.♘e7+

♔h8 31.♕h6 ♖dd8! 32.♖6f5! ♕e2 33.♔g1! Nor can he save the day with 29...♖d7 30.♘h6+ ♔g7 31.♖6f4! f6 32.♖xf6 ♘f7 33.♕f4! ♕b3 34.♔h2! a5 35.e4 ♕c4 36.♘g4.

30.♘d4 ♖xd4 31.♕xe5

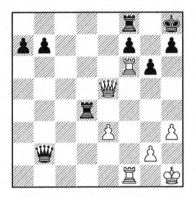

White's strategy has fully triumphed. The pieces disappear from the board one by one, but black's position only worsens. Karpov moved his rook to d2, but his flag fell before he had time to press his clock. **Black lost on time**.

The move 31...♖d2 was the only sensible continuation, but white would still transpose to a winning queen ending: 32.♕e7 ♖dd8 33.♖xf7 ♖xf7 34.♖xf7! ♔g8! 35.e4! ♕c1+ 36.♔h2 ♕h6! 37.e5! ♖f8 38.e6! g5 39.♖xf8+ ♕xf8 40.♕xg5+ ♔h8 (40...♕g7 41.♕d8+ ♕f8 42.e7!) 41.e7 ♕e8 42.h4! h5 43.g4! hxg4 44.h5 ♔h7 45.♕g6+.

A great battle with a tragic finale! The playing hall had long emptied, but the great challenger continued to sit in his rest room behind the stage, trying to calm down and get over the horror story he had just experienced. It was another two hours before the car took him away.

P.S. In spring 1993 at the grandmaster tournament in Linares Karpov beat his sorry record. Playing white, he lost on time thirteen(!) moves before time control. His nemesis in that game was the very same Garry Kasparov.

Game 32

Although the following game was played three rounds before the end of a double round robin involving six grandmasters, the world champion was already assured of first prize. However, intrigue in this game was already assured by the Englishman's win in the first half of the tournament. Garry was desperate for revenge and played what was probably his best game of the tournament, elegantly punishing his opponent for a single positional error.

G. KASPAROV – N. SHORT

Brussels. International grandmasters tournament. 20.12.1986
Queen's Gambit. [D55]

1.d4 e6 2.c4 d5 3.♘f3 ♘f6 4.♘c3 ♗e7 5.♗g5 h6 6.♗xf6 ♗xf6 7.e3 0-0 8.♖c1 c6 9.♗d3 ♘d7 10.0-0 dxc4 11.♗xc4 e5 12.h3 exd4 13.exd4 ♘b6 14.♗b3 ♗f5 15.♖e1

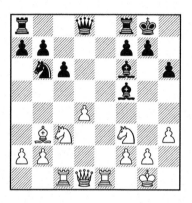

This position became a theoretical battle-ground after game 23 of the second match between the two Ks. At first glance black has no problems – the advantage of the bishop pair, nice squares for his pieces, and a lack of weaknesses. All this should guarantee him equality. However, white's positional threat of anchoring his knights in the center (on e5 and e4) suggests that white's chances are preferable.

15...♗g5

Odd as it may seem, this maneuver was pointless. For now it doesn't matter where white's rook stands (on c1 or a1), but the bishop is better off guarding e5. The path to equality, found by Garry shortly before his trip to Brussels, began with the moves 15...a5 16.a3 ♖e8, and then 17.♖xe8+ ♕xe8 18.♕d2 ♕d7 19.♖e1 ♖e8! 20.♖xe8+ ♕xe8 21.♕f4 ♗e6!

16.♖a1

A nice alternative was 16.♘xg5 ♕xg5 17.♖e3! ♖ae8 18.♕f3!, but Kasparov didn't want to relieve his opponent of the worries of covering e5.

16...♘d7 17.d5!

White changes plan and opens up the center, taking advantage of black's weakened control of d5.

17...♖c8?

This natural desire to avoid his pawn structure being damaged turns out to be black's decisive mistake. Short fails to sense the danger and misses an elementary but effective tactic. He could have fought for equality via 17...♘c5 18.♗c2 ♗xc2 19.♕xc2 ♗f6.

18.♘d4 ♗g6 19.♘e6!

Now white opens up the center in a very advantageous situation. His bishop is now very powerful, while cracks appear in black's fortress. The turn of events now sharpens.

19...fxe6 20.dxe6 ♔h7 21.♕xd7!

The world champion has precisely calculated the following complications and made the right choice. After 21.exd7? ♖c7 22.♗e6 ♗f5! 23.♗xf5+ ♖xf5 24.♕c2! g6!

the chances of both sides gradually equalize.

21...♕b6 22.e7! ♖fe8

He mustn't capture the pawn: 22...♕xf2+ (22...♖xf2? 23.♘a4! is even worse) 23.♔h1 ♖fe8 24.♘e4 ♗xe4 25.♖xe4 and so on.

23.♕g4!

White plans to determine the outcome of the game by marching his h-pawn, for example: 23...♖c7 24.h4 ♖cxe7 25.♖xe7 ♗xe7 26.h5! ♗d3 27.♖d1 ♗d6 28.♗f7! ♖e7 29.♗g6+.

23...♕c5

The dangerous white pawn is doomed, and 24.h4 ♗xe7 or 24.♗e6 ♖b8 25.♘e4 ♕xe7 both look perfectly acceptable for black. In reality, though, he hasn't come a step closer to salvation, as Kasparov elegantly proves.

24.♘e4! ♕xe7 25.♗c2!

This modest bishop move is just as effective as the most spectacular sacrifice. Black is suddenly caught in a web of both vertical and horizontal pins.

25...♖f8 26.g3

Short saw the more direct way to finish him off: 26.h4! ♗xh4 27.♘g3! ♗xc2 (or 27...♕g5 28.♗xg6+ ♔xg6 29.♕e4+! ♔f7 30.♕e6#) 28.♖xe7 ♗xe7 29.♕e2! with a win. However, the path to win demonstrated by Kasparov is more elegant.

26...♕d8 27.♖ad1 ♕a5 28.h4 ♗e7

Black's line of defense appears solid enough. If 29.h5 black had prepared a swindle: 29...♗f5 30.♘f6+! ♖xf6 31.♖xe7! ♖g8 32.♖dd7 ♔h8! 33.♖xg7? (33.♗xf5! was stronger) 33...♕e1+ 34.♔g2 ♕xf2+!!, where white would be left staring at an empty plate. The winner came close to the trap – he used the same attacking mechanism – but his unexpected and, again, quiet first move deprived black of his last illusions.

29.♘c3! ♗xc2 30.♖xe7 ♖g8 31.♖dd7 ♗f5 32.♖xg7+ ♔h8 33.♕d4

Black resigned.

Game 33

The fourth consecutive match between the two Ks was clearly of lower quality than the two previous ones. The younger but more melodramatic player was the first to buckle under the huge nervous burden (in three years they had played over 120 games just against each other). From the start of the match he began to suffer inexplicable crises, and he didn't manage to play any wholesome, truly champion's level games in Seville. In his best win – the conclusive 24th game – Garry made a poor move that almost cost him his crown. The following game could be considered an unadulterated creative portrait of both players.

A. KARPOV – G. KASPAROV

Seville. World Chess Championship. Game 5. 23.10.1987
Grunfeld Defense. [D87]

1.d4 ♘f6 2.c4 g6 3.♘c3 d5 4.cxd5 ♘xd5 5.e4 ♘xc3 6.bxc3 ♗g7 7.♗c4 c5 8.♘e2 ♘c6 9.♗e3 0-0 10.0-0 ♗g4 11.f3 ♘a5 12.♗xf7+!?

This forgotten variation of a popular opening was revived specially for this match by the ex-champion's coach, grandmaster Zaitsev. After this game Seville remained etched in my memory for the beauty of its churches and parks, and the endless chain of variations on the theme of "12.♗xf7", which filled my notebook day after day. Igor Arkadevich, famous for his ability to generate paradoxical ideas, had set our team a devilish conundrum.

12...♖xf7 13.fxg4 ♖xf1+ 14.♔xf1

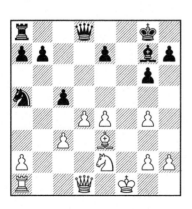

It was from this position, which arose about fifteen minutes after the clock started, that the battle began. White has an extra pawn of questionable value, and a headache caused by the weak light squares in his camp. Zaitsev, however, had found a nice touch that nobody had spotted up until then. Were white, even at the cost of returning the material, to lock the black bishop in a cage with d4, e5, g5 and h4, he would be able to win the game on the other side of the board.

In the following years the move 12.♗xf7 was tested heavily in practice and earned respect, although it didn't prove to be a refutation of the Grunfeld Defense.

14...♕d6!(64)

Such an abnormally long think points not only to a disturbed thought process, but to the player's poor sporting form. This was the second alarm bell that Garry set off in the match: the first was when he "fell asleep" for 81(!) minutes before playing his tenth move in game two.

After painful hesitations, rather

than intensive calculations, Garry chose the continuation that is considered the most comprehensive. Other lines 14...cxd4 15.cxd4 e5 16.d5 ♘c4 or 14...♕d7 15.g5 ♕e6 16.e5 ♕c4 17.♔g1 ♖d8 18.♕e1 ♘c6 are also perfectly playable for black.

15.e5(11)

Despite the exchange of queens, the continuation 15.♔g1 ♕e6 16.♕d3 ♕c4! 17.♕xc4+! ♘xc4 far from simplifies the game. This line was tried in the match in game 11. Fans of sharp emotions can try bursting their brains figuring out the variation: 15.♕a4! ♕xh2! 16.♕xa5 ♖f8+ 17.♔e1 ♕h1+ 18.♘g1 ♗h6! 19.♔d2! ♖f2+! and so on.

15...♕d5(10)   16.♗f2(10) ♖f8(12)

Well, who wouldn't move their rook to such an open line? It was only after the game that we concluded that 16...♖d8 was more promising.

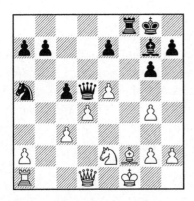

17.♔g1?(05)

Karpov didn't like to spend time on studying ideas proposed by his seconds to the very end, and frequently was happy merely to get familiar with them, relying further on his wonderful innate sense. But that sense could sometimes let him down, as happened here. Instead of gradually building a cage with 17.g5! that could have continued, in white's favor, something like 17...♕f7 18.♕e1 ♘c4 19.♔g1 ♘b2 20.♗e3 ♘d3 21.♕b1 ♕c4 22.♕b3! b5! 23.♕xc4+ bxc4 24.♖b1!, white wastes a tempo that turns out to be sufficient for his opening idea to remain unachieved.

17...♗h6! 18.h4(18)

Further proof that Karpov wasn't sufficiently familiar with the new setup and was still moving guided by his positional understanding and intuition. He always avoided pawn structure weaknesses. However, the only way he could have maintained equality here was to break his pawn chain. After 18.dxc5 the pattern of the game changes radically, for example: 18...♕xe5 19.♕d3 ♕e6 20.h3 ♕f7 21.♗h4 ♘c4 22.g5 ♗g7 23.♖b1! e5 24.♘g3, but neither side would have had an advantage.

18...♕f7! 19.♗g3

Alas, he has to choose the lesser evil. 19.♕f1 ♗d2! 20.♖d1 is met by 20...♘c4! 21.♘g3 ♘e3 22.♗xe3 ♗xe3+ 23.♔h1 ♕xa2 with a clear advantage.

19...♗e3+   20.♔h2 ♕c4!(16) 21.♖b1?!(32)

White has managed to preserve his extra pawn, but at the cost of surrendering the initiative. The black pieces stand on decent squares, and even his knight on the edge of the board is in use, preventing white from forcing an exchange of queens. However, black still lacks the coordination of pieces that would enable him to develop an initiative irrespective of white's action. Therefore, it would have been interesting for white to attempt to open a new front on the part of the board where he isn't yet weaker, pushing his pawn with 21.d5! After 21...♕xg4 22.♘g1 ♗xg1+ 23.♕xg1 b6 (23...♘c4 24.♕xc5) 24.d6! or 21...♗f2! 22.♗xf2! ♖xf2 23.♘g3 ♕f4 24.d6 exd6 25.exd6 ♖d2 26.♕e1 white has gained some counterplay. However, after a long think white decides to continue to play in his usual style – he cannot stand idle pieces.

21...b6(05)

Obviously not 21...♕xa2? 22.♖a1 ♕b3 23.♕d3.

22.♖b2?!(05)

Now it would have been objectively stronger to radically change the pattern of the game with 22.dxc5!, maintaining an unclear position, for example: 22...bxc5 23.♘g1 ♗f2 24.♘f3 ♗xg3+ 25.♔xg3 ♕f4+ 26.♔h3 ♘c4 27.♕d5+ ♔h8 28.♕xc5 ♕e4! 29.♕xe7 ♖xf3+ and perpetual check.

Karpov's choice to retain the elasticity of his pawn chain was mostly a psychological one, counting on black's material deficit, the unclear situation and Kasparov's lack of time to increase his opponent's discomfort. Like in their very first match, you could identify Kasparov's mood easily by a number of external signs that Karpov knew very well. Nevertheless, this clumsy rook move was a dubious idea, as it allowed his opponent to bring his knight into play with tempo. As a result, black's superiority in the center of the board becomes menacing.

22...♕d5(08)   23.♕d3   ♘c4 24.♖b1

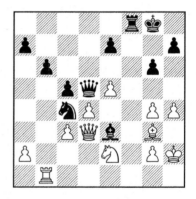

Black has now mobilized his forces successfully and has more than sufficient compensation for the pawn. But how much more? What sticks out the most in this position is his wide choice of promising continuations, which however requires comprehensive thought.

24...b5?(02)

It's hard to place a question-mark against a move that doesn't worsen your position. The speed at which black took his decision is also striking, one which practically offers a draw in an advantageous position.

For whatever reason, the world champion had nobody in this match capable of giving him serious psychological help. Therefore, he was only capable of withstanding the fighting tension when games followed his planned scenario. An unforeseen idea or opening novelty of his opponent would annoy him and make him feel uncomfortable, preventing him from thinking calmly and taking justifiable decisions. His intuition and heightened sense of danger saved him from getting into a nasty mess. However, when the tension reached its peak those qualities were insufficient and a crisis would ensue.

So now, in a moment of crisis, Garry makes a rapid move forcing his opponent to make a choice: either to draw with perpetual check 25.♖xb5 ♘xe5! 26.♖xc5 ♘xg4+ 27.♔h3 ♕d7 28.♕b5 (28.♕c4+ ♔h8 29.♕d5 ♕xd5! 30.♖xd5 h5!) 28...♘f2+ 29.♔h2 ♘g4+ 30.♔h3 ♘f2+, or to continue to fight, which implied greater risk.

At the same time, the logic of events and the active positions of his pieces dictated that the world champion should maintain the tension. The outcome of the battle that was only beginning depended on whether black could get to g2. The tempting path 24...♘xe5 25.♗xe5 ♖f2 26.♖g1 ♕f3 would end in a ditch after 27.♘c1! ♖b2 28.♔h1 ♖xg2 29.♕c4+ ♔f8 30.♖xg2 ♕h3+ 31.♗h2. It wouldn't

have been easy for white to refute the attack beginning with 24...♗f2, but here he had a resource 25.♘f4! ♗xg3+ 26.♔xg3 ♖xf4 27.♔xf4 ♘xe5 28.♕e3! g5+! 29.hxg5 ♘g6+, and as a result the bind would promise nothing more than a draw. Two other hard-to-spot alternatives, demonstrated by Zaitsev, were more effective: 24...♖f2!? 25.♗xf2 ♘xe5! 26.c4! ♕d7! 27.♕xe3 ♘xg4+ 28.♔g1 ♘xe3 29.♗xe3 ♕e6 30.♖b3! ♕xc4 31.♔f2 cxd4 32.♘xd4 e5! and, in particular, the evidently stronger 24...g5! 25.♖d1! gxh4 26.♗xh4 ♗f2 27.♕h3! ♕e4! 28.♗xe7 ♖f7 29.♗f6 ♘e3! 30.g5! ♘g4+! 31.♔h1 ♗xd4! 32.♘g3 ♕f4 33.♕h5 ♕xg3 34.cxd4 ♘f2+.

25.♔h3(17)

This move would normally deserve the "?!" sign, but Karpov, noticing the agitated state of his opponent, deliberately rejected going for a draw and instead took a risk.

25...a6 26.♘g1(04) cxd4(11) 27.♘f3(22) ♖d8

So far, Karpov's decision to continue the fight still looks unjustified. Black has won the pawn back without conceding any activity in his pieces, and his chances of winning have grown. However, the spectators noticed that the approach of time trouble was making the young champion increasingly nervy.

28.a4

Karpov raises the stakes even more by giving his rook some work.

28...dxc3 29.♕xc3 ♕e6! 30.♔h2 bxa4 31.♖b4 ♘d2 32.♖xa4

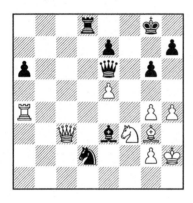

32...♘f1+?

White has lost the threads of the battle. In time trouble it would have been more practical to simplify with 32...♘xf3+ 33.gxf3 ♗d2 and head for a favorable endgame with an outside passer. The partisan operation that black is planning is doomed to failure due to the lack of coordination of his pieces. Karpov was a fantastic gambler, one must admit! He waited for his opponent's crisis, knowing how very hard it is to withstand psychological tension when you lack self-confidence.

33.♔h3 ♖d1 34.♕c2(07)

Leaving himself just a minute on the clock, Karpov continues to take risks, rejecting simplifications. The obvious 34.♖xa6 after 34...♕xa6 35.♕b3+ ♔g7 36.♕xd1 ♘xg3 37.♔xg3 would leave white a pawn up but his opponent would have chances to save the game through enterprising action, for example: 37...♕c4! 38.♕d7 ♗f4+ (he could also play 38...♕f4+ 39.♔h3 ♗f2 40.♕xe7+ ♔g8 41.♕d8+ ♔g7 42.♕f6+ ♕xf6 43.exf6+ ♔xf6) 39.♔h3 ♔f7, when the weakness of the e5 pawn and the threat of the queen invasion would equalize chances. However, white has long staked everything on psychology in this game and now hopes for more.

34...♖c1 35.♕e2 h5 36.♗e1 ♕d7 37.♕xa6 ♖a1?

Kasparov had already come undone, and in the time scramble didn't even see what was happening on the board.

38.♕xg6+

Black resigned. A tragic game.

Game 34

The World Cup was a unique brainchild of the GMA. For the first time, 25 grandmasters from the world chess elite competed in a two-year series of six tournaments for the unofficial title of tournament world champion. As expected, nobody could compete with the two chess titans, and they filled the break between their last and next match with rivalry in the World Cup's tournaments. Karpov's position was more advantageous psychologically, as opening prep didn't play such a big role for him or take up as much time in advance of tournaments as it did for Kasparov. The ex-champion badly wanted to win that cup, as victory would have given him decent moral compensation for his failure to win the Seville match.

The second tournament in the series brought them against each other for the first time in the cup. With one round left, the world champion was a point ahead of his nearest rivals, including Karpov. However, the system for counting points towards the cup as a whole encouraged players to go for a win no matter what the tournament table showed. Therefore, in planning his game against Andrei Sokolov, also born in 1963, Garry decided not to shy from a fierce battle.

G. KASPAROV – A. SOKOLOV
Belfort. World Cup. 03.07.1988
English Opening. [A19]

1.c4 ♘f6 2.♘c3 e6 3.e4 c5 4.e5 ♘g8 5.♘f3 ♘c6 6.d4 cxd4 7.♘xd4 ♘xe5 8.♘db5 a6 9.♘d6+ ♗xd6 10.♕xd6 f6 11.♗e3 ♘e7 12.♗b6 ♘f5 13.♕c5

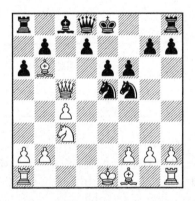

The zest of youth has lit the fire of battle right in the opening. Both players are using psychology well here – each has tested their opponent's daring. In such a test of character the world champion didn't have the right to back down.

This position was already known to theory. White has sacrificed a pawn to gain an advantage in space and has caused black difficulty with coordinating his pieces.

13...d6?!(19)

Sokolov had not played this line before, and his knowledge of its opening subtleties proved to be insufficient for a discussion with Kasparov on equal terms. After a long think, Andrei makes a poor choice. He should have offered an exchange of queens, and although that would have left white with the initiative black would have had more chances of equalizing than he got in the game. The course of a game played later between Ribli and Karpov proves this: 13...♕e7 14.♕xe7+ ♘xe7 15.f4 ♘5c6 16.0-0-0 d5! 17.a3!

14.♕a5 ♕e7 15.0-0-0 0-0 16.f4 ♘c6 17.♕a3

White has completed the mobilization of his forces and is ready to play 18.g4 ♘h6 19.h3 and totally cramp his opponent's pieces. Therefore, black is forced to weaken his pawn structure in the center.

17...e5 18.g4 ♘fd4(06) 19.♘d5 ♛f7(07)

Sokolov has spent far too much time on two obvious moves. Such generosity was leading him to time trouble.

20.f5(23) g6 21.♖g1 gxf5(08) 22.g5!

A very strong move. White needs to liquidate the f6 pawn. Then, after the d6 pawn falls, black's defenses in the center collapse.

22...♚h8(18) 23.gxf6(31)

While white was thinking over this move applause broke out among the spectators – Karpov had won his last game and had caught up with Garry. Therefore, the champion sharply changed his battle strategy. He rejected the aggressive plan that he considered to be the strongest 23.♘xf6 ♗e6 24.g6 hxg6 25.♛h3+ ♚g7 26.♘h5+ ♚g8 27.♗xd4 ♘xd4 28.♘f4! exf4 29.♛h6, and instead decided to play with maximum safety buffers.

23...♗e6 24.♛xd6

The advantages of invading with 24.♖g7 ♛h5 25.♛xd6 ♗xd5 26.♛xd5 were quite uncertain.

24...♗xd5(07) 25.cxd5 ♛xf6 26.♛xf6+ ♖xf6 27.♚b1! ♘d8 28.♗c5!

Sokolov has managed to hold on to his extra pawn, but the white bishop together with the strong

passer create a multitude of threats.

28...♖c8?(08)

Black simply had to liquidate the menacing bishop via 28...b6 29.♗e7 ♖f7 30.d6 ♘8c6 31.♗c4 ♖xe7! 32.dxe7 ♘xe7. Then he would have retained his positions in the center and a couple of strong passed pawns, although after 33.♖ge1! ♘ec6 34.♗d5! white was a bit better. [5] The natural sortie of the black rook with the intent to carry out the same idea proves to be a fatal mistake.

29.♗e7 ♖f7 30.♗d6! ♘f3 31.♖g3

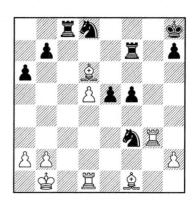

Had the black pawn already left the b7 square (28...b6!), then the intermezzo 31...♘b7! would now have been possible, breaking up white's attack. Now, though, black's position quickly unravels.

31...e4 32.♗e2 ♖f6

Garry had prepared a pretty finale after 32...♖g7 33.♗xf3 ♖xg3

---

[5] Kasparov demonstrates updated analysis in his book *Garry Kasparov on Garry Kasparov: Part II* where he corrects this line to show black equalizes with 33...b5 etc., but white can improve with 30.♗b4 as well as 29.♗xd4 (publisher's note)

34.♗xe4! ♖g5 35.♗e7 ♖h5 36.♖g1 ♖h6 37.♗xf5 ♖b8 38.♗f8, when the d-pawn decided the outcome of the game.[6]

33.♗f4! ♖g6 34.♗xf3 ♖xg3 35.♗xe4!

Admire the strength of these fierce bishops. The rest requires no commentary.

35...fxe4 36.hxg3 ♔g7 37.♖d4 ♘f7 38.♖xe4 ♖d8 39.♗e7 ♖xd5 40.♖xb7 h5 41.♗a7 a5 42.a4

The time scramble was over. **Black resigned**.

Game 35

The first clash at the chess board between the world champion and Vasily was greatly anticipated, in a similar way to the first battle between the two Ks in 1981. However, the game was short of tense battle. The spectators witnessed pretty... confusion. The reason for that was the Ukrainian's flaws of youth.

G. KASPAROV – V. IVANCHUK.
Moscow. 55th USSR Championship Higher League. 27.07.1988
English Opening. [A29]

1.c4 ♘f6 2.♘c3 e5 3.♘f3 ♘c6 4.g3 ♗b4 5.♗g2 0-0 6.0-0 e4 7.♘g5 ♗xc3 8.bxc3 ♖e8 9.f3 exf3 10.♘xf3

The fourth match between the two Ks, which had taken place a year earlier in Seville, didn't bequeath any chess works of art to the world, but had been rich in intrigues, including at the board. This position was one of the big, purely chess mysteries from that match. In game two, Karpov had played the novelty 9...e3!?, after which the defending champion spent almost an hour and a half at the board before making his reply 10.d3, and naturally then failed to withstand the battle tension. However, in his next games as black Karpov didn't repeat his effective invention. So the mystery of the disappearance of the Kasparov Gambit that had worked so brilliantly in the second match was joined by the disappeared gambit line played by Karpov.

10...d5

---

[6] Kasparov demonstrates updated analysis in his book *Garry Kasparov on Garry Kasparov: Part II* where he corrects this line to show black should avoid defeat with 33...♘f7. Therefore, he states white should have played 32.♗f4 instead of 32.♗e2 (publisher's note)

In game four of that match Karpov failed to choose the strongest line, continuing 10...♕e7 11.e3 ♘e5 12.♘d4 ♘d3 13.♕e2 ♘xc1 14.♖axc1 d6 15.♗f4 c6 16.♖cf1 ♕e5 – and after 17.♕d3! he lost without much resistance. Titled commentators tied themselves in knots trying to figure out why Karpov didn't take the path considered to be the most reliable: 10...d5 11.cxd5 ♕xd5 12.♘d4 ♕h5 13.♘xc6 bxc6. One of the ex-champion's seconds, Makarychev, later admitted that his boss intuitively didn't believe in the fortitude of black's position, and his seconds couldn't find any lines to disprove Karpov's intuition.

After the Seville match, Karpov invited the young Ukrainian to several of his training sessions. He badly needed to soak in new ideas, for which Vasily was famous. I'm sure that this contact with the titan ex-champion was also greatly useful for Ivanchuk. Shortly before the USSR Championship, Karpov also shared the unsolved enigma of the move 10...d5 with the young man. Vasily didn't yet have a sharp sense of danger, and there wasn't time for detailed analysis either, but this was more than compensated for by his thirst for knowledge and the move was hence tempting. He decided to take the risk.

11.d4!

This paradoxical move, invented by the world champion, had already been "waiting" for Karpov prior to game four in Seville. The gaping weakness of the e4 square turned out to be imaginary. Moreover, it was in the center of the board that white planned activity, using the open file and fierce bishop pair. Preparing for the game against Ivanchuk, Garry didn't rule out the possibility of a theoretical duel, but nor did he expect his opponent to be so trusting and naive. In any event, he flicked through his cherished notebook.

11...♘e4 12.♕c2!

The other option 12.cxd5 ♘xc3 13.♕d2 ♘xd5 14.e4 ♘f6 15.e5 ♘e4 16.♕e3 f5 led to a complicated and double-edged position. Even back in Seville we assessed it as being second-rate.

12...dxc4

Ivanchuk made this move without thinking, just like all his earlier ones. However, it was hardly the strongest move here and I can only explain its choice as a result of superficial analysis and naivety. Black should have thought about how best to strengthen his center, for example: 12...♗f5 13.♘h4 ♗g6, however, instead he hurries to demonstrate his erudition. Such reckless opening blitz is harmful at the very least because the player as a rule misses the point at which they ought to begin thinking.

13.♖b1!

Vasily had evidently focused his analysis on continuations involving play right in the center of the board, for example: 13.♘e5 ♘xe5 14.♕xe4 ♘g6 15.♕d5 ♕e7. It's perfectly possible that this quiet rook move had at some point occurred to him, but he had failed to figure out the devilish idea that it hid.

13...f5(08)

White's confident handling of the opening only now started to worry Ivanchuk, yet his reply looked natural and strong.

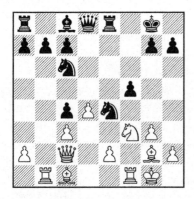

14.g4!!(07)

This unexpected move must have demoralized white's opponent, who suddenly realized that he had stepped on a mine. This is proved by the unusually long think that he then took and his poor reply, after which it was all downhill for black. The impressionable lad was unable to calm down and collect his thoughts at the critical moment.

14...♕e7?(46)

It's dangerous to capture the pawn: 14...fxg4 15.♘e5 ♘xe5 16.♗xe4 ♘g6 17.♗xg6 hxg6 18.♕xg6 with the unpleasant threat of ♖b1-b5-h5. Black should have tried to maintain the outpost on e4 by playing 14...g6!?, although here too Kasparov's analysis proved that white had a solid advantage.

15.gxf5(28) ♘d6

Black wants to use counterplay against the e2 pawn to restrict his opponent's activity, and to use the f5 pawn as an obstacle in the way of the rook on f1. However, the battle was effectively over, having flashed like lightning and compressed in the space of just three moves. The elegant finale is forced and calculated by the champion to the very end.

16.♘g5!(08) ♕xe2 17.♗d5+! (07)

If 17...♔f8 black loses his queen: 18.♘xh7+ ♔e7 19.♕xe2+. The king shelters in the corner, but he will die there.

17...♔h8 18.♕xe2 ♖xe2 19.♗f4 ♘d8(13)

White has a pretty mating attack after 19...♗xf5 20.♗xd6 ♗xb1 21.♘f7+ ♔g8 22.♘d8+! ♔h8 23.♖f8#. Black's position is falling apart – he defends f7, but the weakness of the eighth rank finishes him off.

20.♗xd6 cxd6 21.♖be1! ♖xe1 22.♖xe1 ♗d7 23.♖e7 ♗c6 24.f6!

Mate is unavoidable: 24...♗xd5 25.♖e8+ ♗g8 26.f7 ♘xf7 27.♘xf7#

Black resigned. A nightmare in which black is crushed out of the opening.

Game 36

I have long determined Garry's maximum chess ability at a certain point in time by his number of hard-to-spot but effective solutions. The following game truly contained a flash of genius. At the most tense point of the battle, when white needed to put in an incredible effort to break the desperate resistance of his opponent, Kasparov's idea wasn't even figured out by the grandmasters observing the game with their boards.

Kasparov only twice took a serious think. The first time was when he reviewed the post-opening phase of the middlegame, and the second was when he devised a plan for the decisive storm. Garry carried out a devastating and beautiful attack non-stop, with barely a moment's thought during the process. He saw everything right to the end.

G. KASPAROV – I. SMIRIN
Moscow. 55th USSR Championship
Higher League. 10.08.1988
King's Indian Defense. [E97]

1.♘f3 ♘f6 2.c4 g6 3.♘c3 ♗g7 4.e4 d6 5.d4 0-0 6.♗e2 e5 7.0-0 ♘c6 8.d5 ♘e7 9.♘d2

The approach white has selected to counter the KID setup was perhaps the most solid and deepest one, with something in common with the classical systems of the Spanish Opening. Of course, he faced the risk of being attacked on his kingside, but if he managed to outpace his opponent and be the first to launch an attack, in his case on the queenside, then black would

have greater things to worry about than his own attack. Garry very much enjoyed playing this setup for black, which made it all the more interesting to watch how he tackled the KID with white.

9...a5 10.a3 ♘d7

10...c5 is considered to be an equally valid move, but Smirin sticks to the old rule condemning pawn movements in the part of the board where your opponent plans to attack.

11.♖b1 f5 12.b4 b6 13.f3 f4 14.♘a4(12) axb4 15.axb4 g5 16.c5 ♘f6

We can already clearly see the outlines of a battle in which white is so far more advanced – his pawn on c5 has already charged forward, whereas the g5 pawn is still waiting for reinforcements.

17.cxd6   cxd6   18.b5   ♗d7 19.♘c4(44!) ♘c8 20.♗a3 ♘e8

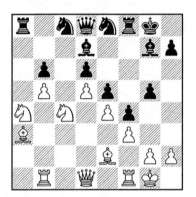

White has managed to tie down his opponent's main forces to defending queenside pawns, and in this way white protects his king for a while from the standard pawn storm. Were it black's move he would surely play 21...h5, but...

21.g4!

A brilliant decision, sharply altering the rhythm of events on the board. Black cannot allow the white pawn to stick on g4, and, in order to gain at least some counterattacking chances, has to force operations on the kingside before he has managed to send reserves over.

21...fxg3   22.hxg3   g4 23.♗c1!(10)

The world champion is carrying out the battle over a wide area. Black cannot hold the outpost on g4, as after 23...h5 24.f4! exf4 25.♗xf4 white has an obvious advantage.

23...gxf3   24.♗xf3   ♘f6 25.♗g5!(10) ♖a7 26.♖f2(08) ♖b7!

Black is demonstrating great defensive skill. Now his queen is free to transfer to the kingside, whereas the hurried 26...♕e8 leads to catastrophe after 27.♘axb6 ♘xb6 28.♘xb6 ♗xb5 29.♗xf6 and then 30.♗h5.

27.♖b3!(05)   ♖a7   28.♖b1(12) ♖b7 29.♖b3 ♖a7 30.♖b4!

The rook has carried out a ton of prophylactic work in this game. Now it defends three white pieces at once, freeing up the queen to go on the attack. It seems that black should have continued his intricate defense by playing 30...♖b7, although after 31.♗h5 or 31.♗e3 his position remained tough.

30...♔h8 31.♕f1!

The point of this strong move isn't yet evident, as black's defensive walls on the kingside appear to be solid. Yet the vastly protected knight on f6 will soon appear to be in a desperate situation.

31...♗xb5   32.♖xb5   ♖xa4 33.♗g2

Obviously, white is increasing the pressure on the pinned knight, yet black's defense appears to be just as obvious. But we don't yet know why the bishop had to retreat to g2...

33...h6 34.♗h4 ♕e8!

Without this move, playing on would be pointless. Passive defense would be akin to resigning.

35.♗xf6 ♖xf6! 36.♖xf6 ♕xb5

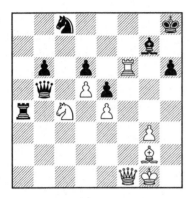

None of the grandmasters observing this game found the following effective continuation of the attack. It seemed to me that, having failed to overcome the stubborn resistance, Garry would force a draw with the trivial 37.♖f8+. However, he had already seen the final position.

37.♖e6!! ♔g8! 38.♗h3! ♖xc4

We still don't see it. Of course, white's moves are very pretty, and they've retained the option of drawing, but why take such a complex path? It was only from the confident and rapid manner in which Garry was making his last few moves that I realized that he had seen something, but I couldn't figure out what...

39.♖xh6!!

It was only now that everybody could see the champion's devilish idea. After 39...♕c5+ 40.♔h1! ♖c1 white's queen looks set to die and his rook is under attack, but it's his move and he has the pretty 41.♗e6!!#. A triumph of spirit over matter on the board!

39...♗xh6   40.♗e6+   ♔h8
41.♕f6+

Now everything ends – time trouble, the battle and the roller-coaster experienced by fans. Mate is inevitable: 41...♔h7 (41...♗g7 42 ♕h4+) 42.♕f7+ ♗g7 43.♗f5+ ♔h8 44.♕h5+ ♔g8 (44...♗h6 45.♕xh6+ ♔g8 46.♗e6#) 45.♗e6+ ♔f8 46.♕f7#. Therefore, **black resigned**.

A work of chess art striking for its beauty and force. In my view, one of Kasparov's best games.

Game 37

I wrote earlier that Garry was particularly strong at playing games whose results were of the utmost sporting importance. This was seen even more so in games against ex-world champions. He won the final game in three matches against Karpov – twice in 1985 in Moscow, and then in 1987 in Seville. In order to win the major grandmaster tournament in Brussels in 1986 he had to win his last round game against Mikhail Tal.

Ljubomir Ljubojevic was in great form during the fifth stage of the World Cup and led the tournament throughout. In order to at least catch up, Garry had to win his last round match against Boris Spassky, whom he had never before defeated. Boris had long given up any ambition in chess and had dropped in playing strength. However, he still retained a deep understanding of chess. He had won only one game in Barcelona, but had drawn all the rest.

Garry now faced a tough test. I think the entire tournament knew he went into this match with the firm intent to win.

G. KASPAROV – B. SPASSKY
Barcelona. World Cup. 20.04.1989
Queen's Gambit. [D35]

1.d4 ♞f6 2.c4 e6 3.♞c3 d5 4.cxd5 exd5 5.♗g5 c6 6.e3 ♗e7 7.♗d3 ♞bd7 8.♞ge2!

White has chosen a rather cunning piece setup in a well-known structure played by Swiss grandmaster Andersson. Ulf, an old friend of Boris, had arrived in Barcelona to catch the final rounds and may well have helped the latter to prepare for the game. Garry and I took this into account in our prep, refreshing our memory with the Swede's favorite openings. Garry had no doubt here that the black knight would move to the edge of the board – Ulf liked to carry out this very maneuver.

8...♞h5 9.♗xe7 ♛xe7

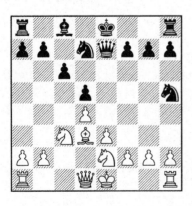

10.g4!

His hard-to-spot subtlety (replacing the trivial 8.♛c2 with 8.♞ge2) allowed white to exploit the drawbacks of 8...♞h5, grabbing space on the kingside.

10...♞hf6 11.♞g3 h6 12.h3 ♞b6 13.♛d2 ♗d7 14.b3 g6 15.a4! a5 16.f3

With his pieces now more logically and aggressively positioned, white can be pleased with the outcome of the opening salvos.

16...h5 17.g5 ♛d6 18.♞ge2 ♞g8 19.e4! ♞e7

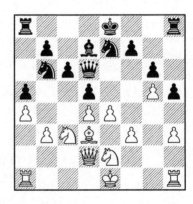

20.♛f4!

The choice of a mature master. With the exchange of queens, the risk of Garry getting hit on the counterattack after all the white pawns had pushed forward is reduced to a minimum, while the gains earned by his aggressive opening strategy remain.

20...♕xf4 21.♘xf4 0-0 22.♘ce2 h4 23.♘g2 ♚g7 24.♚d2

Black's lack of clear weaknesses means the outcome of the game is far from determined. Spassky even believed that his chances were no worse at this point. All that's required from black is patience and some precision in his defending. Evidently, unhurried play with 24...♖ac8 25.e5 ♘a8 26.♘e3 ♘c7 27.f4 ♗f5 28.♗xf5 gxf5 followed by ♘e6 would have posed white the most difficulties in trying to increase his positional superiority.

However, the ex-world champion now makes a positional blunder that voluntarily creates a mobile pawn center for his opponent. His hopes to organize a piece attack against white's pawns prove to be unjustified due to the weak coordination of his pieces and lack of space for maneuvering.

24...dxe4? 25.fxe4 ♖ad8 26.♖af1 ♖h8 27.♘e3 ♖h5 28.♖fg1 ♗c8 29.♚c3 ♖hh8 30.♘f4 ♖d6 31.♗c2?

An unfortunate slip-up while carrying out a wide-scale attack. By exchanging knights 31.♘c4 ♘xc4 32.bxc4 white would further increase his domination of the center.

31...♘a8?

A reciprocal mistake just when black's chances of saving the game had seemed real. Desperately short of time, Spassky fails to find the right plan of defense and in the confusion simply blunders a pawn. After 31...♖hd8 32.♖d1 f6! white has a choice – 33.♘c4 ♘xc4 34.bxc4 fxg5 35.e5 gxf4! 36.exd6 ♖xd6 or 33.♖hg1 f5! (Spassky had missed this trick) 34.♘c4 ♘xc4 35.bxc4 fxe4 36.♗xe4 ♖f8 37.♖gf1 ♗f5 38.♗g2 but in neither case emerged with an advantage. [7]

32.♘c4 ♖dd8 33.♘xa5 ♘c7 34.♖f1 b5 35.♖f3 ♖hf8 36.♖hf1 bxa4 37.bxa4 f6

Black's position after the mistake 31...♘a8 quickly unraveled, and had he not played his last move he would have lost without our bearing witness to the following demonstration of white's combinational brilliancy.

38.♘xg6!

The world champion played this move instantly, relying on his intuition. Analysis after the game proved that this was not only the prettiest, but the most effective path to a win, as 38.gxf6+ ♖xf6 39.♘h5+? gxh5 40.♖xf6 led after

---

[7] Kasparov recommends the immediate 31...f5 in his book *Garry Kasparov on Garry Kasparov: Part II* (publisher's note)

40...♘cd5+!   41.exd5   ♘xd5+
42.♔b2 ♘xf6 43.♘xc6 ♖d6 to an
unclear position. [8]

**38...♘xg6   39.gxf6+   ♔h6
40.♘xc6 ♖d6 41.d5**

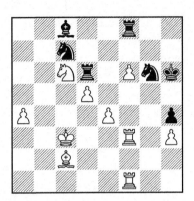

Four passers are more than
sufficient compensation for the
knight. Moreover, black's pieces lack
coordination. Spassky finds the best
practical chance. With an exchange
sacrifice he breaks up white's pawn
chain in the hope of bumping off the
pawns one by one.

41...♖xc6+! 42.dxc6 ♘e6 43.e5!

It's very important to introduce
the sleeping bishop into play. White
doesn't need such a large number of
pawns to win the game.

43...♘xe5

The attempt to drum up
counterplay with 43...♘g5 44.♖e3
♗xh3 is also losing, due to 45.♖xh3!

♘xh3 46.e6 ♘g5 47.e7 ♖c8 48.♗f5
♖xc6+ 49.♔b4 and so on.

44.♖e3 ♘g6

44...♘xc6 falls to 45.♖e4!

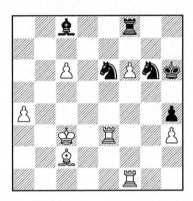

45.f7!

The awesome threat of 46.♖f6!
prevents black from having the time
to consolidate his forces. 45...♔g7
is best defeated by 46.♖g1 ♘ef4
47.♖f3! ♔h6 48.♗xg6 ♘xg6 49.♖f6.
Nevertheless, Spassky's move made
no difference and the rest doesn't
require explanation. [9]

**45...♘gf4 46.♗b3 ♔g7 47.♖e4!
♖xf7 48.♗xe6! ♘xe6 49.♖xf7+
♔xf7 50.♖xh4 ♔e7 51.♖h8 ♗a6
52.h4!**

Black resigned. The two rook
pawns striving to queen cannot be
stopped.

All's well that ends well, don't
you think?

---

[8] Kasparov recommends 42.♔c4 and still winning in his book *Garry Kasparov on
Garry Kasparov: Part II* (publisher's note)

[9] Kasparov recommends 46.♗xg6 ♔xg6 47.a5 as the simplest way to win in his
book *Garry Kasparov on Garry Kasparov: Part II* (publisher's note)

Game 38

Far from all grandmasters when playing against Kasparov attempted to compete with him in his ability to cause confusion. Even such greats as Karpov and Korchnoi would soon regret the challenge if they accepted it. However, there are some players who don't like to simplify the game – and would claim they don't know how to – and their games with Garry were always messy.

American grandmaster Yasser Seirawan's games against the world champion were never quiet affairs. The following game was so confusing that not even its participants were ever able to get to the bottom of it, and they would return to its analysis time and again.

Kasparov's performance at the final stage of the World Cup was challenging, and he found taking decisions at the board tortuous. In such circumstances, it's very important when preparing for games to guess how the opening would pan out. This wasn't so much to economize time, which is always short when a player is out of form, but to gain additional confidence used when taking decisions at the board. The American's opening repertoire was not that varied, and the position which they had on the board after twelve moves was the same as that on Garry's magnetic chess set in his hotel room when he left for the round.

Y. SEIRAWAN – G. KASPAROV
Skelleftea. World Cup. 27.08.1989
Modern Benoni. [E74/A65]

1.d4 ♘f6 2.c4 g6 3.♘c3 ♗g7 4.e4 d6 5.♗e2

That year, Seirawan preferred to attack with the Saemisch setup. However, the same year the world champion had recorded a number of convincing wins with black in that line. Therefore, we had no doubt that the American would reject the Saemisch and return to the variation that he used to play. And that's what happened – that's how openings are guessed.

5...0-0 6.♗g5 c5 7.d5 h6 8.♗e3 e6 9.♕d2 exd5 10.cxd5 ♖e8

Kasparov transposes into a line of the Benoni that is favorable for black. This first modest achievement by black was the result of the champion's huge opening erudition, which enabled him to enjoy great freedom in selecting an opening system.

11.f3(03)

It's hard to come up with a more logical move than this one, as the exchange of pawns with 11.♗xh6 ♘xe4 is clearly better for black. However, we now see an opening setup in which white, it transpires, was too hasty in developing his light-colored bishop. With his fifth move he committed it to a position which only now turns out to be an obstacle to the development of the g1 knight and, consequently, to castling.

11...h5!(05)

Thirty years ago, the careful 11...♔h7 was considered mandatory here. This daring pawn thrust is far from the champion having a bit of fun, and is the modern method of active defense, which has successfully passed multiple practical trials, both in Indian systems and in the Sicilian Dragon. In fact, even in the Spanish. Today, such weakening of the king's pawn protection is no longer automatically condemned, but may be condoned on the basis of dynamic factors that may exercise a considerable influence on the progress of the battle. In moving his pawn far from his king, black not only restricts white's kingside activity but also harbors more aggressive intentions of his own. The trappy move 11...a6 would have been a mistake. After 12.♗xh6! ♘xe4? 13.♘xe4 ♕h4+ 14.g3 ♕xh6 15.♘f6+ black would lose material.

Despite our favorable beginning, I was alarmed at Garry's five-minute think over the pawn's sortie. In the opening, such committal moves are the fruit of carefully considered home solutions. I concluded that Garry was starting to doubt his prep. A self-confident grandmaster properly ready for battle would not

have spent more than a minute here and would have pushed the daring pawn forwards with ostentatious confidence.

12.a4(02) a6(05) 13.a5(19)

A very questionable decision and, as is evident, one taken after much self-torture. It forces white to accept additional commitments. Indeed, if white fails to take advantage of the outpost on b6, the pawn's raid will not only turn out to have been a waste of time, but will also force white to constantly tend to its protection. Seirawan didn't want to weaken control over b5 (after 13.♗d1) and decided to wait for black to make the natural developing move 13...♘bd7, which would block the diagonal for his own bishop and allow white to carry out the typical regrouping ♘g1-h3-f2 and then 0-0.

A more interesting continuation, hampering black's activity, would have been moving the bishop back with 13.♗g5! Events would then have unfolded something along the lines of 13...♕a5 14.♖a3 ♘h7 15.♗f4 ♕c7 16.h4 ♘d7 17.♘h3 ♘e5 18.♘g5 ♖b8.

13...♘h7!(04)

An unexpected and strong reply. The world champion makes a very subtle move, catching his opponent unawares and thereby creates an advantage. Each of Kasparov's moves so far contains deep meaning, aggression and power. Now black, while continuing to prevent white's knight on g1 from developing, displays his intentions to turn to active play both in the center and on the kingside.

14.♗d1(10)

I think it would have been easier for white to solve his problems without admitting the pointlessness of his last two moves. After 14.♘a4! he would have highlighted that his opponent also had problems in development and weak squares. White could have met the natural 14...♘bd7 with the nice 15.♘h3 b5 16.axb6 ♘xb6 17.♘f2 ♘xa4 18.♖xa4 ♖b8 19.♖a2. Yasser however rejects the knight move, evaluating the position after 14...f5 15.♘b6 ♖a7 as unacceptable. Yet were we to continue the line 16.exf5 ♗xf5 17.♘c4!, it transpires that it's white who creates threats in the center first, and at the same time his knight manages to carry out defensive functions while his queen's rook is ready to conduct operations along the third rank. [10]

14...♘bd7(04)   15.♘ge2(02) ♘e5 16.b3

In pre-empting the threat of 16...♘c4, Seirawan is forced to restrict the operation of his light-squared bishop, thereby admitting the failure of his opening strategy. However, one should not overestimate black's achievements here, as white has no obvious weaknesses in his camp and

his king will soon find safety on the flank. Black's advantage is down to the fact that for now he can dictate the course of events.

16...♛h4+!(31)

An interesting idea. Seirawan was worried about the more natural break 16...f5, assessing black's chances as better after 17.♗c2 fxe4 18.♗xe4 ♘f6. Kasparov saw this option, but after a long think chose another, more interesting action plan from the strategic point of view.

17.♗f2 ♛f6

The threat 18...♛xf3 is highly effective even though it is obvious. However, it's not simple to assess its force at the board.

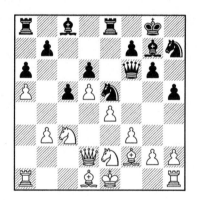

18.♛e3(08)

Yasser condemned this decision, when instead of developing other pieces he moves his queen to a clumsy position. 18.♗e3 looked more logical, after which the lively

---

[10] Kasparov recommends 16.♛c2 in this line in his book *Garry Kasparov on Garry Kasparov: Part II* (publisher's note)

continuation 18...h4 19.h3 ♘xf3+ 20.gxf3 ♕xf3 is only dangerous for black: 21.♖f1 ♕xh3 22.♗c2! ♗g4 23.0-0-0! ♗xc3 24.♘xc3 ♗xd1 25.♖xd1. However, the gradual execution of the blockading plan 18...g5 19.0-0 ♘g6 keeps the initiative in black's hands.

Short castling 18.0-0 appears to be a trivial oversight, however, the evaluation of this natural move may prove critical to the assessment of the overall position. During the game, Seirawan was only worried about 18...♘g5, but after 19.♕e3! (19.♔h1? ♘exf3!) 19...♗h6 20.f4! it's hard to figure out who stands better.

Yasser made his choice guided by his intuitive, safety criteria and belief in his opponent's tactical acumen.

18...h4!(06)   19.h3(06)   g5! 20.0-0(08) ♗d7(10)

Black decides above all to improve the coordination of his major pieces. However, it would have been more logical when following the intended strategy to play 20...♘f8. In that case, to avoid a complete bind, white would have had to take a risk with 21.f4 gxf4 22.♘xf4, although 22...♘eg6! 23.♘fe2 ♘d7 24.♔h1 ♘de5 25.♗c2 ♗d7 would have left him with nothing better than to fight for equality.

Spassky believes that the maneuver 20...♗h6! is also unpleasant for white, forcing him to retreat, for example with 21.♔h1 g4 22.f4 g3!

21.♔h1(05) ♘f8(0)

Logical, but why didn't he spend any time thinking over it? After all, there were other interesting options that black shouldn't have ignored. For example, the unprotected white rook made the following line attractive: 21...♗h6! 22.♗c2 g4 23.f4 ♕g7 (23...♘g6 was also worth considering) 24.hxg4 ♘xg4 25.♕f3 f5 26.exf5 ♘hf6!.

22.♗g1(03) ♘fg6(0) 23.♗h2 (02)

Both players complete their maneuvering and are ready to begin the real battle.

23...c4?!(07) [11]

The world champion stops the logical implementation of his plan and suddenly begins a fight on the queenside, where he has no advantage in forces. He believed that the black pieces located on the kingside had taken up ideal positions, and that he could undermine the threat of f3-f4 by opening the c-file and placing his last unemployed piece on it. However, the cost of hastening the mobilization of the entire black army is too high. His opponent, who was ready to hunker down in deep defence, now gains the chance to activate his pieces previously locked

---

[11] Kasparov recommends 23...g4 in his book *Garry Kasparov on Garry Kasparov: Part II* (publisher's note)

in a cage. As a result, play becomes so sharp that it goes out of control and chaos soon reigns on the board.

The drawbacks of black's move were so obvious that Yasser, deciding that only he had chances of winning, spent the minutes while his clock ticked over this move simply on putting his thoughts in order. His reply didn't require consideration.

24.♖b1(03) ♖ac8(02)

It wasn't too late to stop spreading the fire. Of course, an attack launched by the thrust 24...g4 was now discredited by the careless push of the pawn from c5: 25.f4 g3 26.♗g1 ♗h6 27.♕d4!, however, he could have retained equal chances in a double-edged but no less chaotic position with 24...♕d8!, reminding white of his weak a5 pawn and opening the path for the f7 pawn to push forwards.

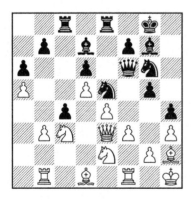

25.♕a7!(11)

It wasn't easy for Seirawan to settle on such a long, albeit tempting queen sortie. At the previous stage of the World Cup he had lost to Karpov straight after making a long queen move, from e2 to a6, in a slightly worse position. His king in that game was only left without serious protection for a single move, but that was enough for the ex-world champion to hit him with a nasty tactic. Such experiences play a role in how grandmasters make decisions, and sometimes serve as major guidelines.

25...♘f4?!(10)

The unexpectedly sharp activation of the white queen seriously unnerved the champion, and he made a hasty decision. So far there was no need to panic in fact, but it's unpleasant for anybody when their peaceful life is suddenly disrupted by unwanted concerns due to their own oversight. Seirawan didn't spend eleven minutes thinking about his last move for nothing.

Nevertheless, moving the queen to a7 had its drawback, too – white had weakened the defensive capability of his powerful kingside fortress, and so it was now that black simply had to turn the screws on the kingside by thrusting his pawn forward with 25...g4!. This was what worried Yasser the most, but he relaxed when concluding that after 26.hxg4 ♗xg4 (26...♘xg4 27.♗g1 h3 28.g3 ♘4e5 29.♗d4 with an advantage for white) 27.♘g1 ♘d3 28.♘ce2 white was on the verge of winning, for example, 28...c3? 29.♗c2. However, his evaluation was too optimistic, as the modest exchange 28...cxb3! retained an unclear situation on the board, for example: 29.♗xb3 ♗d7 30.♕xb7 ♘c5 31.♕b6 ♘e5 32.♗xe5 ♖xe5.

26.bxc4(06)

Without having readjusted to the sudden change from depressing existence to full-blooded living, Seirawan gets all excited and decides that he can immediately set about destroying his opponent's queenside.

After the game, he criticized his choice, believing that first exchanging with 26.♗xf4 gxf4 accorded him an advantage, as it deprived black of any attacking chances. After 27.♕xb7 a critical position arose which both grandmasters assessed as better for white – but they were mistaken. They based their evaluation on the line 27...♕d8 28.♕xa6 ♖a8 29.♕xd6 ♕xa5 30.bxc4, but ignored another option, 27...♖b8 28.♕xa6 ♖a8! 29.♕b6 ♖eb8 30.♕d4 ♖xa5, which in my view gives black counterplay, for example: 31.b4 ♖a3 32.b5 ♕g5 (or even 32...♘d3 33.♕xc4 ♖xc3 34.♘xc3 ♕xc3 35.♕xc3 ♗xc3 36.♖b3! ♗a5! 37.♖xd3 ♗xb5 38.♖b3 ♖b6! 39.♖g1 ♗c4 40.♖xb6 ♗xb6 41.♗c2 ♗xg1 42.♔xg1 ♔g7) 33.♕d2 ♘d3 34.♗c2 ♕e5 or 31.bxc4 ♖c8 32.♗b3 (32.♖b4 ♕g5 33.♕b6 ♖a1!) 32...♘xc4.

Having preserved the elasticity of his pawn chain, Yasser, without realizing it, had placed the game on the path of fantastic complications.

26...♘xc4(0)

The world champion's illogical choice, which sharply altered the nature and rhythm of the battle, presented both players with a ton of new problems and worries and knocked them out of the playing roles to which they had become used since the opening was over. The players didn't have sufficient time left to get into the skin of what was effectively a new game that had begun on move 24. This is the right way to explain the large number of impulsive decisions taken and missed opportunities. In the time remaining to control, the players' thought process was damaged by the tense situation that had suddenly emerged.

The world champion captured the pawn with his knight without thinking, although he had decent alternatives. Seirawan hadn't even looked at this capture, believing that the knight had to remain on e5 to defend the bishop. Yasser believed the only continuation to be 26...♖xc4 27.♖xb7 ♗c8 28.♖c7, correctly believing he was better here.

However, white's position is cemented by the two strongly linked knights, and the exchange of one of them would weaken white's foundations. This suggests two possible continuations:

(i) 26...♖xc4 27.♖xb7 ♘xe2! 28.♗xe2 ♖xc3 29.♗xe5 ♕xe5 30.♖xd7 ♕f4 31.♗xa6 ♗e5, and the more promising

(ii) 26...♘xe2! 27.♗xe5! (27. ♘xe2 ♘xc4 28.♖xb7 ♖a8 29.♕f2

♗b5 or 27.♗xe2 ♘xc4 28.♗xc4 ♖xc4 29.♘e2 ♗c8) 27...♘g3+ 28.♗xg3 hxg3 29.♖xb7 ♕xc3! 30.♖xd7 ♗d4 31.♕xa6 ♕d3, all of which grant black an advantage.

Here it's worth noting the great strength in reserve of both these grandmasters in such a tense situation. Despite their logical errors, the position continued to be equal. Only the initiative swung backwards and forwards.

27.♖xb7?!(07)

Now black manages to further raise the battle tension. Seirawan had his last chance to exchange his bishop with 27.♗xf4 gxf4, safeguarding his king. Then, the pawn capture 28.♖xb7 would have led to an unclear position, as can be seen by two lines, which also serve to highlight their authors' tastes: 28...♖a8 29.♕f2 ♗c8 30.♖a7 ♖xa7 31.♕xa7 ♕d8 32.♗a4 ♖e7 33.♕a8 ♘xa5 34.♖c1 ♖c7 (Seirawan) and 28...♘e3 29.♖g1 ♗b5 30.♘xb5 axb5 31.♖xb5 ♕a1 (Kasparov).

27...♘d2(03) 28.♖g1(06)

Alas, white had no choice. Other rook retreats were more dangerous, for example: 28.♖f2? ♖a8 29.♕e3 ♘c4 30.♕c1 ♘d3. After making his move, Seirawan stood up from the table sure that he was winning.[12]

28...♘xh3!(10)

Yasser had spent his time thinking about how white would gain an advantage after 28...♘d3.

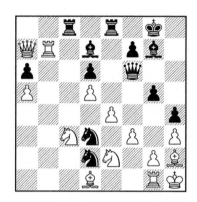

This is what he calculated:

(i) 29.♖xd7 ♖xc3 30.♘xc3 (30. ♖xd6? ♘xe4!!) 30...♕xc3 31.♗xd6 ♗d4 32.♕c7 ♘f2+ 33.♔h2 ♕e3 34.♖d8! ♖xd8 35.♕xd8+ ♔h7 36.♕f8 ♘g4+ 37.hxg4 ♕xg1+ 38.♔h3 ♕h1+ 39.♗h2 ♘f1 40.♕xf7+ ♗g7 41.♕h5+ ♗h6

(ii) 29.♗c2 ♖xc3 30.♘xc3 ♕xc3 31.♗xd3 ♗d4 32.♕xa6 ♗c8 33.♕c6! with an advantage. However, there are always errors in long variations. Instead of 31...♗d4 a stronger move was 31...♕xd3!, and after 32.♖xd7 ♗d4! 33.♕c7 ♗xg1! 34.♗xg1 (34. ♖d8 ♖xd8 35.♕xd8+ ♔h7 36.♗xg1 ♘f1!) 34...♘f1! the game should be a draw.

Kasparov's choice is obviously better based on general observations. His knight has stormed into the

---

[12] Kasparov recommends 28.e5 and places a question-mark against the move played in his book *Garry Kasparov on Garry Kasparov: Part II* (publisher's note)

enemy fortress, capturing on the way an important pawn defending the king. The knight attacks the rook and ties white's queen down to protecting the vital f2 square. Moreover, the players were too short of time to assess even roughly the consequences of capturing the knight.

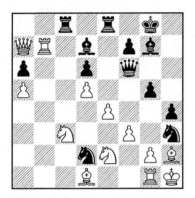

29.e5(0(!!))

It is hard to understand the reason for such a strange and, above all, instantaneous decision taken in a complex position. Seirawan, as he later admitted, had missed black's previous move. His pawn sac was more likely a flash of intuition than a bluff. Yasser believed that the d5-e4-f3-g2-h3 pawn chain had been a strong fence keeping out the black knights, yet once the knights had nevertheless leapt over it the fence was no longer needed. In sending the pawn to its death, white's aim is not so much to use the e4 square for his knight, but,

rather, considering the capture 29... dxe5 to be the most natural one, he plans to liquidate the threats to the c3-e2 knight pair, which he viewed as the foundation of his defense.

Alternatives to the move 29.e5 were analyzed after the game, and several leading grandmasters took part, enthusiastically attempting to get to the truth. Yasser believed that he had missed the chance to save the game by not playing 29.♖xd7 ♖a8 30.♕b6 ♘c4! 31.♖f1! ♘xb6 32.♖xd6 and then 32...♕e7 33.♖xb6 ♘f4 34.♘xf4 gxf4 35.d6. It is indeed hard to assess this position, but it was far from mandatory for black.[13] With the queen sac 32...♕xd6! 33.♗xd6 ♘c4! 34.♗a4 ♘xd6 35.♗xe8 ♖xe8 36.gxh3 ♖c8 he would have retained some advantage.

During the game Seirawan had no inkling of the fantastic position hidden in his variation after 29.♖xd7 ♖a8 30.♕b6 ♘c4 31.gxh3!! and then 31...♘xb6 32.axb6 ♕xf3+ 33.♖g2

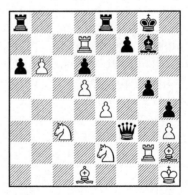

---

[13] Kasparov recommends 33...♗xc3 as winning for black in his book *Garry Kasparov on Garry Kasparov: Part II* (publisher's note)

At the board it would have been impossible to adequately assess the chaotic position imprinted on the diagram. Black captures another piece, but at the same time has to allow the rest of the white army to gain activity and for a short time has to leave his king under fire. Black only has to select the lesser evil of 33...g4 34.♘g1! ♕xc3 35.♖xg4 or 33...♗xc3 34.♘xc3 ♕xc3 35.♖xg5+ ♔h8 36.b7 ♖ab8 37.♖xd6 f6.[14]

These variations could not have been calculated at the board either, so we should admit that in giving up the pawn, Seirawan intuitively again found the best practical chance, one which caused so many complexities that the only compasses showing the way were intuition and... luck.

29...♖xe5?(0(!))

At a critical moment in the battle, when precise moves are worth their weight in gold, Garry takes an impulsive, hard-to-explain and, evidently, erroneous decision. The champion's poor form has made itself felt. Faced with an unforeseen reaction by his opponent, he again loses his way, and his instantaneous reaction when he had a wide choice proves to be quite poor.

At the same time, the paradoxical 29...♖c5 was much more in keeping with Garry's style. In this case, both 30.♗f4 ♕f5 31.♗xd2 ♗xe5 32.f4 ♘f2+ 33.♔h2 ♖xc3 34.♗xc3 ♗xf4+ 35.♘xf4 ♕xf4+ 36.g3 hxg3+ 37.♖xg3 ♘xd1 and 30.♖f1 ♖xe5! 31.♗xe5 ♕xe5 32.gxh3 ♘xf1 33.f4 ♕e3 were to black's advantage, while 30.♖e1 ♘f2+ 31.♔g1 ♘h3+ leads to perpetual check. Moreover, black had great chances to retain the initiative were he to simply withdraw his queen from the attack: 29...♕f5. As the black bishop was poisoned, 30.♖xd7? ♕xd7! 31.♕xd7 ♘f2#, Seirawan would again have had to find a defense to mate, as a result of which another fantastic position would have arisen: 30.e6! ♖a8! 31.exd7 ♖ed8! 32.♕b6 (32.♕e3? ♘c4 33.g4 ♘xe3 34.gxf5 ♘f2#) 32...♘c4 33.gxh3 ♘xb6 34.axb6 ♕xf3+ 35.♖g2 ♗xc3 36.♘xc3 ♕xc3 37.♖xg5+ ♔h8 (37...♔f8?? 38.♗xd6#) where white was faced with a tricky choice between 38.♖c7 ♕e1+ 39.♖g1 ♕e4+ 40.♖g2 ♖g8 41.♗g4 ♖xg4 42.hxg4 h3 43.♖c8+ ♔h7 and 38.♖h5+ ♔g7 39.♗g4 a5! 40.♖c7 ♕e1+ 41.♗g1 a4 42.b7 ♖ab8 43.♖c8 ♖xb7 44.♖xd8 ♕e4+.[15] Finally, the third path with

---

[14] Kasparov recommends 33...♕xh3 as tipping the scales in black's favor in his book *Garry Kasparov on Garry Kasparov: Part II* (publisher's note)

[15] Kasparov recommends 39...♕e1+ in this line in his book *Garry Kasparov on Garry Kasparov: Part II* (publisher's note)

29...dxe5 was evidently the most favorable one for black: 30.♖xd7 ♖a8! 31.♕e3! (31.♕c5 ♖ec8!) 31...♘c4 32.♘e4! ♕f5! 33.♕c5 ♖ac8![16]

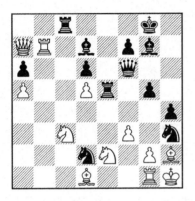

30.♖xd7!(03)

White's decision to preserve his bishop was totally correct, as after 30.♗xe5 dxe5 31.♖xd7 e4! the black pieces would unexpectedly come to life and the outcome of the battle would be unclear, for example: 32.♕e3 ♘xg1 33.♔xg1 ♘xf3+ 34.gxf3 exf3 35.♘e4 ♕f5 or 32.♘xe4 ♘xe4 33.gxh3 ♕xf3+ 34.♖g2 ♕h3+ 35.♔g1 ♕d3!

30...♘xg1(01) 31.♕xg1(01)

Each player had just six minutes left to reach move 40, and the situation remained extremely tense. Yasser's intuition again told him to cherish his bishop, but evidently this was a mistake. After 31.♗xe5 ♕xe5 32.♕xg1 h3 33.♕f2 hxg2+ 34.♔xg2 ♘c4! 35.♔g1 ♘e3 36.♗a4 ♘xd5 37.♘xd5 ♕xd5 38.♕e3! it was not easy for black to find a way to save the day. Prior to this point black had never looked so close to losing.

31...♖ee8

It is hard to recommend a better move, although Seirawan was only worried about 31...h3 and still had no intention of capturing the rook.

32.♖xd6 ♕f5 33.♗a4!(02)

A very unpleasant blow in a time scramble.

33...♕d3

It's catastrophic here for black to spend a tempo on retreating the rook, for example, 33...♖e7 34.♖c6 ♖ce8 35.d6! and so on.[17] Realizing that black would be doomed if he followed such a "correct" and at the same time forced turn of events, Garry found the best practical chance. He unexpectedly "throws" his queen into white's camp ice-hockey style, ignoring the losses it entails. In such a desperate position, his priority was to create a new, unforeseen situation in which either player could easily go wrong.

---

[16] Kasparov doesn't consider this line and insists that 29...♕f5! was the only right move in his book *Garry Kasparov on Garry Kasparov: Part II* (publisher's note)

[17] Kasparov recommends this line and improves it with 34...♖xc6 as maintaining the balance and places a question-mark against his actual 33rd move in his book *Garry Kasparov on Garry Kasparov: Part II* (publisher's note)

34.♗xe8 ♖xe8 35.♖c6 h3!(02)

The world champion decided to head for this position in his attempt to save the game. Seirawan is sure that white had a big advantage here. I also believe that black should be punished for his play – otherwise, where is justice in chess? Yet I failed to find any lines that proved it!

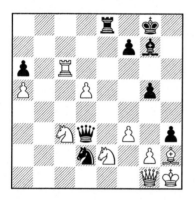

36.♗g3?!

Yasser rightly criticizes this move and explains his choice by the desire to protect e1 from invasion by the black rook, which is especially dangerous when your flag is hanging. He believes that the game is decided by 36.♕f2 and brings the following evidence: 36...♖e3 37.♖c8+ ♔h7 38.♕g3! hxg2+ 39.♕xg2 ♖xf3 40.♘g1! ♖f1 41.♘e2! followed by ♘g3 and ♕h3. However, black can improve with 36...hxg2+ 37.♔xg2 ♘c4!, preserving equal chances after 38.♖xc4 (38.♘e4 g4!) 38...♕xc4 39.♘e4 g4 40.♘2g3 ♕xd5.[18]

36...hxg2+!   37.♕xg2(02) ♘xf3(01) 38.d6

Ignoring the further strengthening of his opponent's attacking potential would be fatal for white. By pure intuition, Seirawan complicates the struggle further. By advancing his pawn, he hopes to break any new attacking wave, for example: 38...♕h7+ 39.♗h2 ♗e5 40.d7 ♖d8 41.♖c8. White later criticized himself for not playing 38.♕f2, but his position after 38...g4 39.♘f4 ♕h7+ 40.♔g2 ♘e1+ 41.♕xe1 ♖xe1 42.♗xe1 is really unclear. Moreover, black could have equalized with 38...♗xc3!? 39.♖xc3 ♕d1+ 40.♘g1 ♘xg1 41.♕xg1 ♕xd5+.[19]

38...♖e6!

With white's flag on the verge of falling, any new threat, even not a particularly serious one (39...♖h6+) is unpleasant at the very least because it is distracting and eats up precious seconds.

39.♕f2 g4?!

A risky and, above all, impulsive decision, dictated by the fact that Seirawan only had a few seconds left to

---

[18] Kasparov states that 36.gxh3! was winning for white in his book *Garry Kasparov on Garry Kasparov: Part II* (publisher's note)

[19] If 38.♕f2 Kasparov recommends 38...♕h7+! in his book *Garry Kasparov on Garry Kasparov: Part II* (publisher's note)

make his last move. However, in such circumstances the most unpleasant problems are those requiring a choice to be made. From that point of view, the move 39...♗xc3! would have done more damage to white, who would have had to figure out the right way to recapture. It turns out that white could not have retained a material advantage with 40.♘xc3, as the line 40...♖e1+ 41.♔g2 ♖g1+ 42.♕xg1 ♘xg1 43.♖c8+ ♔h7 44.d7 ♕xd7 45.♖c7 ♕d3 caused him difficulties. Only the return of material with 40.♖xc3! ♕d1+ 41.♘g1! ♘xg1 42.♖c8+ ♔g7 43.♕xg1 ♕f3+ 44.♕g2 ♕d1+, requiring precise calculation from white, would have led to a draw.

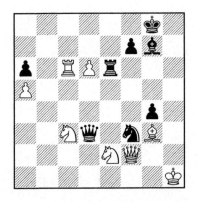

40.♖c8+

Seirawan would physically have not been able to make one more move. He was unhappy with this move, but the majority of grandmasters would have done the same given such a shortage of time. He believes that he again missed the chance to win with 40.♔g2! This move is indeed objectively stronger, and the line that he showed 40...♗xc3 41.♖xc3! ♕d5 42.♘f4! is convincing. However, it's questionable whether white has an advantage after 40...♘e1+!, for example: 41.♕xe1 ♕f3+ 42.♔g1 ♕xc6! 43.♕d2! ♗f6! 44.♕d5 ♕xd5 45.♘xd5 ♗d8 or 41.♔f1 ♘c2! 42.♔g1 ♗d4! 43.♘xd4 ♘xd4 44.♖c5! ♘f3+ 45.♔g2 ♘e1+ 46.♕xe1 ♖xe1 47.♗xe1 ♕xd6.[20]

Without doubt, 40.♔g2! would have enabled white to fight for the full point, but you don't make that sort of move with your last seconds if you can check your opponent instead.

40...♔h7(01) 41.♘f4(37!)

The American's long think convinced him that he could not win here, and, tired of the emotional rollercoaster, he decided to force move repetition.

41...♖h6+(01) 42.♔g2 ♘e1+ 43.♔g1

White cannot take the knight: 43.♕xe1?? ♕f3+ 44.♔g1 ♖h1#.

43...♘f3+ 44.♔g2 ♘e1+

Draw agreed.

A great battle! Fantastic chaos!

This game, like many others in this book, should be played through for its instructive use.

---

[20] Kasparov states that after 40.♔g2 only 40...♖h6+! with the idea of 41...♘e1+! led to an immediate draw in his book *Garry Kasparov on Garry Kasparov: Part II* (publisher's note)

Game 39

Tilburg was the last tournament where I acted as Kasparov's second, and this game was the last one that I could recount as a direct witness providing observations useful for young players on the road to chess Mount Olympus.

V. IVANCHUK – G. KASPAROV
Tilburg. International tournament. 28.09.1989
Sicilian Defense. [B96]

1.e4 c5 2.♘f3 d6 3.d4 cxd4 4.♘xd4 ♘f6 5.♘c3 a6 6.♗g5

Ivanchuk made a decent start to the double round-robin grandmaster tournament in Tilburg. However, his first game against the world champion in the tournament, which the latter again won (this time in a strictly positional style) knocked Vasily out of his stride. He lost several games and found himself hopelessly behind the leading pack. Nevertheless, we expected him to be properly ready for the second game. The only way for him to demonstrate to the world his importance in Big Chess was to take the game to the world champion and hold his own. White's choice of an aggressive opening setup (previously Vasily had preferred 6.♗e2) confirmed our prediction.

6...e6 7.f4 ♛c7 8.♛e2

A second opening surprise. White avoids an excursion through the theoretical debris after 8.♛f3 and plans to launch an attack on a less usual square. He is staking on the e4-e5 break, not being afraid of complications after 8...b5 9.e5 b4 10.♘cb5! axb5 11.exf6.

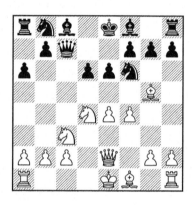

8...♘c6!

Faced with an unexpected move, Garry is of course guided by his experience of studying Sicilian positions. Above all, he focuses on mobilizing his forces as quickly as possible.

9.0-0-0 ♘xd4 10.♖xd4 ♗e7 11.e5?!

White had a wide choice of continuations that would have maintained uncertainty on the board 11.♛d3, 11.♛d2 and 11.♗h4. However, the young grandmaster finds it psychologically challenging to maintain the tension in an argument against such a menacing opponent, and so he chooses to bring certainty. His decision turns out to be premature, as the e5 pawn soon turns into a target of attack.

11...dxe5   12.fxe5   ♘d5 13.♗xe7?!

This new impulsive decision by Ivanchuk makes it harder to protect the unfortunate pawn. He had to exchange knights with 13.♗d2! ♘xc3 14.♗xc3, retaining approximately equal chances, for example: 14...0-0 15.♕e4 ♗d7 16.♗d3 g6.

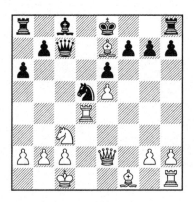

Vasily now poses his opponent a test: 13...♘xc3? 14.♕g4! ♕xe5 15.♗h4 ♕e3+ 16.♖d2 ♘xa2+ 17.♔d1 0-0 18.♕a4, but it's too easy for the champion.

13...♘xe7! 14.♘e4 0-0 15.♕h5

White rightly assumed that the weakness of the e5 pawn would prevent the knight from establishing itself on d6 and hence plans a different journey for it.

15...♘g6

Black is consistent in his attempt to limit his opponent's aggression, and rejects the more committal 15...♘f5, which would lead to massive

complications after 16.♘f6+! gxf6 17.♗d3 ♕xe5 18.♖e4! ♘g7! 19.♖xe5 ♘xh5 20.♖xh5 f5 21.g4! fxg4 22.♖g1.

16.♘g5 h6 17.♘f3

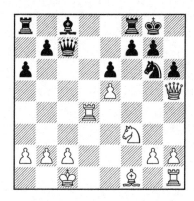

A critical moment in the battle. At first glance, white has rid himself of his problems, as it seems that black has no counter to ♗f1-d3xg6 that would strengthen white's position.

17...b5?

Despite thinking for over 20 minutes, Kasparov ignores the logical 17...♖d8!, leaving all of white's problems unsolved. After the forced exchange 18.♖xd8+ (18.♖g4 ♖d5! 19.♗c4 ♖xe5!) 18...♕xd8 black quickly creates play in the center by getting his bishop to c6, for example: 19.♕g4! (19.♗d3 ♘f4 20.♕g4 ♘xd3+ 21.cxd3 b5! or 19.♗c4 ♕c7 20.♗b3 ♗d7 21.♖e1 ♗c6 22.♔b1 ♖d8) 19...♕a5! 20.♗c4 ♗d7 21.♖e1 ♗c6 22.♕g3 ♖c8! 23.♗b3 ♗xf3 24.gxf3 ♖c5.

18.♗d3 ♗b7 19.♗xg6 fxg6 20.♕xg6 ♗d5!

Kasparov   risks   nothing   in

sacrificing the pawn – his bishop is that strong.

21.♔b1 ♖ac8 22.♖c1 ♕e7 23.♖g4 ♖c4 24.♖xc4 bxc4 25.c3 ♕a7

It was worth considering transposing to an endgame with 25... ♖f4!? 26.♖e1 ♕f7! 27.♕xf7+ ♔xf7, where the activity of the black king heading for f5 compensated for the missing pawn. However, the world champion already wanted to rest. He had already come to terms with a draw and was waiting for peace initiatives.

26.♕c2 ♗xf3 27.gxf3 ♕e3 28.♕a4 ♕d3+ 29.♔a1 ♖xf3 30.a3! ♕d5 31.♕xa6 ♖h3 32.♖g1

The exchange of queens with 32.♕d6 ♕xd6 33.exd6 ♔f7 also led to a clear draw.

32...♖xh2 33.♕c8+ ♔h7 34.♕c7 ♖g2! 35.♖xg2 ♕d1+ 36.♔a2 ♕b3+ Draw agreed.

This was Ivanchuk's first draw with the world champion after three losses. Three years later, he would score his first, wonderful win against Kasparov.

APPENDIX 1

Kasparov's Main Tournaments and Matches

No.	Year	Competition	City	+	–	=	Place	D	C	OE
1	1978	Sokolsky Memorial	Minsk	11	2	4	1	0.5*		
2	1978	All-Union Qualifying Tournament	Daugavpils	6	1	6	1			
3	1978	46th USSR championship (H. League)	Tbilisi	4	4	9	9			
4	1979	International tournament	Banja Luka	8	0	7	1	2	10	2488
5	1979	47th USSR championship (H. League)	Minsk	6	3	8	3-4	*	12	2533
6	1980	European team championship	Skara	5	0	1				
7	1980	International tournament	Baku	8	0	7	1	0.5*	10	2487
8	1980	World Junior Championship	Dortmund	8	0	5	1	1.5	-	
9	1980	24th Olympiad (2nd reserve)	Malta	8	1	3	-	-		
10	1981	International tournament	Moscow	3	1	9	2-4		15	2601
11	1981	International tournament	Tilburg	3	3	5	6-8		15	2608
12	1981	49th USSR championship (H. League)	Frunze	10	2	5	1-2		12	2529
13	1982	International tournament	Bugojno	6	0	7	1	1.5	14	2583
14	1982	Interzonal	Moscow	7	0	6	1	1.5*	12	2545
15	1982	25th Olympiad (2nd board)	Lucerne	6	0	5	-		14	2576
16	1983	Candidates match (1/4 f.)	Moscow	4	1	4	1	-		
17	1983	International tournament	Niksic	9	1	4	1	2.0	14	2590
18	1983	Candidates match (1/2 f.)	London	4	1	6	1	-		
19	1984	Candidates match (final)	Vilnius	4	0	9	1	-		
20	1984/5	World Chess Championship	Moscow	3	5	40				
21	1985	Match with Hubner	Hamburg	3	0	3	1	-		
22	1985	Match with Andersson	Belgrade	2	0	4	1	-		
23	1985	World Chess Championship	Moscow	5	3	16	1	-		
24	1985	Match with Timman	Hilversum	3	1	2	1	-		
25	1986	Match with Miles	Basel	5	0	1	1	-		

D   Distance from 2nd

C   Category

OE   Opponent'sElo

*   indicates where Kasparov won his last game to gain his tournament or match place.

No.	Year	Competition	City	+	–	=	Place	D	C	OE
26	1986	World Chess Championship	London/							
			Leningrad	5	4	15	1	-		
27	1986	27th Olympiad (1st board)	Dubai	7	1	3	–	*		
28	1986	International tournament	Brussels	6	1	3	1	2.0	16	2637
29	1987	International tournament	Brussels	6	0	5	1-2		14	2581
30	1987	World Chess Championship	Seville	4	4	16	1-2	*		
31	1988	International tournament	Amsterdam	6	0	6	1	2.5	17	2674
32	1988	World Cup stage	Belfort	9	1	5	1	1.0*	15	2624
33	1988	49th USSR championship (H. League)	Moscow	6	0	11	1-2		14	2594
34	1988	World Cup stage	Reykjavík	6	1	10	1	0.5*	15	2618
35	1988	28th Olympiad (1st board)	Thessaloniki	7	0	3	1			
36	1989	World Cup stage	Barcelona	7	1	8	1-2	*	15	2615
37	1989	World Cup stage	Skelleftea	4	0	11	1-2		16	2633
38	1989	International tournament	Tilburg	10	0	4	1	3.5	16	2626
39	1989	International tournament	Belgrade	6	0	3	1	3.0	15	2613
40	1990	International tournament	Linares	6	1	4	1	0.5	16	2629
41	1990	Match with Psakhis	Murcia	4	0	2	1			
42	1990	World Chess Championship	New York/							
			Lyon	4	3	17	1	-		
43	1991	International tournament	Linares	6	1	6	2		17	2658
44	1991	International tournament	Amsterdam	2	0	7	3-4		16	2636
45	1991	International tournament	Tilburg	7	1	5	1	1.5	17	2666
46	1991	Int. tournament (active chess)	Paris	5	1	2	2		17	2683
47	1991	International tournament	Reggio	3	1	2	2-3		17	2679
48	1992	International tournament	Linares	7	0	6	1	2.0	17	2659
49	1992	International tournament	Dortmund	5	2	2	1-2	*	17	2659
50	1992	30th Olympiad (1st board)	Manila	7	0	3	1		16	2626
51	1992	European team championship (1st board)	Debrecen	4	0	4	1		15	2616
52	1992	Int. tournament (active chess)	Paris	8	1	1	1	2.0	17	2671
53	1993	International tournament	Linares	7	0	6	1	2.5	17	2677
54	1993	World Chess Championship	London	6	1	13	1			

APPENDIX 2

Kasparov's Records

1	January 1975 11 years 9 months	Debut in the junior (under 18) Soviet championship	7th place +4 −2=3
	No boy below the age of 12 had ever before participated in official competitions in that age group		
2	January 1976 12 years 9 months	Soviet junior champion (under 18)	+6 −1=2
	No boy below the age of 13 had ever before won a national championship in that age group. Bobby Fischer became US junior champion at 13.		
3	July 1976 13 years 3 months	Debut in the world junior championship (under 16)	Shared 3rd place +4 −1=4
	No boy had ever debuted at such an age in official FIDE tournaments for 16 year olds		
4	January 1977 13 years 9 months	Soviet junior champion (under 18)	+8 −0=1
	No junior of any age had won the title of Soviet junior champion twice in a row. His score of 8.5/9 was also a record for such tournaments.		
5	January 1978 14 years 9 months	Made the Master of Sport of the USSR norm at the Sokolsky Memorial with more points than required.	1st place +11 −2=4
	Nobody at his age had won an adult tournament of master's level. Made the master's norm by a record 3.5 points more than required.		
6	December 1978 15 years 8 months	Debut in the Higher League of the USSR championship.	9th place +4 −4=9
	Before that, the record belonged to Botvinnik, who debuted at the age of 16.		

7	April 1979 16 years	Debut in an international grandmaster tournament in Yugoslavia	1st place +9 −0=6
	Before Kasparov, nobody of that age had won a grandmaster tournament, all the more so with a 2695 performance rating. After round 10 he already had 9.5 points! Made his first grandmaster norm with two rounds to spare.		
8	December 1979 16 years 8 months	Third place in the adult USSR championship	+6 −3=8
	Nobody had before won a prize at the age of 16 in the adult USSR championship		
9	January 1980 16 years 9 months	Debut in the Soviet adult team at the European team championship	+5 −0=1
10	January 1980 16 years 9 months	Debut in the international rating list with the highest ever Elo rating for a debutant	
	Nobody had ever before debuted with such a high rating – 2595, making him 15th in the world.		
11	April 1980 17 years	Made his second grandmaster norm with points to spare and awarded the grandmaster title	
	Only Fischer became a grandmaster at a younger age than Kasparov (15).		
12	August 1980 17 years 4 months	World Under 20 Champion	+8 −0=5
	Gaining the title at this age was a record for Soviet players		
13	December 1980 17 years 8 months	Olympic champion as part of the Soviet team	+8 −1=3
	The youngest Olympic champion in the history of chess		

14	December 1981 18 years 8 months	Soviet champion	+10 −2=5
	The youngest Soviet champion in history		
15	September 1982 19 years 5 months	Winner of the interzonal	+7 −0=6
	The youngest ever participant in the candidates cycle		
16	November 1985 22 years 7 months	World champion, defeating Karpov	+5 −3=16
	Youngest ever world chess champion		
17	November 1986 23 years 7 months	World champion for the second time, defeating Karpov	+5 −4=15
	Youngest ever two-times world chess champion		
18	December 1987 24 years 8 months	World champion for the third time, drawing with Karpov	+4 −4=16
	Youngest ever three-times world chess champion		
19	September 1989 26 years 5 months	Winner of the first World Cup, the unofficial tournament world championship	
	So far the only winner [21]		
20	October 1989 26 years 6 months	Sets a world record Elo rating at the super-GM tournament in Tilburg	1st place +10 −0=4
	Exceeds Fischer's previous record rating (2785) set in 1972 by ten points		

---

[21] As of the publication date of the original book (publisher's note)

21	November 1989 26 years 7 months	New record rating of 2800 set at the super-GM tournament in Belgrade	1st place +8 −0=3
	Setting a new historical level. According to the rating system used in the USSR, his rating would have been 2811		
22	December 1990 27 years 8 months	World champion for the fourth time, defeating Karpov	+4 −3=17
23	October 1993 30 years 6 months	World champion for the fifth time, defeating Short (organized without the involvement of FIDE)	+6 −1=13
24	October 1995 32 years 6 months	World champion for the sixth time, defeating Anand (match organized by the Professional Chess Association)	+4 −1=13
25	September 1997	New record rating of 2820	+4 −3=17

APPENDIX 3

What Kasparov's Chess Career in Ratings Tells Us

	Kasparov	Karpov			Kasparov	Karpov	Kramnik
01.07.77	2320	2739		01.01.91	2800	2725	
01.01.78	2381	2716		01.07.91	2770	2730	
01.01.79	2453	2713		01.01.92	2780	2725	
01.01.80	2534	2718		01.07.92	2790	2715	
01.01.81	2625	2690		01.01.93	2805	2725	
01.01.82	2640	2720		01.07.93	2760	2760	2710
01.01.83	2690	2710		01.01.94	2740	2740	2710
01.01.84	2710	2700		01.07.94	2780	2780	2725
01.01.85	2715	2705		01.01.95	2805	2765	2715
01.01.86	2720	2700		01.07.95	2795	2775	2730
01.01.87	2735	2715		01.01.96	2775	2770	2775
01.01.88	2750	2715		01.07.96	2785	2775	2765
01.01.89	2775	2750		01.01.97	2795	2760	2740
01.01.90	2800	2730		01.07.97	2820	2745	2770

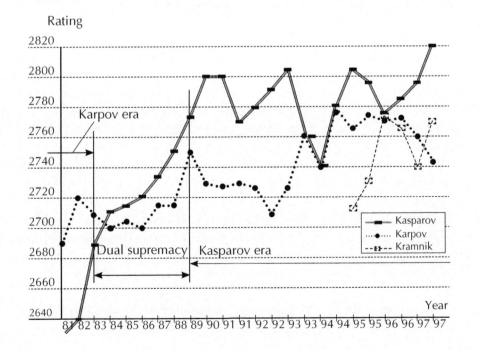

Charts and tables can provide a lot of instructive information if we look at them carefully.

In the period from mid-1977, when Garry first received a national rating (2320), to the end of 1989, he constantly increased that rating.

The first phase of his growth, from July 1977 until the end of 1980, could be compared with the launch of a space rocket, rapidly accelerating. Over those three and a half years, Kasparov's annual rating increase averaged 87 points. There is no other grandmaster who could boast of such a steadily high and lengthy rating increase, especially above the 2500 level.

Further, after he obtained his first international rating based on his 1979 performance, the lad immediately reached 15th place in the world. The following year, already a grandmaster, Garry shot up to number six.

A year later, and the tenacious Kasparov, already a participant in the candidates cycle, had gained the number two spot on the FIDE list. No other player ever got to the number two spot just two years after their first international rating. Many of Kasparov's fans were worried at the time whether he would hold on to such a high ranking. Well, he had other plans...

The final phase of his growth, beginning from the incredible level of 2710, and ending with his new record level of 2800, can be compared with a space rocket reaching its orbit. His continuous presence on that orbit over a lengthy period (seven years) without any periods of decline is perhaps an even more significant indicator than the earlier growth in his rating, as it reflects constantly strong performances in super tournaments.

The new record of 2805, not to mention the Soviet rating of 2811, was 20 points ahead of the previous record set by Fischer in 1972 after he crushed his opponents in the candidates cycle. However, later that year Fischer lost 5 rating points and disappeared from chess, while Garry remained at his record level for an entire year, playing in a tournament and two matches in the period.

His results are best understood in comparison. So how did Kasparov's performance compare with that of his predecessor on the top of chess Mount Olympus?

Karpov achieved his highest rating of 2755 back in 1974, and it slipped just half a year later. Throughout the 15 years shown on the chart, Karpov's rating danced around the average of 2710. We can consider this level to be truly indicative of the ex-champion's ability over a long period in his chess career.

At first glance, such a conclusion sounds unfair for a grandmaster wishing to increase the number of his tournament victories to the impressive record number of 100 and then 150, and who right up to 1983-84 viewed his nearest rivals through a binocular. Yet the figures don't lie.

After 1975, Karpov stopped trying to win every game and began to satisfy himself with first place in tournaments with a minimal distance from second place. Perhaps, knowing how much strength and nervous energy he had in reserve, he wanted to put off a worsening in results for as long as possible. Until the end of the 1970s, no other grandmaster was able to remain for long at the level of 2650, and Karpov was ensured a peaceful life as champion. He was used to that life, and when the young Kasparov appeared he couldn't readjust – his body was no longer used to such a huge workload.

As a result, with the exception of a flash of great performances at the start of the World Cup in 1988, when Karpov attempted to become the world tournament champion, he remained around his usual level of 2710.

The chart showing the gap between the ratings of Kasparov and Karpov leads to interesting conclusions. Their rating rivalry began in the middle of 1980, when the fast-improving grandmaster found himself 150 points behind the blissfully happy champion. Kasparov needed just two years to reduce the gap so much that the world recognized him as the only serious challenger to Karpov's crown. A period of dual supremacy began during which the champion could no longer consider his position on the throne as secure.

The dual supremacy of the two Ks can be considered to have lasted for six years, when the difference in the Elos didn't exceed 25 points – in other words, they belonged to the same rating category. This period began when Kasparov became the challenger, and ended after Karpov's poor performance at the Rotterdam stage of the world cup in the first half of 1989. Karpov began to lag more and more.

Chess fans used to the eternal standoff between the two Ks perhaps missed the moment when a number of young grandmasters first attempted to bridge the rating gap separating them from the two titans. At first, the talented Ukrainian grandmaster Vasily Ivanchuk proved to be the most persistent of them, maintaining an Elo above 2700 for two years and even catching up with Karpov.

So the new chess king has probably not breathed a sigh of relief, seeing his long-terms rival gradually reduce his level. He hasn't needed binoculars to see the young pretenders climbing towards the summit.

So far, the younger generation hasn't achieved much success in candidates matches, but this is down to the specifics of match play, requiring great experience that comes with the years. The young Kasparov was greatly helped to reduce the "waiting time" in a similar situation by frequent encounters (not only over the chess board) with ex-champions and grandmasters of the older generation who had already lived through the bear pit of the candidates cycle. For him, too, though, the process of adaptation to battle at the highest level was far from painless.

The generation of Anand, Ivanchuk and the now fast progressing Kramnik is most unlikely to gain such priceless help, and they will need to build up experience through trial and error, expending an irrational amount of nervous energy. This suggests that the reign of the next, 14th world champion, will be shorter than that of his two great predecessors.

APPENDIX 4

The Benefits of Chess Chronometry
Chronometry of the game Kasparov vs. Akesson, 1980 [22]

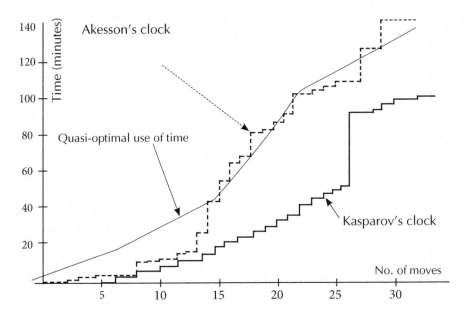

Chronometry of the game Karpov vs. Kasparov, Seville match, game 5, 1987 [23]

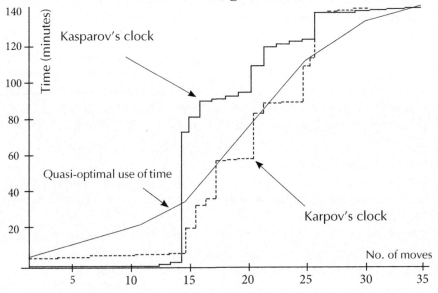

[22] Game 42 in Volume I
[23] Game 33 in the present Volume

Chronometry of the game Kasparov vs. Ivanchuk, 1988 [24]

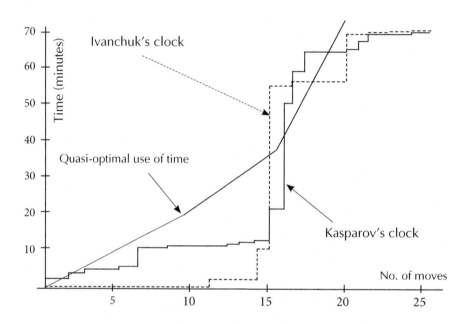

Many chess players attempt to record the time spent on thinking over every move. The simplest and quickest way, without disturbing your focus, is to record the minute hand's position on the score sheet as soon as you write down the move you have just made. Kasparov did just that, starting from the age of thirteen, turning time keeping into a natural continuation of the writing down of the actual move. The elementary calculation of the amount of time spent on each move, consisting of subtracting the previous position of the minute hand from the current position, is best carried out at home before you analyze the game. If, however, you don't have the time (or desire) to analyze the game, chronometry won't be of any use to you, and will be of interest only to a statistician.

Chronometry is no replacement for chess analysis, but enhances it. Being deeply illustrative material, it helps you to identify certain facts and laws that usual game analysis will not find.

Chronometry combined with other graphical methods of analyzing games enables you to draw conclusions that considerably add to your chess analysis and even suggest new areas for analysis.

---

[24] Game 35 in the present Volume

Even ten years ago we could only dream of using graphic methods in our chess analysis. Creating charts was a laborious task even for people with mathematical skills, and for the majority of chess players this task justifiably resembled a monster threatening to eat up tons of time on boring technical work that had no relation to chess. Now however, when most players use computers, it's simple and easy to create such graphs. What used to take several hours doesn't take more than half an hour with the use of the right software.

So what exactly is the use of chronometry?

Chess time keeping allows you to plan the optimal allocation of time spent thinking about moves across various stages of a chess game, and to monitor the deviation from the optimal time on any move. This disciplines thinking and is an effective way to avoid time trouble.

Demonstrating which moves you spend a long time thinking over, chronometry makes you identify the types of position whose understanding and playing need to be improved by additional study at home, so that when you get to the board you take decisions more quickly, more effectively and without unnecessary expenditure of time and energy.

Chronometry is a great help in curing the disease of time trouble well-known to many chess players. Based on its analysis, you can try to select the most effective chess tool able to liquidate the reason for your time trouble.

Time keeping allows you to judge whether it is useful to spend a long time thinking over a move and, counting from which moment in your thinking you need to give yourself a firm order to end your hesitation and make a move on the board. Frequent thinks over moves lasting 20-30 minutes are usually a sign that you lack sufficient discipline in your thinking or need to strengthen your resolve.

At the same time, the curve showing the time spent on thinking over moves can help to identify the player's form, both his readiness for the current game and for the competition as a whole.

Chess analysis with the help of chronometry helps you to identify the player's degree of foreboding of critical moments of the battle. An ability to sense an approaching crisis point in a game is one of the most important qualities separating a good grandmaster from an average IM. Decisions that the player has to make during the game should be not only correct and well thought out, but also taken in a reasonable time scale.

Full analysis of a game intended to correct errors in one's play should include detailed graphic analysis. The latter is based on specific chess analysis needed to build additional charts, such as changes to the evaluation after every move, an assessment of the quality of every move, and so on.

The effect obtained from graphic analysis depends directly on the quality and depth of the actual analysis of the game. There is a direct link between these two types of analysis. Decent analysis of a game provides useful facts and conclusions when combined with graphic analysis, which often points to the need for additional chess analysis in various areas allowing you to reach deeper conclusions and make recommendations for chess study that are of more use to the player. The wide use of chess computers during a player's preparation allows you to recommend such a type of full analysis for constant improvement. In particular, you should subject games that made you think about the reasons for your wins and, above all losses, to such analysis.

Reading the story of Kasparov's games in this book, you may have noticed how the author attempted to explain many moves with reference to chronometry. We will try to obtain some conclusions that you can make by viewing only the main, chronometric chart, from the game Kasparov - Akesson (game No. 42 in Volume I of this book).

The chart shows three chronometric curves. The top and bottom indicate the amount of time spent by each player on thinking over moves. From the very start of our collaboration, I made Garry also write down the time use of his opponent, which proved to be very useful during matches, as it enabled us to uncover weaknesses in the chess thinking of his opponents that they of course attempted to hide.

The middle curve is purely indicative; the optimal expenditure of time according to which time spent on each move is distributed evenly, although there are differences depending on the stage of the game. The parameters of this curve are determined by the players themselves depending on their opening knowledge, playing style and readiness for the tournament. For example, I consider that it makes sense to spend only two minutes on each of the first ten moves of the game, followed by no more than three minutes on each of the next five. The main expenditure of time is usually on the middlegame (from around move 16 to move 25), when there are still no concrete targets to attack and hence there are no concrete action plans, or, alternatively, when a fierce battle is under way whose outcome depends on the quality and quantity of calculations made. I estimate the norm for thinking per move at seven minutes. Then the norm gradually declines back down to two minutes for each of the last ten moves prior to time control. These norms, dictated by my experience, are of course subjective, but they may nevertheless serve as a useful benchmark for a player with a tendency to think too slowly.

For the currently popular time control of two hours for forty minutes, a different timing structure may be more appropriate: to spend no more than fifteen minutes on the first ten moves; another fifteen minutes on the next five moves; then on the most difficult part of the game (moves 16 to 25) no more than fifty minutes; 4 minutes per move on the following five moves, after which you have twenty minutes to make your last ten moves.

Let's return to the chart for Kasparov vs. Akesson. Kasparov's initial expenditure of time points to his great knowledge of the opening and the nuances of the post-opening stage of the middlegame: he spent just thirty minutes on his first 21 moves even though they were high-quality and rich in ideas (as analysis shows).

From an analysis of Kasparov's entire time curve you can reach the conclusion that he was taking decisions with confidence and gradually bringing them to life. So thinking over specific operations (four minutes spent on move twelve, six minutes spent on move sixteen, nine minutes spent on move 22 and seven minutes spent on moves 30 and 31) was followed by a series of one-minute moves, which highlights Garry's confidence that he had selected the right line and didn't need to recheck his calculations.

A lot of time (44 minutes) spent on the decision to sacrifice the bishop (move 27) points to the unclear consequences of such a tempting move. Despite the abundance of pretty variations, intuition made Garry doubt the soundness of his attacking idea and carefully weigh up the degree and need for risk. Indeed, as thorough analysis later showed, black would have saved the game with the best but far from obvious defense.

Kasparov spotted the upcoming crisis in good time (22.♕e2!), which enabled him to take correct decisions (24.d5!) or those forcing his opponent to navigate huge complications (27.♗xf6!?) at critical moments in the battle.

Akesson found the going much tougher than his opponent. Between moves 14 and 28 he expended around 80%(!) of his allocated time searching for equality and counterplay, thinking long over every move, struggling with his doubts and hesitating, rechecking his calculations several times. As a result, when it became his turn to make the right choice in a crisis situation he had neither time nor energy to find the best moves. I think that studying the nuances of the post-opening middlegame was not part of his home prep.

Let's now look at the chart of another game (game No. 33 in the present Volume, Karpov vs. Kasparov), that was played seven years later. Garry's curve contrasts sharply with that of the previous game. His obvious lack of economy with his time testifies above all to his poor readiness for a fight in this game. Indeed, the fact that the majority of Kasparov's curves in his Seville match were wonky demonstrates that he prepared poorly for the match as a whole.

His blitz in the opening (one minute spent on twelve moves) points to an unwanted and pointless nervous excitement preventing him from thinking calmly. His opponent made the same twelve well-known moves at a slower pace (nine minutes) gradually getting into the game.

His opening blitz was replaced by an unusually long (64-minute!) think over move fourteen and another 22 minutes spent on the subsequent two moves. This indicates that the champion unexpectedly found himself in an unfamiliar situation and, having got there, either lost his way or else tortured himself with doubts and unhappiness (in fact, it was a mixture of all factors). He attempted to find a way out, constantly rechecking and rejecting his moves. His confidence was at rock bottom – two short series of rapid moves show up on the time chart. The champion was totally unable to anticipate when crisis moments would arise in the game.

Karpov, at first glance, was barely better at allocating his time, and his time trouble was even worse. However, it wasn't in fact that simple. His opponent's hour and a half spent on what were essentially opening moves together with Kasparov's external signs of being highly strung led Karpov to the conclusion that his opponent was conducting the battle lacking in confidence but while highly anxious. Based on this, Karpov made a decision to maintain the tension and uncertainty of the game situation for as long as possible and using any available means. In some situations he deliberately took a calculated risk, searching for ways to raise the tension even at the cost of worsening his position. This was not a typically Karpovian way of playing, which explains his torture and indecision when deliberately changing his selection criteria for others that didn't match his playing style. This concept will become clear if you now replay the game.

Finally, a few words about conclusions arising from the time chart in the game Kasparov vs. Ivanchuk (game No. 35 in the present Volume), played just half a year after the previous catastrophe. Ivanchuk deployed a highly complex and little-known line, making his moves at lightning speed. That was a big mistake typical of young players. As a result, he not only failed to anticipate but even failed to notice the crisis moment – just when he needed to take a long think and make a mature choice to switch to defending. Kasparov, on the other, hand spent his time quite rationally in that game. His play was close to the optimal time curve in an opening line that he knew pretty well. He was able to take a serious think just at the key moment in the game, where its outcome was essentially decided. As a result, his decision turned out to be very effective and the battle itself was unusually short.

Chronometric analysis of games can be useful both for professionals and young players, and even more so for coaches. An experienced player who adds chronometry to his scoresheet can make a number of useful conclusions even before chess analysis of the game begins. It points to what aspects of play need to be analyzed, which may remain unnoticed without a record of how much time is spent on each move.

APPENDIX 5

Training Game Scoresheets

Тимощенко – ПК   13/VII-82г.

1 e4	c5	22 Cd2 0.06	Ke4 1.11
2 Kf3	e6	23 Abf 0.05	Kae5 –
3 d4	Cd	24 Ab8+ 0.58	Kpd7 1.10
4 Kd4	Kf6	25 Ce3 0.51	KpC4 1.08
5 Kc3	d6	26 Ab1 0.31	d5 1d6
6 g4	e5 1.29	27 Kb5 0.28	Kpc6 1.04
7 Cb5+ 1.25	Cd7 1.21	28 OO 0.24 d4 1.02
8 Cd7+ 1.24	Φd7 –	29 Kd4+ – ed –
9 Kf5 1.23	h5 –	30 Cd4 – Ah5 1.00
10 g5 0.54	Kh7 1.26	31 Afc1 0.10 Cd6 0.47
11 Cd2 0.57	hg 1.23	32 a4 0.16 Ca4+ 0.47
12 Ag4 0.35	g6 –	33 Kpg2 – ef+ –
13 Ke3 0.54	Cpf 1.22	34 Ae2 0.15 Ag5+ 0.43
14 Kg4 –	Kd7 –	35 Kph1 – Ad5 0.37
15 Kb5 0.29	a08 1.26	
16 Ka7 0.23	Ac2 –	
17 Ke3 0.21	Ae2 1.19	
18 CCB 0.20	Ab6 –	
19 Kd5 –	Kg5 –	
20 Kb6 0.15	Kc6 1.18	
21 Ab1 0.14	Ka4 1.13	

Каспаров –   кельн.
16.08.82 Iп V
Владимиров

1 d4 ∞	Kf6 ∞	19 Kd5 82 Cd5 70
2 c4 –	e6 01	20 f4 83 Cb2 81
3 Kf3 –	b6 02	21 f5 88 Kg4 82
4 a3 02	d5 03	22 Aa1 90 Cd4 83
5 Kc3 03	Ce7 04	23 Ad4 – cd –
6 Cd 15	ed –	24 f6 91 Ke6 –
7 g3 –	OO 06	25 Af1 – Cb3 91
8 Cg2 –	Cb7 07	26 Af5 100 Ad5 95
9 OO 18	d5 09	27 g4 114 a5 97
10 dc 27	bc –	28 Ah5 125 Ah5 98
11 Ke5 –	Ka6 15	29 gh – a4 –
12 Cf4 34	Kc7 15	30 h6 126 Kph8 100
13 Φa4 56	Cd6 20	31 Kd4 127 Af8 114
14 Afd1 56	g5 37	32 h4 110 d3 116
15 Cg5 64	Ce5 –	33 ed – Ke5 –
16 Φh4 –	Kc6 46	34 Φd4 134 Ag4+ 117
17 Cd5 48	Kd5 64	35 Kph2 – Ad3+ –
18 Cd8 –	Aad8 68	36 Kpe3 – Ag3+ 119

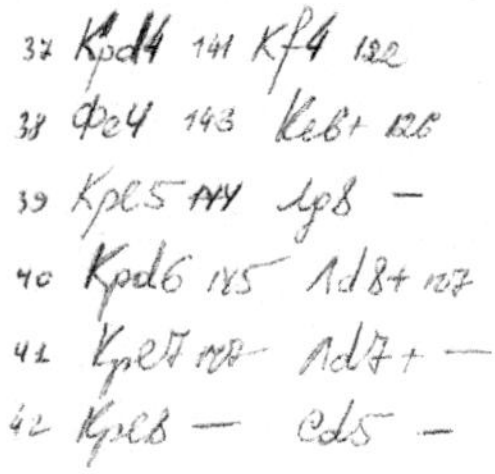

37 Крd4 141 Kf4 122
38 Фe4 143 Kеb+ 120
39 Крe5 144 Лg8 —
40 Крd6 145 Лd8+ 127
41 Крe7 122 Лd7+ —
42 Крe8 — Cd5 —

Владимиров —   Гептель 17.08.82 Ⅱн.
    Каспаров

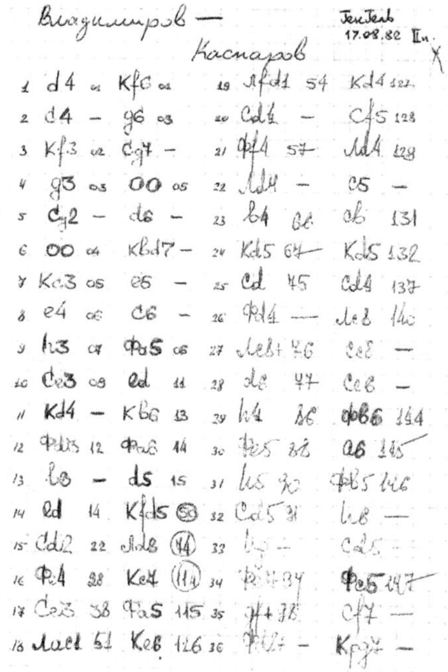

1	d4	01	Kf6	02	19	Лfd1 54	Kd4 122
2	d4	—	g6	03	20	Cd4 —	Cf5 128
3	Kf3	02	Cg7	—	21	Фf4 57	Лd4 128
4	g3	03	OO	05	22	Лd4 —	C5 —
5	Cg2	—	d6	—	23	b4 66	c6 131
6	OO	04	Kbd7	—	24	Kd5 64	Kd5 132
7	Kc3	05	e5	—	25	Cd 45	Cd4 137
8	e4	06	C6	—	26	Фd4 —	Лe8 140
9	h3	07	Фa5	06	27	Лe8+ 46	Ce8 —
10	Ce3	09	Cd 11		28	d6 47	Ce6 —
11	Kd4	—	Kb6 13		29	h4 56	Фb6 144
12	Фb3 12	Фa3 44		30	Фe5 36	a6 145
13	b3	—	d5 15		31	h5 30	Фh5 146
14	Лd 14	Kf5 66		32	Cd5 31	h8 —
15	Cd2 22	Лd8 44		33	b7 —	Cd5 —
16	Фc4 38	Ke4 114		34	Фh7+34	Фe5 147
17	Ce3 38	Фa5 115		35	g4+36	Cf7 —
18	Лac8 51	Ke8 126		36	Фd7 —	Kpg7 —

37	d7	29 Cd5	148
38	Фe8	104 Фd4	–
39		**0**	**1**
40		1ч45м	2ч28м
41			

Владимиров —   19.08.82

Каспаров

1	d4 –	Kf6	03	19
2	c4 –	g6	05	20
3	Kf3	01	Cg7 –	21
4	g3	03	d5 –	22
5	Cg2	04	Фab5	00	23
6	Cd2	10	Фb6	01	24
7	Ka3	21	Cd –	25
8	Ka4	23	Фb6	12	26
9	Cf4	34	Фb4+	11	27
10	Cd2	51	Фd6	+3	28
11	Cf4	04	Фb4+	20	29
12	½	½		30
13				31
14				32
15				33
16				34
17				35
18				36

Каспаров —
Владимиров

1	d4	Kf6	19	Лd5	ed	
2	c4	c6	20	Kd5	Фd8	
3	g3	d5	21	Лd1	Лb8	
4	Cg2	dc	22	Kf4	Cf8	
5	Kf3	c6	23	Ch3	Лc7	
6	OO	Kc6	24	Фc4	Фb8	
7	Фa4	Cd7	25	Cd7	Лd7	
8	Фd1	b5	26	Лd1	Лe7	
9	Фd3	Лc8	27	Kd5	Лee7	
10	dc	Ca5	28	Kc7	Kc7	
11	a3	h5	29	Лc7	Фc7	
12	b4	Ca7	30	c3	Фb6	
13	Kc3	a6	31	c4	Kd7	
14	Лd1	OO	32	Kc5	Kg8	
15	c4	Фc7	33	fg4	Cd2	
16	Фc2	Kb4	34	Фc8	Kph7	
17	Cb2	Kc6	35	Kd7		
18	c5	Kd5	36			

Каспаров —   21.08.82
Владимиров

1	d2-d4	Kg8-f6	19	Cc1-f4	Cf6:e5
2	c2-c4	c7-c6	20	Cf4:e5	Лd6-g6
3	g2-g3	d7-d5	21	Лa1-a3	Kc6-d4
4	Cf1-g2	d5:c4	22	Ce5-f4	Фd8-f6
5	Kg1-f3	Kb8-d7	23	Лa3-e3	h7-h6
6	OO	Лa8-b8	24	d5-d6	f7-f5
7	a2-a4	b7-b6	25	Лe3-e7	Лf8-d8
8	Kf3-d2	Cc8-b7	26	d6-d7	Kd7-f8
9	Cg2-b7	Лb8-b7	27	Лe4-c7	Лd8-c8
10	Kd2-c4	c6-c5	28	Фd7-d7	Лd5-f4
11	Kb1-c3	c4-c5	29	d6-d7	Kb3-d4
12	d4-d5	e6-d5	30	f4:d7	Лc8-f8
13	Kc3-d5	OO	31	Лd4-e8	Лf8-e8
14	e2-e4	Kd7-b8	32	Фd7-e8	Kpg8-h7
15	Лf1-f3	Cb7-d7	33	Лd4-d8	Лg6-g5
16	Kf4-e5	Cd7-d6	34	h2-h4	Лd7-h7
17	Лf1-d1	Kf8-d5	35	Лd8-f4	
18	c4-d5	Cd7-f6	36		

Каспаров —   22.08.82. у
          Владимиров

1	d2-d4	Kg8-f6	19	Kc3-b5	Фd7-e7
2	c2-c4	e7-e6	20	Kb5:a7	Лc8-d8
3	g2-g3	d7-d5	21	Ka7-b5	Cc5:e3
4	Cf1-g2	d5:c4	22	Фe2:e3	Фe7-b4
5	Kg1-f3	c7-c5	23	Фe3-e2	Кa5-c4
6	OO	Kb8-c6	24	Kb5-c3	Кc4:e3
7	Фd1-a4	Cc8-d7	25	Лd1:d8	Лf8:d8
8	d4:c5	Cf8:c5	26	Лa1-c1	
9	Фa4:c4	Cc5-e7	27		
10	Kb1-c3	OO	28		
11	Лf1-d1	Лa8-c8	29		
12	e2-e4	e6-e5	30		
13	Фc4-b3	Kc6-a5	31		
14	Фb3-c2	Фd8-c7	32		
15	Фc2-e2	Cd7-g4	33		
16	h2-h3	Cg4:f3	34		
17	Cg2:f3	h7-h6	35		
18	Cc1-e3	Cc7-c5	36		

ПАРТИЯ №

„23" января

БЕЛЫЕ: Каспаров

ЧЕРНЫЕ: Владимиров

№№ ходов	Белые	Черные	№№ ходов	Белые	Черные
1	d2-d4	Kg8-f6	21	Фe2-a6	g7-g5
2	c2-c4	e7-e6	22	Ke1-f3	Kd5-f6
3	Kg1-f3	d7-d5	23	Фa6-a1	Kf3-g4
4	Kb1-c3	Cf8-e7	24	Лc-d7	Лf-d8
5	Cc1-g5	h7-h6	25	Kf3-e5	Фb1-a5
6	Cg5-f6	Ce7:f6	26	Фa-b2	Фa-d5
7	e2-e3	d5:c4	27	f2-f4	Kg7-h7
8	Kc3-e1	Kb8-d7	28	f4-g5	Лf-d7
9	Cf1-c4	c7-c5	29	Ke5-f7	
10	d4-d5	Kd7-b6	30		
11	Cc4-b5	Kpe8-f8	31		
12	d5-d6	Cc8-d7	32		
13	a2-a4	Cd7-b5	33		
14	a4-b5	Фd8-d7	34		
15	Фd1-c2	a5-c4	35		
16	Лa1-a5	Kb6-d5	36		
17	OO	b7-b6	37		
18	Лa5-a4	Фd7-b5	38		
19	Лa4:c4	Фb5-b2	39		
20	Лc4-c2	Фb2-b4	40		

256

Appendices

№№ ходов	Белые	Черные	№№ ходов	Белые	Черные
41			61		
42			62		
43			63		
44			64		
45			65		
46			66		
47			67		
48			68		
49			69		
50			70		
51			71		
52			72		
53			73		
54			74		
55			75		
56			76		
57			77		
58			78		
59			79		
60			80		

Результат партии: Белые __1__ Черные __0__

Время: Белые _2г 20м_ Черные _2г 0,4м_

Подписи участников: Белые _____ Черные _____

Главный арбитр _____

Тип. МГС «Д» 1974 г. 921- 1000

ПАРТИЯ №

„ 24 “ января

БЕЛЫЕ: _Хаснаров_

ЧЕРНЫЕ: _Владимиров_

№№ ходов	Белые		Черные		№№ ходов	Белые		Черные	
1	d2-d4	00	d7-d5	01	21	b2-b4	83	a5:b4	98
2	c2-c4	–	e7-e6	–	22	a3:b4	–	b7-b5	100
3	Kb1-c3	01	Kg8-f6	–	23	Ka4-c5	36	Kc6:d5	102
4	c4:d5	03	e6:d5	–	24	Qb2:c5	99	Cyc1:f5	–
5	Cc1-g5	–	c7-c6	02	25	Cd3:f5	–	Mb8-b6	103
6	Qd1-d2	05	Kb8-a6	04	26	00	99	Ce7-d6	104
7	e2-e3	16	Ka6-b4	–	27	Qc5-c3	100	Qd8-c7	–
8	Qa2-d1	26	Cc8-f5	14	28	Ma1-b1	102	Kpg8-g7	105
9	Ma1-c1	–	a7-a5	–	29	Mf1-e1	104	Mb6-a6	109
10	a2-a3	27	Kb4-a6	15	30	e3-e4	106	d5:e4	110
11	Qd1-b3	30	Ka6-c7	47	31	Me1:e4	110	Qe7-d1	112
12	Cg5:f6	36	g7:f6	41	32	Mb1-e1	120	Cd6-b8	115
13	Kg1-e2	34	Ma8-b8	57	33	Qc3-f3	128	Mc5-a4	132
14	Ke2-g3	42	c7-g6	60	34	g2-g4	133	La4:b4	–
15	Qb3-d1	45	Kc7-e6	65	35	g4:h5	–	Mb4-c4	129
16	h2-h4	53	h7-h5	72	36	Kpg4-f1	137	Kpg7-h6	118
17	c1-d3	54	c8-d6	73	37	Me4-g4	144	Lh8-e8	–
18	Kg3-f5	61	Cd6-c7	45	38	Me1:e8	145	Qd2-e8	–
19	Qd1-a2	62	Kpe8-f8	76	39	Qf5-e4	148		
20	Ke3-a4	76	Kpf8-g8	25	40				

№№ ходов	Белые	Черные	№№ ходов	Белые	Черные
41			61		
42			62		
43			63		
44			64		
45			65		
46			66		
47			67		
48			68		
49			69		
50			70		
51			71		
52			72		
53			73		
54			74		
55			75		
56			76		
57			77		
58			78		
59			79		
60			80		

Результат партии: Белые __1__ Черные __0__

Время: Белые __2ч28м__ Черные __2ч28м__

Подпись участников Белые _____ Черные _____

Главный арбитр _____

Тип. МГС «Д» 1974 г. 921--1000

ПАРТИЯ №

„25" января

БЕЛЫЕ: *Каспаров*

ЧЕРНЫЕ: *Владимиров*

№№ ходов	Белые	Черные	№№ ходов	Белые	Черные
1	d2-d4	d7-d5	21	Kb3-c5	Kb6-d5
2	c2-c4	c7-c6	22	e4-e5	Kf6-h5
3	Kg1-f3	Kg8-f6	23	Kc3:b5	Lh4-b4
4	Kb1-c3	d5:c4	24	Lad-d1	Lh5-h4
5	a2-a4	Cc8-f5	25	g2-g3	Lh4-h3
6	Kf3-e5	e7-e6	26	Fe3-d2	сдался
7	f2-f3	Cf8-b4	27		
8	Ke5:c4	OO	28		
9	Cc1-g5	b4-b5	29		
10	a4:b5	c6:b5	30		
11	Kc4-a5	Kb8-c6	31		
12	e2-e4	Cf5-g6	32		
13	Ka5:b2	Lf8-b8	33		
14	Ke2:b4	Kc6:b4	34		
15	Cc5-e3	e6-e5	35		
16	Kc4-f2	Kb4-c2	36		
17	Lf1:c2	e5:d4	37		
18	Fe2-d3	Lf1-d8	38		
19	Cf1-e2	d7-a8	39		
20	Ce3:d4	Ld1:d4	40		

№№ ходов	Белые	Черные	№№ ходов	Белые	Черные
41			61		
42			62		
43			63		
44			64		
45			65		
46			66		
47			67		
48			68		
49			69		
50			70		
51			71		
52			72		
53			73		
54			74		
55			75		
56			76		
57			77		
58			78		
59			79		
60			80		

Результат партии: Белые __1__ Черные __0__

Время: Белые __1ч42м__ Черные __1ч52м__

Подписи участников Белые _____ Черные _____

Главный арбитр _____

Тип. МГС «Д» 1974 г. 921--1000

ПАРТИЯ №

„26" января

БЕЛЫЕ: Каспаров

ЧЕРНЫЕ: Владимиров

№№ ходов	Белые	Черные	№№ ходов	Белые	Черные
1	d2-d4 ∞	Kg8-f6 оо	21	a3-a4 105	e7-c8 112
2	c2-c4 —	e7-e6 —	22	b2-b4 ⑫⑧	b5-h5 124
3	Kg1-f3 о4	d7-d5 о4	23	Фd5-c3 13a	Фd5-b8 132
4	Kb1-c3 —	Cf8-e7 о2	24	Ke2-f4 134	Лb8 135
5	Cc1-g5 —	h7-h6 о3	25	Фc3-c6 76	Kb8-d6 135
6	Cg5:f6 о?	Ce7:f6 —	26	Kf3-g5 140	Лe8-d8 141
7	e2-e3 —	OO о4	27	e4-e5 143	c5b5 —
8	Фd1-d2 о?	a8-a6 о4	28	a4:b5 oY	a6-a5 140
9	Лa1-d1 ⑪	Kb8-c6 о9	29	Фc2-b5 145	Лf4-d7 142
10	Лfd1-c2 13	b7-b6 ㉛	30	g2-g3 145	Cg7-f8 145
11	a2-a3 50	Cc8-b7 60	31	Фb5-f1 147	Лd8-c7 146
12	c4:d5 66	e6:d5 —	32	Cf1:h5 44	Лe4-e1 147
13	Cf1-d3 c4	Лf8-e8 ?1	33	Лd1:c1 —	Kc5-c5
14	OO 76	Фd8-d6 ??	34	Лe7-c5 149	a5-a4 148
15	Лf4-e4 76	Лad8-d5 ?5	35	Лe5-c4 —	a4-a3
16	Ke2-b4 ??	g7-g6 83	36	Kg5:f7 —	Фb5-e7 443
17	Лdf1-c1 85	Лc8-c7 90	37	Фc2-c7 —	a3-a2
18	Фa2-b3 93	Cf5-g7 99	38	Cb5-e6 —	Kd2-a1 147
19	Лa3-d1 94	Kc5-a4 105	39	Kg7-g2 —	Kb7-c8
20	Kc3-e2 105	Ka7-c8 107	40		черные просрочили время

31 ... Лd8-a8
32 Фb:a2 и т. д.

№№ ходов	Белые	Черные	№№ ходов	Белые	Черные
41			61		
42			62		
43			63		
44			64		
45			65		
46			66		
47			67		
48			68		
49			69		
50			70		
51			71		
52			72		
53			73		
54			74		
55			75		
56			76		
57			77		
58			78		
59			79		
60			80		

Результат партии: Белые **1** Черные **0**

Время: Белые 2ч29м Черные 2ч30м

Подписи участников: Белые ____ Черные ____

Главный арбитр _____

Тип. МГС «Д» 1974 г. 921—1000

ПАРТИЯ №

„3 " февраля

БЕЛЫЕ: Тимощенко

ЧЕРНЫЕ: Каспаров

№№ ходов	Белые	Черные	№№ ходов	Белые	Черные
1	d2-d4	d7-d5	21	Фc6:c8	Лa8:c8
2	c2-c4	e7-e6	22	Лb7-d7	Cc5:e3 49
3	Kb1-c3	c7-c5	23	f2:e3	Лe8:e3 50
4	c4:d5	e6:d5	24	Лf1-f7	Лe3-e2 51
5	Kg1-f3	Kb8-c6	25	Лf7-g4+	Kpg8-h8 52
6	g2-g3	Kg8-f6	26	Лd7-f7+	Kph8-g8
7	Cf1-g2	Cf8-e7	27	Лf4-e4	Лc8-c4 53
8	OO	OO	28	Лf7-f4	Лe2-b2 54
9	Cc1-g5	c5:d4	29	Лe4-h7	e6-e5 57
10	Kf3:d4	h7-h6	30	e4:b5	a5-a4
11	Cg5-e3	Kf6-e8	31	Лh7-e7	Лc2-b5 58
12	Фd1-a4	Cc8-d7	32	Лe7-a4	Kpe8-f7
13	Лa1-d1	Kc6-b4	33		
14	Фa4-b3	a7-a5 06	34		
15	a2-a4 03	Ce7-c5 (12)	35		
16	Kc3-d5 (14)	Kf8-d5 30	36		
17	Cg2:d5 —	Kb4-d5 40	37		
18	Фb3:d5 —	b7-b6 41	38		
19	Kd4-c6 (15)	Cd7:c6 —	39		
20	Фd5:c6	Фd8-e8 42	40		

ПАРТИЯ №

„4 " февраля

БЕЛЫЕ: Тимощенко

ЧЕРНЫЕ: Каспаров

№№ ходов	Белые	Черные	№№ ходов	Белые	Черные
1	d2-d4	d7-d5 —	21	e2-e3 69	c6-c5 (99)
2	c2-c4	e7-e6	22	Лe4-d1 77	Лb8-c8 90
3	Kb1-c3	c7-c5	23	Фe3-d3 80	c5-d4 —
4	c4:d5	e6:d5	24	Фd1:d4 81	Фd8-c7 87
5	Kg1-f3	Kb8-c6	25	Kc8-a6 88	Cc4-c5 —
6	g2-g3	Kg8-f6	26	Фd4:d5 90	Фc7-c6 (14)
7	Cf1-g2	Cf8-e7	27	Лc1-c3 103	Лd8-d5 127
8	OO	OO 02	28	Лc5-f5 106	Лd8-d4 130
9	Cc1-e3 04	c5-c4	29	b3-b4 (13)	Лc6-d4 132
10	Kf3-e5	h7-h6 06	30	Лd2-f1 140	Лc5:b4 143
11	b2-b3 (10)	c4:b3 12	31	Kа2-b4 147	a5:b4 —
12	Ke5-c6 30	b7:c6 —	32	Лc6-c3 146	g7-g6 146
13	a2:b3	a7-a5 33	33	Фf5-e4 149	Фd5-f5 —
14	Ce3-d4 32	Лc8-b4 34	34	ничья предложена	
15	Kc3-a4 35	Cf8-c5 35	35	Ничья	
16	Cc4-d2 40	Лc8-a6 (39)	36		
17	Лf1-e1 41	Cb4-f5 41	37		
18	Фd1-c2 (12)	Kf6-e4 (15)	38		
19	Ka4-c5 65	Ke4-d2 —	39		
20	Фc2-d2	Cf8-b4 —	40		

№№ ходов	Белые	Черные	№№ ходов	Белые	Черные
41			61		
42			62		
43			63		
44			64		
45			65		
46			66		
47			67		
48			68		
49			69		
50			70		
51			71		
52			72		
53			73		
54			74		
55			75		
56			76		
57			77		
58			78		
59			79		
60			80		

Результат партии: Белые _0_ Черные _1_

Время: Белые _2ч30м_ Черные _2ч27м_

Подписи участников Белые _____ Черные _____

Главный арбитр _____

Тип. МГС «Д» 1974 г. 921—1000

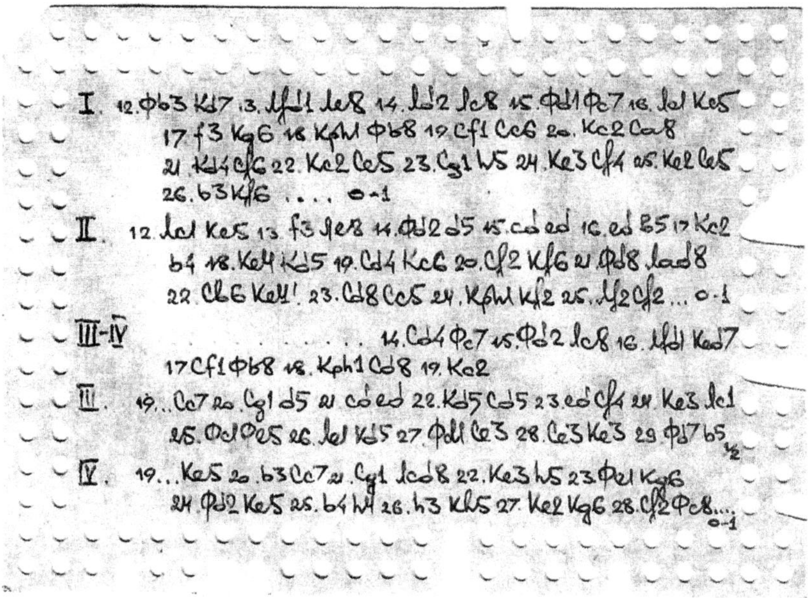

I. 12.Фb3 Kd7 13.Лfd1 Лe8 14.Лd2 Лc8 15.Фd1 Фc7 16.Лc1 Ke5
17.f3 Kg6 18.Kph1 Фb8 19.Cf1 Cc6 20.Kc2 Ca8
21.Kd4 Cf6 22.Kc2 Ce5 23.Cg1 h5 24.Ke3 Cf4 25.Ke2 Ce5
26.b3 Kf6 0-1

II. 12.Лc1 Ke5 13.f3 Лe8 14.Фd2 d5 15.cd ed 16.ed b5 17.Kc2
b4 18.Ke4 Kd5 19.Cd4 Kc6 20.Cf2 Kf6 21.Фd8 Лad8
22.Cb6 Ke4! 23.Cd8 Cc5 24.Kph1 Kf2 25.Лf2 Cf2 ... 0-1

III-IV 14.Cd4 Фc7 15.Фd2 Лc8 16.Лfd1 Kcd7
17.Cf1 Фb8 18.Kph1 Cd8 19.Kc2

III. 19...Cc7 20.Cg1 d5 21.cd ed 22.Kd5 Cd5 23.ed Cf4 24.Ke3 Лc1
25.Фc1 Фe5 26.Лe1 Kd5 27.Фd1 Ce3 28.Ce3 Ke3 29.Фd7 b5 ½

IV. 19...Ke5 20.b3 Cc7 21.Cg1 Лcd8 22.Ke3 h5 23.Фe1 Kg6
24.Фd2 Ke5 25.b4 h4 26.h3 Kh5 27.Ke2 Kg6 28.Cf2 Фc8.... 0-1

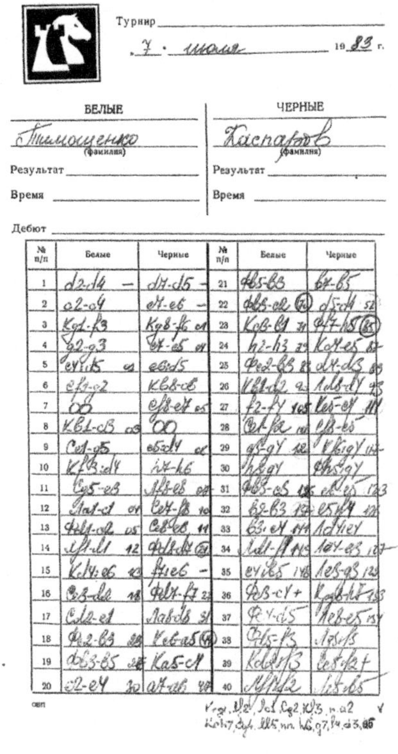

Турнир ________
"7" июля 1983 г.

БЕЛЫЕ: Тимощенко (фамилия)
Результат ________
Время ________

ЧЕРНЫЕ: Каспаров (фамилия)
Результат ________
Время ________

Дебют ________

№ п/п	Белые	Черные	№ п/п	Белые	Черные
1	d2-d4	d7-d5	21	Фb5-b3	b7-b5
2	c2-c4	e7-e6	22	Фb3-c2	d5-d4
3	Kg1-f3	Kg8-f6	23	Kc3-b1	Фf7-h5
4	g2-g3	c7-c5	24	h2-h3	Kc4-e5
5	c4:d5	e6:d5	25	Фc2-b3	d4-d3
6	Cf1-g2	Kb8-c6	26	Kb1-d2	Лd8-d4
7	0-0	Cf8-e7	27	f2-f4	Ke5-g4
8	Kb1-c3	0-0	28	Ce1-f2	Cf8-c5
9	Cc1-g5	c5:d4	29	g3-g4	Kf6:g4
10	Kf3:d4	h7-h6	30	h3:g4	Фh5:g4
11	Cg5-e3	Лf8-e8	31	Фb3-c3	e6-e5
12	Лa1-c1	Ce7-f8	32	b2-b3	e5:f4
13	Фd1-a4	Cc8-e6	33	b3:c4	Лd4:e4
14	Лf1-d1	Фd8-d7	34	Лd1-f1	Лe4-e3
15	Kd4:e6	f7:e6	35	c4:b5	Лe3-g3
16	Ce3-d2	Фd7-f7	36	Фc3-c4+	Kpg8-h7
17	Cd2-e1	Лa8-d8	37	Фc4-d5	Лe8-e5
18	Фa4-b3	Kc6-a5	38	Фd5-f3	Лg3:f3
19	Фb3-b5	Ka5-c4	39	Kd2:f3	Cc5:f2+
20	e2-e4	a7-a6	40	Лf1:f2	Лe5:b5

Kpg1, Лf2, Лc1, Cg2, Kf3, п. a2
Kph7, Фg4, Лb5, пп. h6, g7, f4, d3, a6

Турнир

„8“ июля 1983 г.

БЕЛЫЕ	ЧЕРНЫЕ
Каспаров (фамилия)	Тимощенко (фамилия)
Результат 1	Результат 0
Время	Время

Дебют

№ п/п	Белые	Черные	№ п/п	Белые	Черные
1	d2-d4	Кg8-f6	21	Кa4:c5	Кa6:c5
2	c2-c4	e7-e6	22	d4:c5	Сd6:c5
3	Кb1-c3	d7-d5	23	a2-a3	Лf8-b8
4	Сc1-g5	Сf8-e7	24	Лf1-c1	Фa5:a3
5	Кg1-f3	h7-h6	25	Фb3:a3	b4:a3
6	Сg5:f6	Сe7:f6	26	Лc2:c5	a3-a2
7	e2-e3	0-0	27	Лc1-a1	Сb7-a6
8	Фd1-d2	b7-b6	28	Сe2:a6	Лb8-b1+
9	Лa1-c1	Сc8-b7	29	Лc5-c1	Лb1:c1+
10	c4:d5	e6:d5	30	Лa1:c1	Лa8:a6
11	b2-b4	Сf6-e7	31	Лc1-a1	Лa6-b6
12	b4-b5	Сe7-a3	32	Кf3-d2	Лb6-b2
13	Лc1-c2	a7-a6	33	Кd2-f1	Крg8-f8
14	Сf1-e2	c7-c6	34	g2-g4	Крf8-e7
15	b5:a6	Кb8:a6	35	Крg1-g2	Крe7-d6
16	Фd2-d1	b6-b5	36	Кf1-g3	Крd6-e5
17	0-0	Сa3-d6	37	Крg2-f3	d5-d4
18	Фd1-b1	b5-b4	38	e3:d4+	Крe5:d4
19	Кc3:a4	Фd8-a5	39	Кg3-f5+	Крd4-c3
20	Фb1-b3	c6-c5	40	Кf5:g7	Лb2-c2

ОБП

№ п/п	Белые	Черные	№ п/п	Белые	Черные
41	Кg7-f5	Крc3-b2	66		
42	Лa1:a2+	Крb2:a2	67		
43	Кf5:h6	Лc2-c7	68		
44	g4-g5	Крa2-b3	69		
45	h2-h4	Крb3-c4	70		
46	Крf3-e4	Лc7-e7+	71		
47	Крe4-f5	Крc4-d5	72		
48	f2-f4		73		
49			74		
50			75		
51			76		
52			77		
53			78		
54			79		
55			80		
56			81		
57			82		
58			83		
59			84		
60			85		
61			86		
62			87		
63			88		
64			89		
65			90		

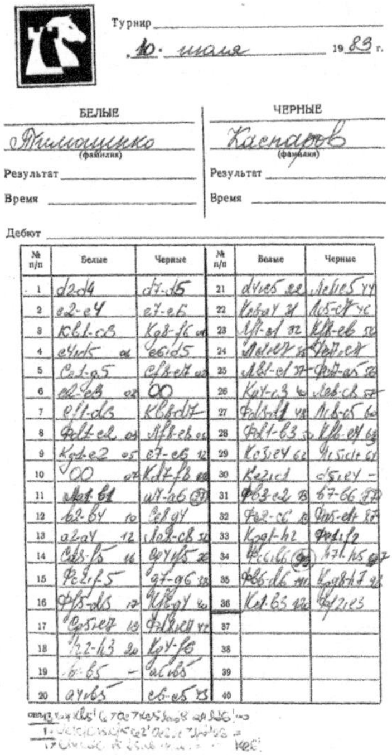

Турнир

10 июля 1983 г.

БЕЛЫЕ	ЧЕРНЫЕ
Тимошенко (фамилия)	Каспаров (фамилия)
Результат	Результат
Время	Время

Дебют

№ п/п	Белые	Черные	№ п/п	Белые	Черные
1	d2-d4	d7-d5	21	d4:e5	Лe8:e5
2	e2-e4	e7-e6	22	Kc3:e4	Лe5-e7
3	Kb1-c3	Kg8-f6	23	Лf1-e1	Kf8-e6
4	e4:d5	e6:d5	24	Лe1:e7	Фd7:e7
5	Cc1-g5	Cf8-e7	25	Лb1-e1	Фe7-a5
6	e2-e3	0-0	26	Ke4-c3	Лe8-c8
7	Cf1-d3	Kb8-d7	27	Фd3-d1	Лc8-c5
8	Фd1-e2	Лf8-e8	28	Фd1-b3	Ke6-e4
9	Kg1-e2	c7-c6	29	Kc3:e4	Фa5:c1+
10	0-0	Kd7-f8	30	Ke2:c1	d5:e4
11	Лa1-b1	a7-a6	31	Фb3-e2	b7-b6
12	b2-b4	Cc8-g4	32	Фe2-c6	Фa5-e1+
13	a2-a4	Лa8-c8	33	Kg1-h2	Фe1:f2
14	Cd3-f5	Cg4:f5	34	Фc6:b6	h7-h5
15	Фe2:f5	g7-g6	35	Фb6-d6	Kg8-h7
16	Фf5-d3	Kf6-g4	36	Kc1-b3	Фf2:e3
17	Cg5:e7	Фd8:e7	37		
18	h2-h3	Kg4-f6	38		
19	b4-b5	a6:b5	39		
20	a4:b5	c6-c5	40		

Printed in Great Britain
by Amazon

26624663R00150